LOUISE BL...............low. Her
husband George........................; a short
battle with bowel............................English
and French at W........................,.......Mars Incorporated as a
graduate trainee in 2006 and worked in various sales and marketing roles
in a career that spanned eleven years. After George's death Louise left the
corporate world to raise awareness of bowel cancer in young people and
discuss the existence of God. The 'George Blyth Trust' funds scientific
research and educational programmes associated with bowel cancer in
younger people. Louise still lives in Nottinghamshire with her young sons
Charlie and Jamie and continues to challenge herself each day to practice
gratitude and create spiritual connectivity through prayer.

From the reviews of *Hope is Coming*

'[Louise] writes beautifully and compellingly and I was immersed,
involved and cared massively, from almost the first page. I wanted to
place every bit of my emotional investment in her and George. This does
not happen often. For me how engaged I feel and how much I care are
the most important elements of a novel and in my opinion [Louise has]
achieved this brilliantly.'

GILLIAN STERN Editor and Lucy Cavendish Fiction Prize, Judge.

'In death George has shown us life. [This] story is going to change
destinies. Lives will be turned around. People will be stopped in their
tracks. I've learnt so much more about God in reading this book. I feel
richer because of it. Because of [Louise's] honesty'.

JANE ELIZABETH KIRBY Rebel Hearts Rebel Girls Founder.

'I have never read anything like this utterly wonderful book. This story
will change lives. What a beautiful gift [Louise has] given to the world;
the most precious love story. Truly Amazing. THANK YOU.'

RACHEL HAYNES Author of *What Doesn't Kill you..*

Hope is Coming

LOUISE

BLYTH

Wonderfulness
of life

First published in Great Britain in 2020 by Wonderfulness of Life.

Copyright © 2020 Louise Blyth.

A CIP catalogue record for this book is available from the British Library.

 @wonderfulness_of_life

www.wonderfulnessoflife.com

Cover Design by Naomi Tipping www.naomitipping.com

ISBN Paperback: 978-1-9163329-04

Author's note

This has been an incredibly difficult yet beautiful book to write. I have relied on memory to recall a series of real-life events that have been documented as authentically as my memory will allow.

What I am about to share unfolded during a time of trauma. I have therefore consulted with some of those who walked with us for accuracy. Their names, personal descriptions and details surrounding their lives have been changed.

Characterisations in this memoir with the exception of George, our respective families and myself are therefore composite. These alterations do not alter the truth of what happened to us both and the very real feeling of what I felt in my heart.

My greatest wish is that this story makes you stop and think. It makes you wonder if there's more to life than what meets the eye. Ultimately my prayer is that our love story opens your heart to the magic of the beautiful universe we inhabit. I pray that it empowers you to awaken your soul and rise up to live in freedom and bear witness to the spectacular love that surrounds us all.

This is also for you my Gorgeous George. This is the astounding legacy you leave for our beautiful boys. This is how our love story will never be forgotten. This is how love always wins.

Louise x

Prologue

I'm here. Snuggled up under the duvet. The covers surround me like a cocoon. I'm hiding, just like I used to with him. I'm trying to drown out the shouts and giggles of my young children. Their energy is beautifully relentless. I'm exhausted. Grief and the endless responsibility it brings, makes me feel tired in a way that sometimes drowns my soul. It hurts. Sometimes it engulfs every part of my being. It's taken some time to pass but I accept now that some memories will never leave my bones. Some memories will always sneak out of my eyes. Some memories I will carry with me forever. It's like that when you lose a part of your soul. I realise now though that you can never fully lose someone you love. All that you love is part of you forever - like salt in the sea and sand in the desert. I'm not drowning in the salty waves of sadness today. Those days are behind me now, although I still have to watch out for the rough seas. This is because I've learned what I need to do to keep afloat when the stormy waters of grief brew.

A few hundred days into this new life I've been forced to learn this. To know and respond to how I survive. How I reset. How I feel what is part of me.

This spot is exactly where I used to lie when I was a little girl. The familiarity of Dad's side of the bed makes me feel safe. It's a space he never knew. A memory he never inhabited. I feel protected. I breathe into the duvet and take comfort knowing that I lived for many years without him. I know I can and I will live for many more. I close my eyes and dance in this moment. He won't be by my side. I know that for certain now. He won't always be here in the way I thought he would be. I push out the duvet and come up for air. I hold back the tears and let myself be distracted by the view out of the window. The trees moving in the breeze ground me. I stare and I nestle my head deeper into the comforting smells. They bring peace. I breathe in the distant memories of childhood. They're delicious; nectar to my soul.

I recognize the feeling as soon as it lands; it's happiness. I let it float over me. I close my eyes and go back to who I was before. Before I fell in love. Before my heart got blasted and cut wide open. I relax. I feel. I open my mind and I start talking because I'm ready now, ready to ask Him to come. I begin to mutter and then I feel. It's not immediate. It's not straight away. But I recognize his force. His peace. He gently pours into my heart. I feel it. He makes my body shudder and my soul feels light in a way I never expected. He's nothing like I imagined. I lie flat and let him wash over my spirit.

The refreshing powers soothe me. I can carry on with my day

now. He's filled my emptiness and woven around the hurt. I lift the covers and watch the winter trees as they sway. The universe is amazing. Spring will be here soon, another season without him another season with him. It's all so confusing. The green shoots make me feel expectant though. I get up and move to the window. I stand tall and wipe away my tears. I know the sadness will never leave me. I know this grief will be curiously interwoven around my heart forevermore. But I have a new love that both lifts and gives me a sense of purpose. I never thought it would go this way and that I would live life with this sort of connection on my side. I stand firm and look at myself in Mum's mirror. The woman standing in front of me is someone different from who she was before. I know this sense of direction would have made him proud.

So here begins our love story.

A chocolate factory is where we lay our scene.

A pair of star-crossed lovers will meet,

and several years later face mutiny.

He will lose his life, yet both will be freed.

From the fatal loins of death,

This is how the unseen became seen.

Love

I hadn't been properly in love until I met him. If I'm honest I think I was just in love with the idea of being 'in love,' before that. The older I get I realise that many people are just so focused on the ideals of romance and not the heart that beats in the space in between. Once you've felt that electric and magnetic connection though, you know it's real. You know why they call the person you think you're searching for 'the one.'

When you meet your match, it's more than just butterflies in your stomach. It isn't just wanting to talk to them until the early hours of the morning. It's when their presence alone grounds you. It's a type of safety and security that envelops every part of your being; you feel protected and safe in a way you've maybe never felt before. When you feel love like this everything else pales into insignificance because you know you're OK. You're protected by a force-field of energy that binds the two of you as one and makes you better together than you can ever be on your own.

For us, it wasn't love at first sight, not at all. We used to laugh about how far from the truth this was.

I met him before we had even done our first day of work at the chocolate factory. We'd both earned a place on the prestigious graduate training scheme there, a programme that I had busted my gut to get into and had already been rejected from once before. On the day I saw him for the first time I felt desperately out of my comfort zone: scared about the situation I had found myself in, scared of who I would meet, scared of what they would think, scared to be lined up next to other future hotshots and potentially get found out for not being good enough. There was so much fear in the pit of my stomach that day and the anxiety blind-sided me so that I barely even noticed him sitting in the reception area. When I looked up to nervously survey my surroundings he was there. He was wearing a bold red tie and reading the newspaper. I could tell from the way he sat that he was self-assured. He looked at home; almost like he was in his grandparents' front room content in the environment he had found himself in with his body laid back at ease looking like he'd always been there. I could see that he was handsome but there was no lightning bolt in my heart or somersault of emotion in my stomach. My thoughts were too rooted in trepidation.

I spoke first. It was a little mumble whilst looking at the floor. I was hugely conscious of my new suit which felt itchy and stiff like I was wearing cardboard. I opened and closed my mouth a few times before any words would even come out.

'I'm Louise,' I said, 'are you here for the induction too?

I saw his dazzling smile first, then his electric blue eyes, serious and playful all at the same time.

'Yes,' he said, 'only they didn't tell me the start time, so I've already been here for ages.'

There was a definite hint of comic irony and mocking in his tone and I was amazed that he was criticising the organisation we were going to be working for.

'Pleased to meet you,' he said, holding out his hand for me to shake, 'I'm George.'

I had never observed such strength and fortitude in anyone else before. The way he continued to relax into his seat, the armchair that was owned by the company that had misinformed him, said it all. I took his hand and his eyes lit up and twinkled.

'Well Louise,' he said, 'I'm just so glad someone else has finally arrived.'

His voice made me feel safe and welcome. I watched as he put the newspaper down, moved his empty coffee cup and the various chocolate bar wrappers the firm had left out for us, and made space next to him. I sat down by his side and breathed.

More of the inductees arrived. All of them walked through the door looking as anxious and nervous as I felt inside; all of them hiding those nerves with the same broad smile and confident stride. Our group was seven in total, but we didn't know that at the time as we simply sat waiting expectantly, making small talk about the summer and where we had gone to university, whilst looking at the door and wondering who would walk through next. A couple of guys I had been interviewed with sat either side of me. Recognising their faces was reassuring in such an alien environment. One of them was so tanned it looked at odds with his new suit and shoes and it made me smile.

'Been away?' I politely asked, desperately trying to make it look like I didn't feel all of the fear that was pressing on my chest. He just nodded and said,

'Yeah,' whilst keeping his eye on the front door.

I watched this guy George with curious envy. He greeted all seven new starters in the same way he had met with me. Somehow he made them all feel like they were his best friend and it was apparent that he was a total charmer. Everyone warmed to him and to his curious and magnetic energy.

After waiting for what felt like forever in the reception area the seven of us were ushered into a meeting room. The fear of feeling like a child in an adult's world reared its head again inside my stomach and after the introductions and niceties, the knot started to twist as I heard the lady from HR talking about our placement locations. I desperately didn't want to move away from home again but, as I mentally told myself to toughen up, I also knew that if I was serious about this new career then I might have to.

My biggest fear was that I'd be placed in Scotland. The thought of having to go there so far from home, completely on my own and start over, was blindsiding me. My heart was pounding in my chest as I waited to hear if I'd get the short straw. To my utter surprise, George spoke up before the HR manager had even taken her laptop out of the bag.

'I would like to go north,' he said boldly as he sat squarely at the table, his blue eyes wide with expectation and wonder. 'It will be good for me!'

I tried hard not to spit out my water. Who was this guy, his attitude was comical. Did he even know where the north was? He spoke about it as a place of bleak discovery, an environment that was so far removed from his sphere of experiences that he must go to gain some level of life-altering encounter. Was he actually for real? It was certainly at odds with his plummy southern accent.

I looked around the table and could see the gleeful glances being exchanged by HR and the scheme manager. They were relieved that someone had the balls to volunteer themselves up for the furthest 'northern adventure'. George's comedic bravery changed the tone of the meeting immediately and I could visibly see the weight being lifted off other people's shoulders in the room, staff and new recruits. As the meeting went on, it became obvious that George was infectious. He spoke to everyone as if they were his long-lost family and he had this unassuming way of telling people what he wanted. Somehow his presence and his ability to use his pitfalls to his comedic advantage helped all the group that day. I'd even go as far as saying that it bound us. Maybe that's why we're all still such good friends because of him, because of the way he showed up.

That evening I called my parents, I was an excited daughter talking to her loving and anxious mum who was keen for me to enjoy all that this new adventure would bring. What stood out though was the fact that I could hear myself talking about George.

'There was this complete posh idiot,' I told her, 'a southerner.'

This was relevant information for my parents: they'd been raised as hardy northerners and delighted in this part of their identity. They had raised me much the same way too.

'Can you believe that he outright asked to go to Scotland? To go north. I'm not even entirely sure he knows where it is. I don't think he has any idea what he's let himself in for.'

We laughed about this man I had met, who didn't know what the north even was. We found him funny. Somehow even back then he comforted my parents too and the ripples of his impact were already being felt amongst us. Changing the subject Mum wondered how much free chocolate I'd been given and if I'd seen any real-life chocolate rivers. George wasn't mentioned any further but his charm had impacted my heart beyond surface-level that day.

Very quickly it became apparent that George was entirely sure of what he was doing. That's when he began to get under my skin. Even though he did it with such apparent spontaneity and a lack of fear that was enviable. I went on to discover that most of the declarations he made were almost always very well thought through. He could somehow look into the eye of something incredibly scary and turn it on its head. Make it OK. That's what he did as we trained together, mastering our craft in the art of selling chocolate bars and generally having a great time with all of our new colleagues.

The two of us became the best of friends; that's really where our relationship started. I found his energy infectious, his jokes funny and how he viewed the world enlightening. He was good energy to be around. Even in those early days, I'd go as far as to say his presence made me be a better version of myself. He gave me the confidence to believe in myself in a way I hadn't ever really dared to before. He also made me belly laugh and lifted my soul in a way that was new ground.

As a group of seven young men and women, we spent our first month living together in a hotel in Slough. It wasn't at all glamorous but more luxurious than the university halls we'd come from. We'd travel together, train together, do our homework together, we'd even eat together. George was always at the heart of what was going on arriving early to get the evening underway, requesting wake-up alarms to be changed by the concierge in our teammate's bedrooms and ordering joke meals. But while he brought and gifted the fun factor, it was also crystal clear that he was going to be incredibly successful at his job, he just had this way of getting people to believe in him and want to be around him. He was infectious.

George and I were in many ways chalk and cheese. He was massively last minute. Back then I was always fearfully organised and on time. He didn't seem remotely interested in how others perceived him and he wasn't ever wracked with guilt, or wishing he'd done things differently in the way I did after each training activity. I think it was because he spoke to so many of my insecurities and made me see a way past them that we clicked. We both valued authenticity and joy. He would incessantly pull my leg and use humour to distract me. At the time I thought this is what it truly is to have a best friend who is a boy. I knew pretty quickly I'd met someone who understood me and felt lucky that there was never any awkwardness between us, no strings attached. We were just mates, pals who could laugh together, help each other out and have a great chat at the end of each day. I was ecstatic to have a new best friend.

After four weeks of training, we all went off to our various jobs across the country. He was in Scotland and I was in Birmingham but despite the geographic distance between us, our friendship grew.

We were both working as entry-level sales reps, positioning new products in the right places in-store and talking to retailers about what exciting chocolate products our company would be launching next. It was high energy. Work hard, play hard, became our mantra as we drove around in our new company cars – 'go karts,' as George used to call them. It became our new normal to gather together over the phone lines, and between customer visits we'd check in with one another on our Bluetooth headsets.

'Ring your team and chat between your account calls,' the chocolate factory would say. 'Share best practice with each other,' we were regularly told.

And so we did – sharing our vulnerabilities, laughing at our follies, supporting each other every minute of every day. But increasingly there was one person more than anyone else that I was spending my time talking to. The calls within work hours led to chats in the evening.

George and I genuinely liked to talk. We called it hanging out on our walkie-talkies. Talking about our day, dissecting what had happened and then moving on to other more pressing affairs such as wondering if we were going out at the weekend and what crazy treats we could buy with our pay that week. Before we knew it the festive season came upon us with its wrapped-up version of romance. This was the first time I felt my stomach flutter as we danced like crazy at the Christmas party.

'Do I *like* him?' was the only thought ricocheting around my mind for the whole of December.

A few days later, I found myself back home in Nottingham, removed from this new world I had discovered. That morning as I opened my presents, I couldn't help but wish there had been something from him. I sat on the sofa that day, the various Christmas TV specials washing over my soul as I simply stared at my phone willing it to ring. He was like a magnetic pull on my heartstrings and I realised then that my day didn't quite feel complete without hearing his voice. I tried to think of a valid reason to get in touch. I blankly wondered if maybe we could have some banter about bad presents. As I sat looking at my phone it dawned on me that he made me feel complete in a way no one else had ever done before.

As the day unravelled and I had drunk a few glasses of Christmas sparkle my heart felt like it would burst. It nearly did when I went back to check on my phone and it turned out he was the one to have sent a text. It turned out he wanted to be in touch just as much as me. I felt heady and weak at the knees as I skimmed over the simple words he had written and was surprised that they created a physical response unlike anything else.

'*Hope you've had a lovely Christmas? Miss you! x*'

It was the best present ever and it made me feel everything: hopeful, expectant, loved, scared. I breathed it all in. Could I bring myself to believe that he wanted anything more? He was mischievous with everyone he met; his character was flirtatious. It was important for him to build connections and charm others. I knew we could talk about life together, but could we do life together? I was scared and I hesitated before I responded. Should I send him my usual jokes as a reply or did Christmas warrant a less playful and more serious tone? As I sat and pondered it was as if my heart knew the way and answered for me. Before I knew it I was punching the letters into my Nokia phone and pressing send.

'*It's been great, but I've missed speaking to you. I've been thinking about you so much! x*'

The text he'd sent sparked a new type of conversation between us. It was less comedic and more caring and connected in a way we hadn't been previously. It was also more urgent and frequent than it had ever been before albeit careful to not unsettle the beautiful friendship that had grown between us. In the days that followed I spent the entire time wanting to text with him and as soon as I sent a message would get a reply back. It was as if the flame that so many later told us they saw burning between us, had finally been lit. We both wanted more than friendship but neither of us knew how to say it.

And then the chance arose. Way back, on the very first group email that George had sent after we'd all met that summer, he had started to plan his Hogmanay party. In true George style he'd sent an open invite to a house he didn't yet live in, to a group of people he had just met. Six months later true to his word he delivered on the promise of a Scottish New Year in the fun way that only he could. That December he crammed almost thirty people into the flat he shared with his housemate. It was outrageously epic, just like him.

Hogmanay 2006 was one of the wettest New Year's eves on record for Edinburgh. Yet, despite the hideous weather and the number of people in such a small space, our spirits weren't dampened. We danced, we played silly games, we wore Scottish hats and even plastered temporary Scottish tattoos on our bodies.

Close to 4 am bedtime came around with the midnight moment long behind us. It had evaporated without even the slightest hint of romance. It was at that point that our friends took the situation into their own hands. Everyone was sleeping everywhere. Any conceivable space had been turned into a bed for the night, even the bathroom floor was taken. Yet I was gifted the coveted spot of sleeping in George's bed. A mattress was a big deal when almost everybody else had a wooden floor. So willingly I donned my tartan pyjama suit and took everyone else up on the offer. I made a huge show about the fact that nothing other than sleeping would be happening. I didn't want anyone to know how much I really liked him and I certainly didn't want him to see that I'd already fallen in love.

14

Once we were in that room though on our own and fuelled by the confidence that only WKD Blue mixed with wine can give you, we had our first kiss. He was the one that instigated it pulling me into his arms and hugging me tightly. Despite having given it so much thought previously when I kissed him for the first time I didn't even have a moment to think about what we were doing. It just felt right. It was love. It was respectful. It was passion. It was every part as lovely as I'd hoped.

He pulled the duvet over our heads and made a tent over our clothed bodies; we were on our own then. Even if his flat was full of more people than it had probably ever held, we were together by ourselves. Our bodies fitted. His lips felt so good and soft. I felt small in his arms and I loved the feeling of the weight of his body pressing against me. He was soft and powerful all at the same time. This was the start of feeling like I was finally at home and the beginning of falling head over heels in love. It was the start of us and our great adventure of becoming one.

Nothing else happened that night. We were such good friends that we wanted to honour the connection we both knew was there. This is genuinely how it played out. However much passion there was, there was also an infinite amount of respect for one another which was evident from the outset. This was because we were both already so mindful that there was a powerful connection between us. We'd known it for a long time so we kissed, we talked and we drifted in and out of sleep in each other's arms. I wore my pyjama suit the entire time. It was lovely. It was deep contentment and pure joy. I felt safe in my heart that night

15

in a way I'd never even dreamed about. I went to bed with a best friend and woke up with a boyfriend. We didn't even have to tell anyone else when we woke up around midday. They'd seen the sparks of love flying between the two of us long before we had and had already guessed our evening had ended with a kiss. They whooped with joy almost as much as we did when we confirmed what they thought.

True love is every part as beautiful as you imagine. It makes you feel like you're walking on air. It makes you feel like you're living your life outside of your own body. It makes you feel utterly in the moment. It grounds and soars you to new places in your heart.

But after our first kiss, I didn't allow myself to simply believe that this was it. I was hesitant. The transition from friend to boyfriend felt a little awkward at first but George had this way of speaking to situations and just making them OK. He didn't even ever ask me to be with him he just made an announcement. He told me he'd called his Granny.

'What on earth did you say?' I asked sort of not wanting to know, but desperately intrigued all at the same time.

'I told her I've met the girl I'm going to marry,' he said.

'How do you know that?' I asked squirming inside.

'I just do,' he teased, 'I've never kissed someone like that before and then spent the whole morning fist pumping!'

My cheeks went red and I smiled. He smiled straight back. He always knew exactly the right thing to say. We were both in love before we'd even kissed but that moment was the symbolic declaration we had both needed to let go of our hearts and let our souls begin to wrap around each other's.

The love that we had for each other as friends changed very quickly into romantic love. It was electric in the way I had read about and always dreamed of. It was a love so crazy that we advance booked flights to Scotland for the whole year. We both knew that this was more than a fleeting romance, it was the type of love that could endure a lifetime. It felt like we were invincible together and life felt simply wonderful.

They say absence makes the heart grow fonder and for us, the distance between us somehow made us closer. The love we had for each other was powerful. It was wanting to be near each other magnetism. It was knowing what the other was thinking, or feeling, without them even uttering a word. On some level, we knew from the outset that it was meant to be. We didn't actively believe in God, but the power of our relationship made us question if there was more. We would often lie in bed late at night and muse over this together, but it was a fair few months into our relationship before we did this for the first time.

We were under the duvet again; that was always where we'd go when we wanted to shut ourselves off from the world. My head was on his chest listening to the rhythm of his beating heart. That was always my favourite place to lay down my head, I always felt so content being snuggled up against the softness of his skin and listening to the workings of his body. It made me feel happy, connected and yet so worried as I found myself wondering about the precariousness of life. It was so incredible to be alive and to be so in love, yet miraculous that it was seemingly one rhythmical beat keeping it all together.

The divine wasn't something of huge importance to either of us back then but we did talk about it, often in these moments of safety and togetherness.

'Do you believe in God?' I asked him that day as he lay back in bed, stretched out looking so relaxed and peaceful, his long legs meaning his feet were peeking out of the bottom of the covers.

I could see his eyes roll even though they were closed. He used to get cross with me always in a nice way when I asked him big questions as he was about to go to sleep.

'I think so,' he said. I wrapped my legs around his and buried my head deeper into his chest. 'I think there has to be something more, I just don't think that this life can be it. It can't be. Life is too brilliant. Too connected.'

He opened his eyes and looked straight into mine. I always felt myself fall in a little deeper when he did that as his blue eyes were always so beautifully hypnotic.

'I mean, take us, I know the connection we have isn't normal. It's a once in a lifetime type of energy. This makes me know that we're supposed to be together. Our energy is connected in some way. I can feel it. It just has to be, otherwise, it wouldn't all be this right.'

His answer floored me but spoke to my soul simultaneously. It's because I knew it too. It was meant to be that we were together. Even if we couldn't articulate the power of love which moved between us.

But God, the divine, the universe, whatever you want to call it, wasn't a subject we ever pursued. We thought we didn't need it. We were desperately in love. We had each other and we were successful in our careers. We had an incredible group of friends and a wonderful family. We thought we had it all. So we did what so many others do and we cracked on with life – achieving, dreaming, chasing the increasingly obscure rainbows that we believed would bring joy and contentment. Our love for each other always propelled and bound us though. It was irrepressible.

Before we knew it our lives were intertwined. He had met my parents over a laid-back curry and watched cricket on TV with my Dad. My parents, retired teachers, had hit it off with him instantly. A few months later, I had found myself in Oxfordshire knocking on the front door of his Mum's quirky country home. I had already met his dad by this point, we were staying at his huge house just down the road whilst he was away in America with work.

As we walked down the road to meet his mum, we both knew without saying that what we were feeling was serious. I was so nervous the first time I met her, but as soon as our eyes locked and I saw her strolling to the door peacefully wearing an apron smattered with flour and a smile that lit up her entire face, I knew that we'd like one another. I recognised the love and charm that oozed from her immediately, it was the same as her son's. She too was quietly mischievous and full of such joy as she welcomed me into her home, threw plates on to the table and served up four different types of cake. I felt at home immediately.

'Will you have another dearest Lou?' she said putting a huge slice of chocolate cake almost into my lap as her dogs gleefully barked around her legs.

I felt connected, I felt included, I felt like this was another space where I was supposed to belong.

Our backgrounds were on paper so divergent. George's parents were divorced whilst mine were still married. Their stories and their lives were markedly different. My parents had met as teenagers whilst working in a department store and followed one another into careers in teaching. George's parents had met in their twenties; by this time his dad had already begun to forge a hugely impressive career in the world of audio engineering, his mum had a beautiful heart and so many wonderful stories of caring for others.

George was the oldest and one of three siblings, with a sister and brother whom he loved and looked out for. I was the youngest of two with a big brother who looked at any potential suitor aggressively if he didn't deem them good enough. George had been raised in a huge house in Oxfordshire, educated privately in his secondary years and was well travelled. I had been brought up in the suburbs of Nottingham, attended the local comp and spent all of my summers camping in France. Despite all of this what was staggeringly beautiful was the way we still connected. We met as equals, even though our circumstances and stories were so different. This was because at our core, as we got to know one another more deeply, we realised we were full of the same love and values.

Almost four years to the day after our first kiss in Edinburgh we bought our first house. Soon after we were engaged and then married. In 2013 we welcomed our first little boy, Charlie. In 2015 we welcomed our second son, Jamie. Our boys were healthy dynamos of energy. We'd moved further north to our dream house to be closer to my parents in Nottinghamshire.

We were on to a good thing. Life was exhausting; as it is for many balancing careers and a young family, but we loved each other to our core. Our relationship was still magic but in a new way, a different way. A more-everyday-normal-kind- of-way.

We were in the middle of redefining how to live as four instead of two when it happened.

We were going through what countless other thirty-something's go through. It was messy and at times hard work. It was arguing about household chores and wondering what we would watch on TV, but it was our messy and we loved it. We didn't want to change it and felt so lucky, so very thankful for every last drop of goodness. We didn't want to alter a note.

If I'm brutally honest though I'm not sure I was always truly comfortable, truly happy in my own skin. I relied on George for so much; too much some might say. He was my everything, my God. He would listen to me at night as we'd go to bed and I'd unload my anxiety on to him, continually seeking reassurance and his recognition. It was gruelling and even though he was always there to wipe away the tears and tell me he loved me, I still had lots of anxiety. I think it's because I always kind of felt that something bad was going to happen. It all just felt too perfect.

I remember telling my best friend this, on the front lawn of our new home, shortly after we had just moved.

'I can't believe this is my life,' I said as I gazed into the rolling garden of our forever-home. 'I just know it can't last.'

As I looked at her and then towards George playing on the garden with our kids, I knew I had spoken my fear out loud to someone other than him for the first time ever.

'It all just feels too good to be true,' I said.

It was hard to say stuff like that out loud back then because I found the worry exhausting and all consuming. But then just a few months later all the fear I'd felt reared its ugly head in a way I could never have anticipated. The niggling anxiety couldn't be buried any longer. In an instant our lives got flipped upside-down. I was on my own with Jamie when it happened, he was an eight-month-old baby impressively enjoying his bouncer, whilst our little Charlie Bear played with his friends at Nursery and George was in London. That was the scene when I got the call that would be the start of a very different season. A time when we would be forced to live in a life-altering fear and live through events that would impact the course of all of our destinies and force a very different existence.

Invictus

Before kids, I thought that I knew the meaning of the word tired but really I knew nothing. If you are lucky enough to move into the season of having children, you start to understand what it means to 'feel' tired. I would describe parenthood as a permanent state of exhaustion. It has many beautiful, amazing love-filled parts, but the brutality of sleep deprivation is simply awful. It makes you cherish ten minutes of lying down and the smallest of mistakes can send you into a crying state of despair. Even the most loving of couples will fight about whose turn it is to go to the crying baby. We did. It used to be the start of so many arguments when we were both so set on winning a few extra minutes hiding under the duvet for the sake of our salvation. It was hiding in a very different way from the tents we used to create together when we first fell in love.

George and I joked before we had children that lack of sleep would be our nemesis and we were SO right; it was the part of parenthood we struggled with the most. Neither of us coped well without sleep before we had children so having the boys was a complete baptism of fire. But when George first started complaining – and I mean really complaining - of being tired, I quite simply didn't want to hear him. I was tired. Life was one big feeling of tiredness.

When George told me he was tired, he was working full time and commuting every day from our new home in the Midlands to London. I knew he was just as exhausted as me but then I'd also given him the highly coveted, 'get out of jail free card,' of sleeping in the spare room. Our crying baby Jamie who was very much waking me, was not waking him. I didn't like going to sleep in a different bed and I desperately missed the safety of going to sleep in my husband's arms. It hurt my heart that this is what we had to do to survive in those days.

'It won't be forever,' Mum said to me as I told her between tears. Little did she know.

The tiredness that George felt wasn't something that he one day just woke up with. It crept into his spirit over months. This is how his body tricked us. It was so gradual that it went on for a long time relatively unnoticed. It got brushed off as the reality of having young children and I would sit and bite my tongue as he would tell me how he needed to rest ahead of yet another big meeting in London at work. This was although I'd maybe had the grand total of three hours sleep in shifts of approximately forty-five minutes. No makeup available was ever going to cover the dark circles under my eyes. It was tough and I mean really tough and it tested our relationship and our love for each other in new ways.

Eventually we managed to turn a corner and settle into a rhythm of rest. Jamie started to sleep a little better and we moved back into the same bed for a short while. But George still felt tired and that feeling of waking back up to the world after six months of caring for a new-born baby never came. He was cycling lots which was his passion. He was working hard in his job in marketing and commuting a long distance. The boys were healthy balls of energy twenty-four hours a day seven days a week. There were always just so many other reasons that he was exhausted. Being really sick wasn't something we ever thought about. We were young, fit and healthy. Other people got life-altering diseases. Not us.

Quietly simmering in the background, the other shit that hit the fan was George's toilet habits. In the world of being a parent alone time even on the toilet, was and still is highly prized! Having a moment to do what you *need* to do in private was as closely sought after in those early years as the delicious extra moments in our bed. Going for a poo took on a whole new sense of freedom for us both when we didn't have little people around. Whenever I got a moment to open my bowels on my own and have a moment to breathe, listening to the chaos loudly unfolding behind the door - the portal to real life, that was most definitely locked - it always felt like freedom! I remember even joking with other mum friends about how long your other half could spend on the toilet. How the much-coveted five minutes of peace we all so desperately wanted was found whilst doing our business on the bog. So I put the increased time George was spending on the toilet down to this. Down to his quest for freedom.

However much we tried to bury it we knew something wasn't quite right. I think he wanted to conceal it more than I did. All I do know is we didn't really talk about it. George cycled the coast to coast and it was only when the GP decided to take a blood test and the results came back slightly awry, that we began to pursue the idea that something bigger might be going on inside his body.

Months of tests then ensued; it seemed like we were looking for a needle in a haystack. It was only when George took matters into his own hands and opted for a private blood report that he was encouraged to take a colonoscopy. After discussing with the consultant some other symptoms he'd been experiencing – those that our GP had brushed off with the diagnosis of piles and a large tube of bottom cream– we decided that this was the best course of action. It would give us the green light that everything was OK.

Stupidly, courageously, or maybe even selfishly, we decided that George would have this procedure on his own in London. This would mean he could go and get the all-clear on his way back home from work. Life was so busy that even fitting in the time for health care wasn't prioritised in the way that it should have been. Work was just as important. Even more so in fact. At every opportunity all the health care professionals had also reassured us that at such a young age George was just doing his due diligence, ticking a box and making sure he was OK.

The moment that I will never be able to erase from my memory is the day I got the phone call no one wants. I'd taken a moment to start decorating our Christmas tree and was feeling optimistic and light-hearted about the festive season that lay ahead. I was quite literally rocking around the Christmas tree holding far too many fairy lights and not believing my luck when my phone started to vibrate. Jamie was gleefully bouncing in front of me. Life was good.

As soon as George started talking, I could tell there was something wrong. His tone was strained but calm all at the same time.

'What are you doing?' he asked.

'What do you mean,' I replied, confused by his question. 'How did it go? Are you alright?' There was panic in my voice now and then a long pause.

'I've got cancer,' was all he said.

And in that moment my world stopped. It felt unbearable to even stand up. Hearing someone you love say that they have cancer is a space-time continuum moment. The only other rite of passage I can liken it to is having babies and getting married. The reason I compare to these moments is not that you feel happy. It's because of that feeling of disbelief, being utterly overwhelmed, wondering if you're prepared and wanting to pinch yourself because you can't believe that this is happening, right here, right now, to you. You feel cloudy, blurry and so disjointed, that you have to pinch yourself to check that it isn't a dream. You feel everything and nothing. You feel like you're watching your own life in slow motion and in third-person. All I remember about this out-of-body moment is physically crumbling down on to the floor, gripping on to a box of baubles as I sobbed. The sobs were audible down the phone to him as Jamie looked on, still bouncing and wondering what was happening. My heart felt like it had been ripped out of my chest and I couldn't control it. My whole body shook with fear, hurt and hate. How could this be happening? Why was this happening to us? Did they not realise who George was? He was my husband. He was a dad. He couldn't get cancer! He was a real-life superhero. Then I managed to get a sentence together.

'How do you know? I asked, both wanting more information, but simultaneously wishing for the moment to end.

'Look Louise the guy who does these procedures knows his stuff. He looks up people's arseholes all day.' He waited to see if there was anything I would say back. I couldn't even find the words.

'Louise, are you still there? It's important that you hear me, that you know that he is certain. This guy knows what this kind of evil shit looks like. I've got cancer.'

Even in this moment of sheer pain and terror, he was still being ironic. Using the same comedic, accepting tone, that he'd use to talk about a problem at work, or reassure me after a hard day at home on my own with the kids. He was hurting too, but he was calm and thoughtful with his emotions and measured with his response. That's how he managed himself in moments of pressure. He just knew how to focus.

'I've called your parents, they're on their way over so you don't have to be on your own,'

I was quiet. Stunned into silence.

'It can't be cancer though,' I said 'it just can't. You're so fit and so well.' I was getting desperate now, I was in total disbelief. I've since learnt that plausible denial is the route lots of people take in times of trauma.

'But I'm really not.' he said, 'am I?'

We finished up the disjointed phone conversation with him telling me he was going to get on the next train home. I was also under strict instruction to call no one and do nothing until my parents arrived. He knew how emotional I could be.

As soon as I had managed to get up off the floor I went into shock. I was in control but out of control all at the same time. Whilst waiting for my parents to arrive I remember wanting to take charge of things that were within my sphere of influence. I cancelled a party I had planned with my friends. I even rang the online call centre for the grocery delivery that was due to arrive at our house. I was very clear that I no longer needed the cocktail sausages. I told the guy at the other end of the phone quite plainly, with no emotion whatsoever, that the cancellation was because I'd just found out my husband had cancer. There were no tears. I was just numb.

What happened next remains a bit of a blur. I remember everyone's instant reaction was to try to convince us it wouldn't be that bad. People wanted to tell us we'd most likely caught the cancer early and that maybe the massive tumour the specialist had just photographed in George's bottom wasn't evil at all. How could it be? How could someone so healthy get cancer? Optimism was how everyone we told, dealt with the bleakness of our news. But to me it felt suffocating, as I didn't have the strength left to feel anything but blackness. I pushed down the anger and hurt I felt when the news I was delivering to family and friends was met by shock and then hope. In that moment we couldn't allow ourselves to hope or think anything other than the worse – it had already been unofficially confirmed. The evil cells were there and we had to get our heads around them sooner rather than later, despite the rallying cries from those around us. We knew that if we allowed ourselves to believe anything otherwise we would be in for far more hurt and anguish.

After we had got our heads around the initial shock and made the necessary appointments, we had to figure out what to do next. Part of living with cancer is the shadow of doubt and uncertainty that it casts into every crevice of your life. In the initial aftermath, the minutes, hours and days felt like decades as we waited for more news and appointments to roll around and figure out what the hell we were supposed to do next. Cancer had taken away any certainty we'd previously focused on. It had stolen our plans for the future and our hope.

During that time when the world as we'd known it felt utterly unrecognisable and the hours and days that moved by felt like decades, I started to feel a profound appreciation for everyday beauty and joy. It wasn't a technique I'd ever read about but soon realised that looking at life in the way my children did was the only

30

way I actually felt like I could function. It was a technique I learnt very quickly that would become rooted in all of our survival.

I would find myself putting the kids to bed and whilst washing their feet with bubbles and tickling their toes, would consider the countless times I'd done this before and never really truly appreciated how happy we all were.

As I would look around the bathroom, I became aware that I'd missed so much of what had been happening around me up until this point and recognised that for the largest part of my life, I'd always been thinking ahead. Ironically worrying about what might be, rather than looking to the now and thinking about what was. Despite having only known the disease a very short while cancer had already shaken me awake. It showed me that I had never really lived my life in the moment before and almost immediately it made me appreciate everyday joy and moments with my children in a way I never had before.

In those first few days post-diagnosis, when I was desperate and completely lost, I'd look at my boys' faces, particularly whilst they were sitting in the bath and they would ground me unlike anything else. Their awe and wonder at life would give me hope. As I moved the bathwater around their bodies and stared into their innocent faces, I would feel angry that George's cells had been conducting invisible warfare inside his body.

'How could this awful disease be living with us and neither of us have a clue?' I'd wonder. 'How long had his cancer been there? Living our lives with us, lurking in the background, waiting to pounce.' These thoughts made me feel sick.

It was like a stranger had moved into our house, a stranger who had surreptitiously been stealing everything we owned as well as re-arranging and displacing the furniture of our future. Really, I had no other choice but to take pleasure from the every-day at this time. It was the only beautiful moment to focus on. I'd think things like:

'George has cancer, but I still can smell my kids' hair after a bath. George has cancer but I can still stand in my house and it is still my home. George has cancer but I can still eat my favourite food. I can still hold his hand. I can still tell him I love him.'

Post-diagnosis wasn't just an emotional roller-coaster, it was the ride of our lives. Every single part of our beings had been knocked into a different perspective. I felt sad as well as helpless. Overwhelmed as well as isolated. I jostled with the desire to fight versus the desire to run.

I wanted to be an inspiration. I also wanted to curl up into a ball and make life stop. I desperately wanted to go back to how life was before. I wished with every fibre of my being that it wasn't happening to us, that it wasn't my husband who had the tumour, that it wasn't my kids who would have to live out this chapter at such a formative time. It was all just so hideous. It was so exhausting and the early reality was I no longer knew what I wanted. Everything was so uncertain.

There's never a nice time to find out that the big C has turned up to the party of your life uninvited, but for us it landed on our doorstep just as the entire world wanted to proclaim their happiness. Christmas.

The distant memories of that text message and our first kiss, couldn't have felt further removed from the shock we now found ourselves in. The cancer diagnosis we'd just received also felt remarkably at odds with how everybody else was feeling. The pain and hurt were tangible for us and yet we couldn't go out of the house without being thrown in front of adverts bursting with family moments, romance, delicious food and versions of the most exquisitely wrapped presents; all of which we should have supposedly been buying for each other. That Christmas I felt at odds with the world's emotions in a way I never had before and everyone's delight and happiness at the upcoming festive season felt like the largest pieces of salt imaginable being rubbed into our gaping wounds.

Forty-eight hours after George's diagnosis I found myself in the shops, trying to distract myself from the words ricocheting in my mind from that phone call. As I fingered the clothes and looked at the endless gifts on display, everything felt so pointless.

As I waited in line at the tills, I looked at the floor and let the Christmas music wash over me. I didn't want to sing, or dance along. I didn't feel excited. I just felt the loss and hurt. As I got to the till it was as if I was in a foreign country and the entire environment felt so alien to how I felt inside. As I fumbled for my purse and looked at the floor I wondered what the assistant thought about me. The next thing I knew she was passing me my receipt and eagerly wishing me a, 'merry Christmas.' I looked back at her straight into the eyes. I wanted to scream, I wanted to shout,

I wanted to lie down on the floor and burst into hysterical tears. How was my life ever going to be 'merry' again after this?

'Merry,' was not going to cut it anymore. Life was utterly awful. It felt black. My universe felt utterly unrecognisable, as I stood surrounded by people who all looked happy. I pushed down the daggers starting to rise in the back of my throat and ran to my parked car outside. As I opened the door and sat in my seat, I felt like I could breathe again. I was safe as the hot tears rolled down my cheeks.

To all of those around me that day I looked happy. To them, I was simply a woman doing her shopping and I didn't have a sign on my neck that told the world my husband had just been diagnosed with cancer; although at times I did find myself wishing that I had one. As I sat in my car watching the world clamour for their Christmas presents and others hustle for parking spaces, I realised, that if I was going to cope, I had to see that perhaps everyone I had ever met and would meet in the future, had a story too.

In that moment, I wondered if this was the ultimate lesson in never assuming anything?

To the outside world I looked OK. I was dressed, I was put together. I had a huge amount of foundation concealing the hurt and tears I'd cried. But this façade was also disguising everything else. It didn't show the fear or the hurt or the loss I was feeling for the life that would no longer be mine. It didn't show the permanent sick feeling I had in the pit of my stomach, swirling with relentless concern and trepidation over how I was going to cope.

How I was going to care for a baby, a two-year-old and a sick husband. It didn't show the mental pain I was feeling deep inside. I had made none of this visible to the unassuming shop assistant when she'd wished me 'Merry Christmas'. I quite simply didn't know how.

That evening, after my first foray of stepping back out into the frenetic world I began to rationalise my emotion. As George attempted to distract himself with a football match on TV, I soaked in a hot bubble bath upstairs and wondered if I could really feel mad at a shop assistant who I didn't even know? How could she be expected to know about George's cancer if I hadn't told her and hadn't had the vulnerability to show what was really on my heart. I didn't like the rage that her simple festive greeting had made me feel and as I let the hot water comfort me, I knew that I wasn't really mad at her. I was mad at cancer.

As I lay flatter into the water with all of my body submerged the bubbles up to my nostrils and covered in soap, I started to recognise a familiar emotion bubbling up. I still felt angry. I still felt scared but I also knew this feeling well too, it was much better and was something I could do good with. I took a deep breath and turned over in the bath submerging my face under the water. I opened my eyes under there although knowing that this too felt alien. It was hope.

Yet I couldn't quite articulate or understand where I was getting it from, it seemed there was no natural explanation, but I'd figured out in that very moment that we all have a story. That at times we're all at the mercy of others' free will or the misconduct of our own bodies, regardless of whether we like it or not. As I turned my body over in the water and looked out of the bathroom window, I took comfort from this feeling of luck. It was much like the dark night outside; so unknown.

George's cancer was no one's fault. We obviously didn't want it to be there, we hadn't been acquainted with it that long and we already knew how much we loathed it. But I realised as I lay in the bath that I couldn't change that it had happened or make it go away in an instant.

What I could do though and what I knew we were both extremely good at, was formulating a come-back plan. In my mind's eye not living our lives because of this disease was simply not an option. It was up to us now, as to how we would show up, and we had to choose what type of attitude we would stick our fingers firmly up into the face of cancer with.

I let my toes stick out of the water and thought about our early days together in Edinburgh. I let the care-free images of us walking hand in hand, lying in bed until midday and discovering new depths to each other's characters dance in front of my eyes like an old movie. It hurt my throat. But back then our relationship had taught us to understand and respect love. What struck me as so odd now, as a mother to two young children and a wife to a husband with cancer, was that these emotions I was feeling were much the same, but the total opposite of those first feelings of togetherness.

Cancer was something neither of us could escape, it was just like our love. I recognised that the changes both cancer and love could cause, were unexpected, unprecedented and immeasurable. The difference was though, that cancer was bringing pain, not joy. I knew then that we had to choose. That we were going to have to make a choice as to how we mopped up this mess and it would be up to us to choose whether we responded with joy, anger or hurt.

I pulled the plug out of the bath and stood up, naked and vulnerable to reach for my towel. It was slowly starting to come together that we would have to be deliberate about how we would get George better. We had to show up with love.

As I wrapped the towel around myself, dried my body and looked at myself in the mirror - red-faced from the hot water mixed with tears - I realised, that this festive season wasn't going to be about Christmas pudding, or the gifts under the tree. We couldn't buy our way out of this disaster. More than ever it would be what was inside our hearts that would pull us through. I finished drying myself off, put my pyjamas on and went downstairs.

In the living room, George was laid on the sofa watching the football. He looked so well – weary maybe, but content. I went and sat next to him but we didn't hug. Since that dreaded phone call, we had both been struggling to understand what each other was thinking and also to articulate what we needed from each other. George's cancer had made us feel isolated in our relationship, even though it had only been a matter of days.

This was the first time in both of our lives that news had quite literally floored us, as well as driving a tangible divide between our hearts. As the adverts flashed up upon the screen, George sat up and looked at me.

'What do you think we should do?' I said.

We had already made all of the medical appointments we needed to make.

'We need to make a plan' he said, 'they've always loved telling us at work how much all of the best decision makers do that. We need to force ourselves to emotionally detach and look at what is happening pragmatically and logically.' George's gaze remained fixed on mine. 'Let's go to Reeth,' he said. 'I can always think more clearly there.'

The old saying goes that in moments of despair you fly, or you fight. It seemed now was that time for us to fly and before we could come back to the world and think about putting on our fighting faces, we had to run away. Reeth had always been a safe space for George. He had holidayed there from a young age and more recently his mum had left Oxfordshire and set up home with her partner in this peaceful village nestled in the north Yorkshire dales.

The next day on our way into hiding, George decided that we needed a project name. He wasn't going to have cancer. He didn't want the blackness that this word alone brought into our lives. Instead, he wanted to have a project that would be entirely focused on getting him better. This project would be how we would refer to the disease moving forward. Small as it seems this first step was a very deliberate move on George's behalf. As a marketing manager, he had read many books on positioning and unsurprisingly naming conventions always featured highly in terms of how an individual subconsciously responds. When he suggested doing this whilst speeding north in our car and listening to music that was pumping out of the stereo, I knew that the boy wearing the red tie was speaking to me once more.

He was back. He would show up in the way *he* wanted to, not in the way the word cancer forced him to. I smiled as I realised we'd both had the same idea. He just knew how to execute it better than I did.

We bounced project names off one another like some surreal sort of episode of 'The Apprentice.' The music was somehow drowning out the reality of what was happening in our lives and this felt like our first way of fighting back. It was cathartic to be driving fast in a direction we had chosen, with the music blaring and making a conscious choice around how George would be labelled. This was our life. We knew that it didn't belong to cancer and we wanted to make that clear to anyone who met us. It felt like the first delicious taste of freedom and hope. It was amazing.

After all of my name suggestions were shot down for being too cheesy or feminine, George smiled and sort of winked at me.

'I've got it,' he said, his eyes twinkling. 'What about Invictus?'

The name pierced my heart instantly. It was thunderous. I felt the power as soon as the word came off his lips. It gave me goose bumps. But for whatever reason I didn't show this to him, instead I laughed!

'Isn't that the name of an aftershave, or that sports event Prince Harry runs?' I said.

'Google it,' he replied.

The search results asked me if I wanted to buy an aftershave from Amazon, showed me pictures of the multi-sport event which had begun a few years earlier, but below that, I saw the Ernest Henley poem entitled Invictus.

'Wow,' I said, utterly mesmerized as I scanned over the words. 'Did you know that there was a poem about this? Have you seen it before? Did you read it at school or something?'

George didn't say anything; He didn't need to. In that moment his look told me he had no clue what I was talking about.

'I'm not sure how you know this,' I went on, 'but this poem is beautiful, it's amazing, it's unbelievably apt! Let me read you the words,' I said, almost falling over myself with excitement. 'I think what we're going through is utterly *Invictus*! I don't know how you knew it but somehow you did!'

I commanded my best reading voice and as the car continued to hum and the boys slept, beautifully unaware of the chaos unfolding around them, I read the poem aloud for the first time.

INVICTUS

"Out of the night that covers me,
Black as the pit from pole to pole,
I thank whatever gods may be
For my unconquerable soul.

In the fell clutch of circumstance
I have not winced nor cried aloud.
Under the bludgeoning of chance
My head is bloody, but unbowed.

Beyond this place of wrath and tears
Looms but the Horror of the shade,
And yet the menace of the years
Finds and shall find me unafraid.

It matters not how strait the gate,
How charged with punishments the scroll,
I am the master of my fate,
I am the captain of my soul."

ERNEST HENLEY.

When I finished reading the silence in the car was palpable.

'That's it,' he said. 'That's the project name. I don't have cancer now. We have a life project. This is project Invictus.'

'Do you feel it?' I asked filled with hope. 'Do you feel that feeling in your heart?'

'Yes,' he said with a firmness that was unflinching. 'I can really feel it.'

I turned the music back up and looked again at Google. Search engines can be the biggest nemesis when you're diagnosed with a life altering illness – there's just so much information about all the bad things that can happen. We had deliberately been on an internet search ban to protect ourselves, but I couldn't help but want to know more about this poem and its author. I typed ferociously into my phone and discovered through Wikipedia that Henley had written this whilst facing the cancer of his time - tuberculosis.

The more I understood about this man, the more I felt like someone understood how we were feeling. The combination of courage and steadfastness inspired us to know that if this guy, all those years ago, had felt and known what we were feeling today, then so too had so many others. The poem made us realise we weren't as alone and isolated in our emotions as we thought. Invictus gave us hope. It was more than just a project name. It would be our mantra for the days, weeks and months to come. It would be the words we lived by and when things got really, really tough, it would be the scripture that would see us through.

As I look back, I reflect that it's so interesting seeing how you can know but not know all at the same time. How could George have known about this poem? How could he have known that it would speak to both our souls in a way that we couldn't articulate? Surely that couldn't all be from an aftershave advert, or having seen Prince Harry's Invictus games? Later that evening we high fived his thought process as we sat around his mum's kitchen table, filled with a variety of cakes just as it had been in those early days and excitedly told her about our re-brand. It was all ours for the making, we never plausibly thought it was possible that words could be given to you from a more distant and supernatural source that at this point was not even on our radars.

With a project name in place and in the safe confines of George's mum's hospitality, we felt ready to look at the next part of the plan. After a good night's sleep and even better breakfast, we set up our new office on the kitchen table and waved the boys off with their Granny to a day of playing in the snow. We needed to establish who George should appoint as his doctor and what help we both needed to survive.

Ever the pragmatists and focused on the end goal of getting the 'all clear,' we sat in front of our laptops and began sending emails. We were determined to contact anyone we knew who might be able to offer us help and insight into what he needed to do in order to survive. People we knew who had experienced the walk of cancer.

As ever it was George who had the top trumps of connections. Through his work he was lucky to be connected to a very commercially successful, straight-talking and astute soul; he had fondly nicknamed this guy the Bertster.

The nickname was very George. After a short spell at the chocolate factory, George had gone on to join a food company in order to follow his gastronomical dreams. When the job came up at this organisation and George was successful at the interview, we both knew that he had to take it.

Fast forward a few years later and as he had grown in position and stature at the firm, so too had the brand. The Bertster, was brought in as the eyes and ears, to steer the board of directors in a season of unprecedented growth. He was well-known as a heavy hitter in the industry we worked in and both of us were massively excited when we realised George was going to have the opportunity to work with him on the board.

As their relationship developed, George also discovered that this business extraordinaire had the personal experience of helping care for someone with cancer. This man it seemed, knew something about the path we would be walking.

So on that day from the confines of his mum's delicious-smelling home in the country, a time when we still had no clue as to what the future would hold, George got in touch. I wasn't there for the call; I was made to go and stand in the adjoining room so as not to distract him. I don't think he ever called him Bertster to his face either. It wasn't a nickname George openly broadcasted beyond his close friends, even he wasn't brave enough for that.

On the phone that day Bertster's advice was clear, concise and unbelievably useful. It's something that I still always talk to people about when they're in the early stages of living with a cancer diagnosis. 'Big B's three-point plan,' as George called it, was something we quoted to each throughout his treatment.

What George learnt that day became our mantra just as much as the Invictus poem. At the time we felt incredibly *lucky* that the connections we had meant that we could open up conversations with someone as insightful as him. Looking back, I now *know* that we were supposed to be connected. This is because his advice was the first part of our salvation, I know without a shadow of doubt that he was positioned into our lives to speak wisdom over George's soul. It was meant to be.

All too regularly personal interactions and the conversations that fall out of these relationships are linked to the person's wisdom, experience or your own luck for knowing them. This perspective is very true if you don't view your network as connections you're *supposed* to have. That you don't see your community as having been *given*. I'm not saying that the universe makes you have your friends. I'm saying that they are *positioned* for you to make. It is then your choice if you want to pursue the relationship or not. Being in the right or wrong place, at the right or wrong time is something I hear quoted so often. What I've learnt and have had a huge amount of time to reflect on since this day, tucked away in the cosy snug and hum of a country kitchen, is that maybe our connections are far more deliberate than any of us really know. They have to be, when I think how useful this advice would be for our future.

So back to the Bertster and his pearls of wisdom. Gem number one was that we should put care in place for the carers. The primary carer for the cancer patient is so often so easily overlooked. All of the focus is always on the patient, quite rightly so, they should always be the number one priority because cancer treatment creates more warfare and pain on the body than initially the disease maybe does itself.

But I know first-hand that for the person who is living with the patient, caring for their physical and emotional needs, as well as keeping 'life' on the road for the family, a cancer diagnosis rocks their world in a very, very different way. When George told me later that day what the Bertster had said I felt like I could actually breathe. It felt so good to be noticed, that the weight on my chest which had been there for days, finally lifted.

A few days later when we got home from Yorkshire and decided to put plans in place to support me in looking after the children with a nanny, it helped more than I could have believed was possible. It was so obvious, but not obvious in terms of advice, and helped protect George too. This was because I was able to be present for him and give him the support he needed, without crippling my well-being.

The second piece of magical advice was to put psychological support in place for the patient. The cancer bomb had made us both so preoccupied with George's body and all the minutiae of his cells that we would spend hours willing the cancer to be chopped out, imagining the rogue bastards being flooded with toxic chemicals or being burnt with radiation to annihilate their growth track.

In the midst of this internal, imaginary warfare, despite the fact that we could both permanently feel it, it was very easy to overlook the management of the most important faculty under attack, our minds.

A permanent preoccupation with the body leads to a hard-wire change in thought patterns which for us were inescapable. Death loomed in a way that it never had before however much we tried to deny it, or desperately chose our mindsets over it. The shift was universal and we rapidly discovered that getting help with this change was imperative.

The Bertster told us that getting George a good psychologist was as important as getting the right treatment. Dutifully, around five days after this conversation, George employed a psychologist. He also had a kinesiologist, a specialist who worked with him on every aspect of his health and he worked with both of these professionals extensively on positive mental mind-set.

The work was hypnotic and allowed George to market his own cancer fight, not only to himself but also to those around him. For him, there was only ever one line of conversation. That was survival. There were no ifs. No buts. Only ever certainty that he would make it.

Fast forward a week or so after our car journey up north and we were parked on our driveway at home ready to depart for another day at the hospital. We sat in the car looking forward in the quiet, neither of us actually wanting to set off. George hadn't even got as far as switching on the ignition yet somehow we both needed to take a moment to breathe energy and power into our spirits in the peace of the car. We knew that if we did it might equip us to better deal with yet another day of poking, prodding and unending ambiguous news that lay ahead. It was in this moment that I heard for the first time the real truth behind his diagnosis. His bright blue eyes couldn't look into mine and he was deliberately positioned so I couldn't hold his hand. I knew when there was something big he had to say, it was always remarkably obvious.

'You know the other night, when you popped out of the appointment to take the call about the kids?' he asked.

47

I sat up in my chair then, I knew there was something else coming.

'Well, I finally asked about what the stats were. I finally got them to tell me. I needed to know. I needed to hear them.' He breathed in as he released the words, like a guilty secret he'd been holding. He was referring to the statistical chance of him being cured or surviving. Our Google ban meant that we deliberately hadn't looked at these numbers ourselves. We'd made a pact not to as the advice we had overwhelmingly been given was that this was dangerous. It would protect our mental well-being they said because George was more than just a number.

'Why did you do that?' I asked, my insides feeling like they were in a food mixer. 'I thought we'd decided to not find out.'

I could see him looking at me but not looking at me. I could also see the determination written all over his face.

'We know that these numbers don't really carry a lot of meaning, on a case by case basis. They're sort of meaningless,' I went on, but he was still looking forward. I knew that there was more to come.

'Are you mad with me?' he asked, his eyes were now fixed on mine and looking into me in a way that only he could.

'No,' I said, I genuinely wasn't, 'but you do know that you're now going to have to tell me what they said? You can't keep it a secret?'

He rubbed his hands on his blue jeans to smooth out the creases. They were the same jeans that he'd worn for years and were part of his persona as much as his smile and the sparkle in his eyes.

'I've got a seven per cent chance,' he blurted. 'I've got a 'seven percent chance of living another five years.'

Sometimes you can't help your bodily response. My reaction in that moment was that I felt physically ill. My stomach started flipping, my palms became sweaty and the familiar ball of hurt reared an ugly head in the back of my throat. I couldn't control it. He saw it. He saw the look of physical hurt on my face before I could even open my mouth and answer back. That's when he moved forward in his chair. He grabbed me by the hand and jolted me back to life. He was looking at me directly in the eyes now, just as he had when he told me he was going to marry me all those years ago. He was holding both of my hands firmly in his, wrapping his fingers over mine protectively. Stoically and completely authentically he said;

'But it's not really as bad as it sounds,'

I was struggling to compute how this was the case at this point. How was this not bad?!

'If I was in a room with one hundred other people,' he went on, sitting bolt upright and speaking with absolute authority, 'and you had to pick seven to survive. Who would you pick? Go on, who would you pick?!' .

I couldn't reply. I was stunned.

'You'd pick me' he said. 'I know you would. Just as much as I know that I would be in those seven. I feel it in my heart. I know it. Talking about not surviving this disease is ludicrous. Do you think an Olympic medal winner goes into the games thinking he might not win? Do you think he actually believes that the best-case scenario is that he'll get Bronze? No. The gold medal winner goes to the games knowing he has the capability to win. This isn't something he just says. He knows it. He feels it. His body is capable of it. Getting the all clear is my Gold medal. I will do this. I can get better.'

As I sat there doing my goldfish mouth all over again, I was in awe of him. I remember him quite pointedly putting the address of the hospital into the satnav and accelerating off the drive with a deliberate force. I was never scared or unnerved by George but I also knew when not to mess with him. Now was most definitely not the time for back-chat. If mindset alone could cure cancer he would have annihilated his disease there and then.

That very day in the hospital would be when we needed the third and final piece of the Bertster's prized advice more than ever before. He had told us to work with the medical team as if they were our teammates, our equals. We were also told to never assume anything, to always ask questions and remind ourselves that the medics, however educated and knowledgeable they were, were still only just as human as us both. Like all teams we had found ourselves in at various points in our lives, George's medical team still wanted to be known on an individual basis. They needed motivation, inspiration and a reason to go over and above to help us. Ultimately we knew it was up to us to make a lasting impression and be someone that they thought about even when we weren't there.

One of the first rules we had learnt about selling all those years ago when George had outrageously charmed his way through training, was that people buy people. We learned that personal relationships were so central to how much gets done in life. Most of us already know this, I know for instance, that if I like someone and feel a connection to them, then I'm more likely to help and care for them.

Now I'm not saying that we ever got preferential treatment, or that we got bumped to the front of queues in waiting rooms. But what we did do was make an effort to build human relationships with the entire village of trained professionals that cared for George.

It wasn't easy to start this off but we both set our minds to it. If I'm honest, it was extremely hard work and sometimes we were known for all of the wrong reasons. This is what lay ahead of us on the day we sped off, with George focused like a laser on winning gold.

The appointment that would happen that day was another moment in time that will stay with me forever, for all the wrong reasons. It was the moment we would find out that George's primary tumour wasn't just bad, but really bad. So bad in fact that it was utterly inoperable until the hospital had pumped his body full of the highest dose chemo in the hope it might shrink. I'm only as human as the next person and even though I desired to win others over and separate my emotion from the task in hand, just as George and I had agreed, sometimes feelings get the better of me. In these moments there's nothing I can do, other than just roll with it.

We all know that at times when you're often actively trying, the behaviour you want doesn't come as easy as you may have hoped. What I've come to realise since then is that maybe the reason why you can't behave in the way you've planned is because you're supposed to experience the fall-out of that emotion. We often don't see the good stuff when it happens in the most awful of moments. Maybe that's just how it's supposed to be, or maybe we're just too focussed on our own ego? Either way, I didn't see the good forces around me that day. I was too wrapped up in fear.

On this day when we found out that George's cancer couldn't be chopped out, I was already exhausted. The boys weren't sleeping and they didn't know what was going on because we still hadn't found the words to tell them. What they did know was that they were unsettled by the sadness surrounding our hearts and the unplanned periods of absence they'd been forced to have from us both. I wasn't sleeping all that much either because I'd just found out my cheerleader in life only had a seven percent chance of being with me for another five years. All I could feel and see was blackness and hurt. Naively we walked into our appointment hoping to find out about an operation. We walked out of there broken and were told, in the same way a mechanic tells a driver about the need for new brake pads, that the standard route of treating bowel cancer wasn't applicable in George's case. He was in the category of the worst of the worse-case scenarios.

That evening we were talking to a surgeon. These types of doctors are amazing at chopping people open and fixing them, but not always as amazing at the gentle chatting part. It takes an awful lot of skill to go from being amazingly dexterous, wielding scalpels inside the human body, to then telling someone that they're most likely going to die sooner than they have ever anticipated. I'm not sure if any level of training ever equips anyone for that. There's no way of wrapping it up nicely.

The moment we were told surgery wasn't possible was a standout one because I couldn't control my emotions or follow the advice the Bertster had given us. At that moment the world seemed to stop all over again, just as it had every time we'd heard bad news since the diagnosis. I looked at the awful 80's print curtains surrounding the window in front of me and willed myself not to scream or shout at the poor surgeon sat in front of us. I was so angry, it was just like the episode with the shop assistant all over again. I was mad that he could tell us something so life-altering, with no apparent glint of emotion or empathy for our circumstances, and it hurt my heart in a way that I'd never before experienced.

Before I'd even had a moment to process the magnitude of the news, the surgeon was wrapping up the meeting and asking George to go and get his bloods taken. I took my gaze from the garish curtains and looked at this man straight in the eye. Between gritted teeth, with tears silently rolling down my cheeks, I simply said,

'Are you actually joking?'

My bottom lip was most definitely wobbling and my fists were clenched by my sides. Going to get blood taken now, in a moment where I couldn't even get off the chair for hurt and upset was the last activity I wanted my husband to undertake. I wasn't playing to the three-point plan on any level. All the grace and manners my parents had worked hard to instil into me over the years evaporated in that very instant.

George looked at me in absolute disbelief. I remember the surgeon going to get the paperwork and breaking with convention and taking George's blood in the consultation room.

At some point amid this emotion fuelled moment, I was asked to step outside.

Standing in the hallway whilst crying my eyes out, I made my way over to the receptionist who was sitting behind the desk. She handed me a tissue.

'Are you OK love?' was all she said as I burst into tears with an uncontrollable response.

I didn't realise it at the time but what I now find so interesting is that her being there was such a gift that evening. I was meant to meet her by her reception desk when I was in an emotionally vulnerable place. I cried hysterically in a way I hadn't with anyone else. I told her that my husband was most likely dying. I told her I had two babies at home and I wasn't sure how I was supposed to cope. I told her how much I loved him. I said everything I was so desperately trying to keep contained. She hugged me, she passed me more tissues and then said something that will stay with me forever as she looked at me with a mix of compassion and fire.

'The team here are the best you could ever meet, you know, if I had your husband's diagnosis, I would want to be treated by the team in this hospital. They're amazing. They're brilliant. They're some of the best people you could hope to meet. Treat them like your family. That's what they will become. You're going to need them, and they will help you, even if it doesn't always feel like what they're telling you is help.'

I was stunned into silence by her kindness and amazed that she had spoken such truth into my heart. In that moment I had walked away from our three-point plan but it was as if she'd been sent there to remind me of what I was supposed to be doing. I notice more and more now, that often it's the strangest of people, in the most bizarre situations, who deliver messages of truth to your heart; even if they themselves don't realise that this is what they do.

As I wiped away my tears George came back along the hospital corridor. It felt so at odds to watch the man I loved walking back towards me in this environment. He looked the same as he'd always looked; his bright green garish coat was at odds with the hospital corridor we found ourselves in and his confident stride didn't make me feel hopeful in the way it usually did. All I could see was the cancer bombshell surrounding him like an orb. Looking at him as he walked towards me with his whole persona bloodied made me feel frightened in a way I hadn't ever felt previously.

He looked up and smiled and reached out his hand to mine. He nodded and smiled at the receptionist who squeezed my hand as a goodbye. We walked hand in hand back to the car park in the winter darkness. He started the engine and started to drive us home. No words were spoken until we were winding on the country lanes back to our house.

'What did she say,' he asked.

I looked at him puzzled trying to hold back the tears; I knew he was talking about the receptionist.

'Oh, not much,' I responded. I didn't know how to tell him that I'd just poured my heart out to a complete stranger, told her all of my fear and confided the truth that was shadowing my heart.

'She seemed nice,' he said.

'Yeah she was,' I replied as I looked off out into the dark night, wanting to close down his conversation.

'I will beat this you know,' he said reaching out to grip my hand.

I didn't reply and simply just held his hand back, quietly looking out of the window with tears softly streaming down my face. He turned the radio up and we sat in silence until we got home and fell into bed exhausted and broken. As I tried to fall asleep that night I thought about how kind the receptionist had been; she genuinely seemed to care for my well-being. In all of our many hospital visits that ensued I always expectantly looked for her, hoping to see her warm smile again. But sadly it would be another few months before our paths would cross again. Her soul had most definitely made an imprint on mine that evening and I wondered what she thought about me as I drifted off.

It's Terminal

The next morning as I woke up and tried to process the news we had been told the night before, it hit my thoughts like a steam train. It wasn't cancer I was scared of. It was death. As humans, we know a fair amount about death and cancer but still so little. They are both an enigma for very different reasons. It's in our nature to find justification and reasoning behind tragedy, all of us to lesser or larger scales are looking for it and are often subconsciously seeking life and living as the solution. It's all we know as humans to look to life as hope, it's kind of how we're wired.

I realised quite early into project Invictus that we had to keep hoping there was more life to be lived if we wanted to find a way to keep going. Life also equalled hope in my mind back then and the only way I could function on a daily basis, was by looking each day in the eye as it unfolded and telling myself that I could survive. Before cancer, we were so addicted to knowing our next destination and wanting to understand where we were headed that this new-found way of viewing the world was alien. Previously hope had always looked like a better job, a bigger house or another holiday. There was just so much consumerism in our life that we disregarded where our actual life was happening. The moment George was diagnosed all of those ways of thinking went out of the window. Our hope became centred on two new things. Daily life and a cure for cancer. That's what I had to focus my mind on the next morning when I started about my day.

I knew I was not the kind of person who ever just accepted the status quo – I always liked to think that I had the skills within me to course correct – that had been indoctrinated into me in the corporate environment I lived and breathed during my twenties. In the beginning, this is how we both approached our Invictus project and all the appointments that came with it. We decided to learn and to challenge and that was exactly how I'd approached the dreadful appointment that had come crashing down around me the night before. Our conversations were always about what we could do to beat George's disease, rather than what we could do to be accepting of it. After all, no human is ever accepting of death, right? We had been educated along with the rest of the western world to defy age at every turn; wrinkles and grey hair for us were both signs of something we had learned to actively avoid and evade. Cancer it seemed was much the same and we didn't want to accept it might be here to stay.

Somehow I survived the fallout after that dreadful night with the surgeon and just a few days later we found ourselves back in the hospital as we sat in yet another appointment, with another doctor. We asked the same question we had already asked multiple times before, despite knowing that the prognosis was bad.

'What could George do to give himself the best possible chance of surviving?'

This was because our intent was grounded in some amazing logic but we had failed to recognise you need to accept the cards you have been dealt, however awful they are.

At this point we were not in the space of acceptance. That hideous evening with the receptionist had shown me that I was not at all OK with what was happening; all that we wanted was to find solutions as we thought they would bring us hope.

That day, this doctor's particular response to our question was a standout one. It was so far removed from what we had already been told that it made me sit up in my chair and really listen. This particular consultant was someone that we saw fairly frequently and were also beginning to get to know a little better.

She was quirky, she liked our jokes and talked to us both as human beings, not just to George as a cancer patient and me as his suffering wife.

As she sat there that evening, deeply meditating on the question we had asked her and leaning back in her office chair, you could visibly see the reflection washing over her. She closed her eyes, removed her glasses and put her fingers on her forehead, almost as if she was massaging out the thoughts inside. After a few seconds, she began to clean her glasses and then sat upright. She looked different without her spectacles and it seemed almost deliberate that they had been removed. It was as if she wanted to show us another side of her personality;

'This isn't really medical advice,' she said, 'it's more soul advice. But something tells me that the two of you are maybe open to hearing what I have to say.' She paused.

George and I looked at each other and then back at her.

'If I could tell you one thing, give you one piece of advice to truly live by, it would be to accept the circumstances you find yourself in,' my mind raced as I tried to hear her words.

'Find a way to peacefully manage them into your life. Don't be aggressive in how you cope with them.' The doctor breathed and I breathed with her as she looked into our souls for a response.

Interestingly her thoughts didn't jar our mindset and we weren't angry with what she had said. This was because she was completely correct in her estimation that we were both open to new ideas; it was always how George and I looked at situations.

She also most definitely sensed that we were both already completely exhausted by our project to get better, despite the fact, it had barely even begun. Acceptance wasn't something we'd even ever thought about at this point. Neither of us really had any idea about *how* we could find it, the wiring in our brains just didn't know how back then.

If acceptance could bring peace though, I wanted a slice of it. But I knew of no process to get from A to B, in terms of finding acceptance in something as big as: 'Your husband has cancer, a type of cancer so bad that his days on earth are potentially numbered and the only way out of this is to trust and accept your fate.'

Acceptance just wasn't something we did. We knew how to laugh, how to be positive, how to make a plan. We would only ever accept things if they were on our terms.

Acceptance of cancer felt like a defeat, it felt like we were acknowledging that death had won and that was something neither of us wanted. The conversation continued.

'What do you mean?' I asked not really understanding what she was telling us.

'Well,' she said, 'there was this woman, a number of years ago, who did just that. But I really shouldn't be telling you about this.' Her voice sort of faded as she looked out of the window.

It was George who said,

'Please. Go on.'

She quietly nodded and replaced her glasses on to her nose, 'Well, there was this woman in America. I actually spoke with her doctor over the phone. I know that her diagnosis was genuine, I know that the disease she had was severe. She had been graded as incurable and given weeks, maybe even days to live. I don't know all of the details, but I do know she trusted and accepted.'

I abruptly interrupted her flow.

'How did she do this?' I was sitting on the edge of my seat willing her to be more precise. She looked at us thoughtfully and simply continued.

'Through her acceptance of what would be, through her trust in the bigger picture, she was cured. Her cancer disappeared. No one could explain it. I've spoken at length with her doctor over the phone. He doesn't know what happened, it was an extraordinary case and the only plausible explanation was her acceptance. Her faith in something bigger. I've never met this lady in person, but her case deeply intrigues me. I believe that maybe her remarkable cure was linked to her acceptance.'

I was stunned.

'Well, how do we get that. I mean where do you even start with that!?'

My question shattered the peaceful atmosphere in the room. At the time I couldn't bring myself to believe in something as remarkable as real-life miracles. I believed that what this doctor was telling us was true, she had come to us highly recommended by the Bertster as an expert in her field. But if miracles were real how did I get one and why didn't the whole world know about them. Why weren't they more widely documented and shared and why was I only hearing about them now George had cancer?

I don't remember how the appointment wrapped up, it was probably fairly awkwardly given the conversations we'd had, but I do remember it was the first time I left a doctor's meeting room not feeling like another piece of my heart had been ripped from my chest. It was the same feeling the Invictus poem had given me. It was hope.

But yet, although we both heard this remarkable story and I had heard for the first time that others had managed to find acceptance in these horrendous circumstances, I still couldn't believe that this level of mystical, supernatural belief could ever be real. It all just seemed so intangible and beyond my logical reach.

Even though *I loved* the sound of what acceptance, faith and trust could offer, the very concept of it was just too difficult to grasp let alone buy into or actively participate in. I just didn't get it. George didn't either. He brushed these comments aside just as much as I did.

This story of the miracle was, therefore, something we were told and yet, even though it deeply impacted my thinking, we did nothing about. My human instinct was to help George get better but I really didn't believe that spirituality was something that could actually save him. We definitely weren't as ready for miracles as the doctor had maybe thought, so instead we looked at our situation scientifically as that was what we knew.

We decided to throw out carcinogenic foods, we began to filter our water and cut down on the consumption of red meat and sugar. We did anything that had a plausible proven link to helping George get better. If it made pragmatic sense to us, then we attempted to activate it in our life. It was George though who ultimately made the decisions about what he would and would not put into his body; he never put that decision-making on me. From the outset he said that he wanted to go for the medical approach,

'I'm no Steve Jobs,' he would say. 'I like to be a little bit hippy every now and again, but I don't truly believe I have the power within me to heal this bastard. I need science! I need all the drugs they're prepared to pump into my veins. I'll take all the drugs I have to. I'm ready!'

So with George firmly in the driving seat, it was decided that we would do his treatment the full-throttle medical way. We believed this was the only route capable of saving him.

The way he directed himself into his treatment programme was with the same force he'd driven the car off the drive on that statistic pep talk day. The era of 'George's marvellous medicine' is what came next as we knew there were only two sure-fire ways to kill cancer – cut it out or, 'nuke the bastards;' the latter being a George Blyth original one-liner mimicking some Armageddon-esque alien invasion style film, that by proxy was so bad it was good.

George was prescribed a large dose of chemo to shrink his primary tumour and liver Mets; (cancer club lingo for secondary tumours.) His dose was twelve rounds. We were told it was pretty much like putting bleach into his veins. But we wanted that bleach, it was something we wanted SO badly that by the time the chemo came around we were ready to fight back. The moment that first drop of medicine hit George's blood system and brought him out in a hideous allergic reaction, we breathed a sigh of relief. We felt like we were finally doing something. Despite the fact that the drugs made George feel disgusting it felt brilliant that we were finally killing them off.

That first round of chemo was our way of finally getting back at the cells that had ruined our lives from the inside out. We sat next to each other all day knowing that our boys were safe with their grandparents, clutching on for dear life and watching short films from a group of our friends that they had recorded to encourage us.

Chemotherapy was and is every part as awful as you think. And while I was never intravenously attached to the magic medicine, I had one of the best seats in the house. What I quickly realised was that every part of the cancer journey was full of such dread, but paradoxically such bleak joy at the same time. The fragility of life made the everyday a wonderful gift and opportunity to live, even if it meant living all day whilst having a twelve-hour chemo infusion. The amount of time spent receiving the marvellous medicine also meant that by proxy, the nursing team became more than just medical staff. Our chemo ward was a place full of desperately ill people, but the human spirit that resided there was enough to stir a passion in the darkest of depths of our hearts on the saddest of days. There was humour, there were bald jokes, there were the knowing glances of support and love from total strangers. And there was kindness. SO much kindness. At the time, I thought that more people should hang out on chemo wards because if you can get over your personal fear of death, they're full of people who truly appreciate every last drop of life. People who appreciate the small stuff. People who know that this is a battle of love, not hate.

For me, the scariest part of walking into the chemo ward that day was feeling sorry for all of the people with no hair – particularly the women. Looking back, this was because I was still struggling to make peace with what was happening. The bald head and waif-like figure combo have become part of what we think of as the cancer 'look'. It's somewhat prisoner of war-esque, because it's what you think death looks like. What I've come to realise is that what people look like bears no resemblance to how healthy, or how close to death they may or may not be. Cancer is an inside out battle – just because people look well on the outside doesn't mean they are well on the inside. My stint on cancer wards has taught me that it's often the people that look the most well that have the least time left to live.

I also quickly learnt that living with cancer is synonymous to living with the bereavement of your old life. Just because you look OK on the outside, it does not mean that you are OK on any level whatsoever inside. So the next time you want to tell someone who is sick that they look well, don't. Tell them they look beautiful, tell them they look strong, tell them you can see their courage in their hairstyle and clothing. Don't tell them they look well. No one who is sick in the mind or body wants to hear that. It's like being told that someone ate your last Rolo, because you know you can't get it back and being well might not actually ever be possible again.

It was our boys who made us look into the eyes of chemotherapy with such courage and normality. It took a few weeks for us to tell them that George had cancer; not because we didn't believe it, but because we simply didn't know what their little brains would understand and compute around the news that we had been given. After all, Charlie was still only two and Jamie just eight months old. On the day George was hooked into his marvellous medicine we knew it was time to break this silence, largely because the hospital had informed us that one of the treatments he would be given would be inside a pump that would then be taken home for forty-eight hours. The contraption looked a little like a sports bottle and had a clear tube that ran up to the port he'd had fitted just a few days earlier. It was a very outward projection of the disease brewing inside him and there was no way of us not communicating this to our children.

We had decided to tell them about the cancer together with the pump as our hard evidence. Somehow this seemed like a visible indication of the disease that's so difficult for adults to comprehend, let alone children. They were running around in their pyjamas, dutifully and beautifully prepared for bedtime by Mum. Charlie saw the navy-blue case that protected the pump first, 'What's that Daddy?' was all he asked.

George looked at me and I stepped forward, we hadn't rehearsed what we were going to say, but we'd read about what we should and shouldn't say online, in this instance Google had been very helpful.

'Daddy is very, very, very poorly in his bottom,' I said breathing in the hurt. 'He's got something called cancer. Cancer is when your body tries to break itself.'

Charlie looked at me, then at George and laughed. It was not at all what we were expecting or how we were feeling,

'Silly cancer,' was all he said.

I looked to George, unsure as to what to say or do next, he spoke up.

'You see this bottle,' he continued, clearly showing the pump to our totally bemused two-year-old, 'it's got medicine in it.

Medicine that will help me get better and it's connected into my body.'

Charlie looked mesmerised, taking in the tube that travelled from the bottle hooked on to George's belt at his hip and up to his chest. He fingered it delicately, I didn't even need to tell him to touch gently, he just knew. He turned around with his chubby face glowing and simply said,

'Pol?' We couldn't help but laugh.

We knew exactly what he was asking, he was wondering if the chemo was Calpol, his only real experience of medicine at this stage in his life. George and I looked at each other,

'No,' I said firmly even though I wanted to laugh with him. 'Daddy needs medicine that is much stronger than Calpol to get better. This will help him,'

I breathed in the hurt but somehow Charlie knew how to respond better than anyone else had up until this point. He looked up at George, back to me and threw his arms out towards George,

'Poor Daddy,' was all he said.

It was the most simplistic response we had received from anyone on the cancer journey so far. As he hugged us both with Jamie laid out on the floor cosily kicking and cooing in his baby grow for the night, I knew I had to adopt Charlie's attitude to this medicine. What would it be like if I just thought of the medicine as Calpol too? Would it make this disease more palatable to digest?

Another fourteen days later, back at the hospital and plugged into the machines once more one of our favourite chemo nurses, Rachel, told us to look out for the gifts that cancer would give us.

It made me think of Charlie just a few days earlier, padding around in his pyjamas thinking chemo was Calpol and I knew right then that this was one of the most paradoxically perfect pieces of advice that we would receive. Cancer made us see our life so differently and because it was so brutal, it made us appreciate everything in life so much more. In some respects, it forced us to see the world in the way our boys did.

We appreciated George not feeling nauseous. We appreciated being able to sleep. We appreciated being able to hug our kids and do the small stuff, like pick them up from nursery school and sit and read with them. Cancer made the small stuff become big stuff. It completely made us re-evaluate every part of our life as well as realise what was really important. After living in this new world for some time, we soon realised that it was love and hope that powered us through, not our car, our holiday plans, or the latest gadget I may or may not have bought online. Love really was all we needed.

Seven out of twelve rounds into treatment our Invictus team were feeling overwhelmingly positive. Scans showed that both the primary and secondary tumours had shrunk considerably; we were on to a winner. The team wanted to move George into radiotherapy – I'm pretty sure that he's maybe the only cancer patient ever that asked for his full twelve doses of chemo. I'll never forget him sitting in the doctor's room wearing his shorts and flip-flops despite the fact that the daffodils were only just about re-emerging after winter and rather outlandishly saying,

'Please can I have some more?'

Everyone laughed. The medical team adored the courage and fun he brought. All of our laughter that day felt like we were finally headed in the right direction, towards being victorious over life.

We bounced from the world of chemo into four weeks of radiation treatment. Our Invictus routine got mixed up. We weren't in the hospital every eleven days, but every weekday instead. The radiotherapy nurses were a different crew, another group to win over and get to know. This change threw us both off our course temporarily but we soon adapted. We made the treatment routines work, we came to know the drill and were prepared for symptoms almost by the hour. We knew when our boys could be tickled by Daddy and laugh in the way that only he could make them. The strange painful rhythm of all of this disgusting medicine weirdly gifted us peace. It also gifted us reassurance that we were doing something helpful. In our minds, because George could feel the side effects so brutally we convinced ourselves it must be doing some good inside. We were certain it was wiping out the cells that were trying to screw with our lives.

Once out of radiotherapy we were into a season of watch and wait. This was our opportunity to get our lives back. We both returned to work, we spent time with friends, we went away on a romantic weekend together. We did all the stuff that we should have been doing. It felt wonderful. We were living again and were not having our lives dictated by sickness. In many ways it felt like energy was slowly returning to our souls. A couple of months later George was told that it was time for the first of what we hoped would be two major surgeries. Stage one was to chop out the rogue cells from his liver. If that went well, stage two would be to chop them out from his bottom. George managed to fit a sneaky one-hundred mile bike ride in around London and raise £20,000 for charity. We then confidently walked back into the hospital for the next step of our treatment plan- a liver resection- whilst George's mum waited patiently at home with the boys baking chocolate cakes and wrapping them in her love.

The surgery was hefty and dangerous – cutting away two-thirds of the liver is pretty major stuff, but he went into it like he was having his tonsils removed. This was part of the reason all of the family wasn't with us, it was because he genuinely knew no fear, he believed with all of his heart that he would survive.

'They don't need to be here,' he'd said the night before.

'I'm going to be fine, I'll go to sleep for a few hours, get the cancer cut out and then wake up and see you. They needn't worry, I've got this.' He was so bold with his response as he packed his pyjamas into the hospital bag in readiness.

The day of that surgery was a big one. For months, I'd managed to contain my anxiety because somehow it seemed like we were winning the war. That day though all of those gut-wrenching, throat hurting, armpit sweating feelings came back. It was scary. Having to watch the love of my life be wheeled off down the corridor to be cut open and have part of one of his major organs chopped out. Part of me wanted to lie on the bed and go with him, part of me wished I could take his place and once he had gone, I felt bereft that no one else had come with us.

As I sat in the car park staring at the concrete hospital building in front of me and wondering exactly where he was, I decided to go over to my parents. I knew my boys were safe with their Granny and she was safe with them back at our house. I needed to be with my mum that day and feel her love around me. The clock ticked by so slowly and I kept calling the hospital on repeat trying to get an update as to where he was and how he was doing. Eventually, around 4 pm, I got the news I had been waiting for; he was on the intensive care ward and I could go and see him. I ran out of my parents' house, briefly calling his mum and sister to let them know he was OK en route.

Ringing the doorbell to go and see my husband on a high dependency ward was overwhelming. I wasn't sure what I was going to see and how it might be and was full of trepidation. As I got close I could see that he was sat up in his bed and his eyes were wide open in an opiate-based drug haze. I had never seen him surrounded by such a large team of people before. There was the lady at the end of his bed writing everything on a large clipboard. There were two people either side of him. There were so many scary looking machines. But in the middle there was him. He was wearing his glasses and looked incredibly pale but when he saw me I got his best smile and my heart leapt. I squeezed myself between the team of people, so I could sit down and hold his hand.

'He's been talking about you ever since he woke up,' said the nurse.

We sat there together, surrounded by people we didn't know, holding hands, listening to the rhythmic beeps and whirs of the machines around us, waiting. Breathing. Winning.

We sat hand in hand for what felt like hours. It was just like when we'd first got together and walked the streets of Edinburgh, wanting to tell the whole world how much we loved each other. I leaned into him, I couldn't hug him, it would have hurt him too much. Instead, I kissed his neck but it wasn't warm in the way it was usually - it was cold. But behind the unfamiliar smell of the hospital gown and iodine was *his* smell. The gorgeous scent that I recognised as safety so I held his hand tightly and whispered into his ear,

'This is it. This is the start of the rest of our lives. This is the first time since December that you've been cancer-free. We're on the road to getting this beaten!'

He clenched my hand back and smiled. He was still so pale,

'I hope so,' he said, as he gripped tighter, 'I love you so much Louise. Thank you. Thank you for doing this with me.'

The days when he was laid out in intensive care were hard. He still had this way of making them beautifully full of life and normality though. He spent his day writing meal and drink requests to both me and his mum and insisting I sent messages to all of those who wanted to visit him, telling them he was fine. A couple of days later I rang the bell to the ward and requested to be allowed in; visiting was limited to immediate family and was only two people at a time. To my surprise I was told that he was busy.

'Busy?' I repeated absolutely incredulous as to what I was hearing through the intercom. What on earth was he doing!

After being made to wait on the bench outside I was finally allowed in twenty minutes later and saw him immediately sitting on his chair and smiling with a cheeky glint in his eyes.

'Look, they've figured out how to turn the disco lights on!'

I looked up and over his bed were various multi-coloured lights; their brightness mirrored the infectious zest for life that he had beaming out of his eyes.

'They switched them on so I could have reflexology,' he said, laughing and holding his wounded stomach.

The boy in the red tie was always there when I needed him most, looking for the fun and the sunshine. He always looked for the positive, even if that meant sweet-talking the nurses into giving him reflexology on an intensive care ward. Only George could do this.

Before we knew it, he was out of the hospital and recovering well from his surgery. He went back to work a second time around. He trained rigorously on his indoor turbo trainer to get his fitness levels up and his cycling legs spinning with our boys watching him incredulously as he rode his bike in our spare room. Just six weeks after being laid on the operating table he completed another bike ride; this time it was London to Paris. We celebrated this victory as much as all of our family and friends around us. It felt like he was a real-life super-hero as we walked hand in hand under the Eiffel tower and face-timed our delighted children who were safely back at home with their Granny and George's brother and sister. The feelings we felt that day were pure happiness and pride. We couldn't quite believe how far we'd come and were so thankful that he seemed to be winning the war.

Unbeknown to us though even on that day in France, as his liver quickly regenerated sadly so too did cancer. Once we were home from Paris, George had what seemed like a cold and felt run down. Then he got severe shoulder aches. The aches led to horrendous heartburn. This led to not being able to eat properly. We didn't know what was wrong. We couldn't figure it out. After an emergency scan and several hospital visits later, we finally got the news that was so disgustingly awful we didn't even want to believe it ourselves.

The cancer was back and there wasn't an option to cure it. George could have more chemo; it might buy him some more time, it might not, no one really knew. The only certainty was that his days in his earthly body were now most definitely numbered and our future together was not going to be for as long as we had previously hoped. There was now no way of him ever beating this disease.

The word terminal was never actually used in the appointment we sat through. Lots of polite conversations happened with us about how some people were successfully living with cancer. I remember it being the first time I was ever handed a box of tissues and the nurse who I wished was Rachel was desperately embarrassed when she realised the box was empty. I remember thinking that this couldn't be it. This couldn't be happening. Surely?! Didn't they realise we'd figure something out, after all we'd only been stood under the Eiffel tower a few weeks ago so this couldn't really be happening, maybe it was even a mix-up?

The appointment we had that day was clear and unclear. George wasn't going to get better. There was never going to be a cure or a life without cancer for us. We didn't have any indication of timing – with hindsight, I genuinely think the medical team didn't think it was going to be as fast as it actually was. I will never know.

That's the whole thing with cancer, you never really know anything. You never really know what curveball you're going to be thrown next. The only certainty you have is that all assurances you had previously known, have been thrown out of the window. Your life becomes utterly unrecognizable and every time you start to pick the pieces up and put them back together, along comes another blow which forces you to fall to the floor all over again, leaving you bereft, scrapping around and refocussing on what you've still got to cling on to.

It was only when we couldn't go back home to our boys who were being cared for by the nanny we'd dutifully employed following Bertster's advice, that we cried. We howled in fact. Our cups of energy and positivity were utterly depleted. We drove to my parents' house as it was plausibly the nearest place we could take ourselves that felt safe. We quite literally didn't know what to do or where else to go, I can't even remember telling Mum and Dad what had happened as we walked through their front door. I have no recollection of the words used; if I told them or if it was

George. All I remember is that I could barely speak. I was utterly inconsolable.

Dad drove us back to our house because neither of us was safe to be behind the wheel. I still don't know how he managed to do that. When I got home, I couldn't bring myself to go inside and look at my beautiful children's faces knowing their lives would be ruined. I was just so hurt. I didn't know how to go back into the fray of teatime and gently carry on, until we were ready to find the right words and the right time to tell them. To tell our little loves that my gorgeous husband, their beloved daddy, wasn't going to live to tell the tale. That they were going to have to live their lives without him and he was going to die.

By this point, Charlie was three and Jamie had turned one, they had no idea what death even meant, it wasn't something we had ever even spoken about. I remember Dad desperately trying to console me as he sat with me on the wall outside our house, calming me down and helping me to breathe through the hysterical tears. He told me that somehow, someway, we'd find a path through the shit storm that was ahead.

'You will find a way through this,' was all he kept saying over and over again as he gripped his arms around my shoulders.

I just sat with him and cried. I didn't know which way I was supposed to turn and what I was supposed to think. It all just felt so black and so numb. The only certainty I now knew was George's death and it was hands down the scariest challenge I'd ever looked into the eyes of. No God walking with me that I knew. All I was going to have left from my love story were my kids, who

I clung to. George was terrified, he knew he was going to die. I was terrified, I knew I was going to be a widow in my thirties. My boys didn't know it yet but they were going to be father-less. It was hideous, it was a nightmare, it was inconceivable that this had become our life. But my Dad is a wise soul though, he was very right to think that there would be a way through, it would come in the way I least expected it.

Searching

It's a strange thing hope. It's funny how even in the darkest of moments you want to find it. You want confirmation that it's not as bad as you think it might be and you anticipate that something amazing or miraculous might happen to save you. When George was diagnosed as being terminal, we were hysterical, broken and dazed, but the bubble that was hope quickly resurfaced. It was completely inexplicable.

Maybe it was because the whole situation we had found ourselves in didn't feel real. It's strange how you can be told something so devastating, cry your eyes out, barely be able to speak, then pull yourself together and walk into your house and drink a cup of tea.

When George found out he was terminal he didn't feel well, but we also knew he wasn't going to die that afternoon. He was tired, he was suffering from cold-like symptoms and back pain, but he wasn't bed-bound. Even though he was desperately uncomfortable, he wasn't dying. Not yet anyway.

They say that seeing is believing. This was the case in the first few days after we were acquainted with the news that death was coming. To be told that your best friend is going to die from the disease that has taken up residence in his body is surreal. To then have to go home, put your boys to bed and still have the opportunity to watch your favourite TV show together is surreal. However selfish it sounds it immediately leads you to question your mortality. We all know that we're going to die, it's the only certainty of life, however scary it is to hear, and that evening I found myself wondering what I was really so scared about anyway.

In those first few days, I remember trying to convince myself that until something really dramatically altered, nothing had really changed. We were both going to die before cancer had shown up, so why was I so scared now, he wasn't going to die just yet, he still seemed sort of alright and was OK. Simply speaking this was my way of surviving.

I would tell myself that yes George is sick, but he'd mostly been sick for the last ten months of our lives together. Being sick had somehow become the new normal and I was used to living with it now. Maybe he could be the person who would live with incurable cancer for longer than anyone else. I truly believed that anything was possible where George was concerned. That was what I hoped.

So we went home. We organised with the hospital to start more chemo. We were optimistic that it might buy him an incredible amount of time. We were hopeful that it might give us more time than it's brought any human in the world ever. We miraculously hoped that in the time George responded to his treatment science would find a cure for cancer. That way we could still live our happily-ever-after and not be as terminal as the doctors thought. And so we desperately clung to our fairy tale because we didn't know what else to do.

At this time I remember George sitting in his pyjamas in our living room eating chocolate and seriously talking about having his liver resected again. He wanted the cancer to be chopped out. He wanted to be cut open and cured in a way that no one else had ever even experienced before.

'Wouldn't it be amazing,' he said, as his animated face took away from his insipid colour and drawn-in cheeks, 'if I could be the person to defy odds and science?'

I desperately wanted to subscribe to every madcap idea he had.

I desperately wanted to believe that there was something somewhere that maybe we hadn't yet discovered that could help us. Somewhere in my heart I just believed that this had to be true. I believed in him which made me believe in hope.

Our daily reality quickly became talking about how George might defy death as we bounced into a TV episode of 'Grand Designs.' Whilst watching we'd talk about what we might have for tea; this would be something he could eat that would potentially soothe his stomach pain. The everyday mundane juxtaposed next to life and death conversations became a beacon of comfort and every additional night that George got to kiss the boys to sleep allowed our hope to burn brighter. We appreciated each moment, each memory, even though we were absolutely petrified as to what may or may not be ahead.

I felt so alone and isolated at this time as I looked into the eyes of George's impending death as a young mother and realised I was going to have to raise our children on my own. It was incredibly frightening at a time when I felt like I had to be brave for him. Imagine being told right now, that the person who is the one you do life with, the one who knows all of your secrets and flaws, the one you count on as well as being the one who always cheers you on, isn't going to be there for the rest of your life. That they won't be there to help you nurture and develop the children you've made together or roll over and wake up next to you in your shared bed. They won't stand at your side as you brush your teeth at night or bring you a cup of tea and smile to start your day in the morning.

Growing old won't be what you thought it would be, they won't be the one who sees you go grey and get a little doddery and still love you all the same because they remember you when you were twenty. These thoughts were utterly terrifying to comprehend.

No one ever wants this as their reality and it is why countless people told me time and time again that they couldn't even imagine my reality. This is because even conjuring up the parallel universe of what this would look like for them is too painful to bear. But this is what we were forced to do, along with countless others who have gone before us and countless others who will go after us. We had to imagine what our lives were going to be like knowing he wasn't going to be there at the centre of it all. He had to imagine it; I had to imagine it and plan for it. I can tell you now it's every part as hideous and unpleasant as you think it might be.

Before George died, I'm pretty sure we'd even asked ourselves the question,

'Would you rather know that you're dying, or just be shot dead?'

As a side note, this wasn't because we were crudely preoccupied with death; it would have been part of some silly drinking game, after one too many adult lemonades. Before life with cancer, I would have opted to be shot or for George to be shot. It seemed easier to not know what was going to happen.

I now know that having the opportunity to say goodbye, even if it is brutal and painful in a way your soul finds hard to bear, is incredibly powerful.

But maybe death, just like God, himself, meets us where we are? I recognise this is a BIG statement to make and that just like birth, there are one thousand and one different ways that you may or may not leave your human clothes. But having to think about *how* it was going to happen was a thought that was increasingly on our minds. This was because we knew it was going to happen much sooner than we'd ever anticipated.

Just before George had been diagnosed as terminal I decided to get therapy. Bertster had told me way back in December that I needed help, but I'd put it off up until this moment. The terminal diagnosis had caused such a relentless hurricane of hurt, pain and confusion that I'd finally decided it was time to seek some professional support.

Making this decision, (as well as agreeing to marry George) was hands down one of the best choices I have ever made. I was propelled into action after we were told that more treatment would be needed just a few weeks earlier. I had literally been so floored by the news, that I had taken to my bed for two days in a state of shock and utter exhaustion. It was all just too much.

The sleepless nights with Jamie. The strain of being a mummy to two very little boys who were confused and unsettled and needed more comfort than ever. The pressure of being a wife to someone who was dying and needed both physical and emotional support. The struggle of being at work and holding down a job, 'just in case.' The pressure and responsibilities were endless. It was awful. I knew I was going to be the only one who could provide for the family.

Looking back, I don't even know how I showed up to work in my job which was still at the chocolate factory. It turns out my corporate role was in fact therapy too. It was so far removed from the nuclear-sized bomb that was detonating in my life that talking about the latest product developments and profit margins seemed easy. It was definitely more palatable than death.

Getting a psychologist felt amazing. I had someone who I could go to every week and tell all of my thoughts to without any judgement whatsoever. I didn't have to pretend I was OK. I could just be. I could unravel my fears and I could openly talk about George's impending death. A conversation which he had very much kept off the table at home. I could talk about how I felt; I could do some level of scenario planning. I could genuinely show my fear to someone who wouldn't have a sleepless night and worry about the agony and trauma my soul felt. It was liberating in a way I never expected it to be, this was because even when we were told George was going to die, he still didn't believe it himself.

He was an overcomer. He believed that he was Superman and unflinchingly supposed that if anyone could defy the odds, he would. I know that he believed way more than the next person in his abilities, it was part of why I'd fallen so madly in love with him all those years ago. But even when he was dying, George wanted to pretend that it was all OK - that he wasn't feeling as poorly as I knew he really was. He was a gifted sales and marketing director; so much so, that he was selling and marketing the concept of his own life and determination to live as much to himself as anyone else. It was hard to live and cope with, as well as being incredibly difficult to observe. I needed an outlet for my grief and knew at this point that I wasn't going to find this in him.

George and I didn't really row. Like all married couples we had arguments and we disagreed about where we should spend our time and our money. We'd also bicker about what our priorities were in life, but up until his impending death, we'd always pretty much been on the same page about the big stuff. Since the beginning of 'us,' whenever we had a really tough decision to make, we almost always found ourselves agreeing. If we didn't, we respected the other person's strengths, perception and opinion so much so, that we would take a leap of faith and trust in our own decision making and side with the other. There is one moment though that will always stand out as an almighty disagreement and this happened in the few days after George had been diagnosed as terminal.

We were at home in our kitchen. He was desperately trying to pretend he wasn't in an immense amount of pain. It was a weekday approaching early evening, and the light was beginning to fade as it does on those autumn nights in early October.

On that day George's amazing mum had come to visit and had made what felt like one hundred tiny cupcakes for the boys in our kitchen. She loved her biggest boy in a way that only a mum can and I was SO thankful for her help and support. I visibly remember the relief I felt when she came through the door with her warm smile and toys for the children. It was the same way she had always greeted us, the same way she'd walked towards me for the first time ten years earlier when I'd eaten cake with her for the first time.I knew that George's mum could talk to his soul in a way that I couldn't. The beautiful bond that existed between the two of them was something I always looked up to and hoped to have with my boys.

They were close, not in an annoying way but in a lovely, caring kind and protective way. So that evening when George's mum announced she was going home I felt like the rug had been pulled out from under me. I desperately wanted her to stay because she brought a hope unlike anyone else that was tangibly felt across our home. She also shouldered the responsibility of caring for George which brought an unmistakeable calm and peace.

That night, I wasn't angry with her for going back home. I was angry with George for not telling her like it was and not being vulnerable enough to ask her to stay.

I was angry that he was pretending he was alright to protect her and was leaving me to pick up the pieces. I was mad that he was in denial about what was happening in his body and wouldn't ask anyone for help. There was so much rage inside I couldn't bear it, but most of all I felt angry that he was dying and would be leaving us to muddle through life without him. I felt like a volcano, on the verge of a Vesuvius level explosion. It was awful.

So later that evening, after she had returned home, I told him. George had been the victim of my temper tantrums many times before, but that night I was SO unbelievably outraged that he wasn't asking for any help, that I screamed.

I felt so wronged that I yelled. I was mad, so, so mad. But I felt like he didn't hear. The tears burned my face. The hate burned the back of my throat. He just stood there and took it. He knew me well enough to know there was nothing else he could do. I was so mad that night that I did something that I'd never ever in the history of our time together done before. I got in my car and l left. I left my sick husband on his own with our boys. And I didn't even tell him I was leaving; I just slammed the door behind me, stomped outside and got in my car. I didn't answer his phone calls. I wanted to make him realise that he couldn't manage without me. I wanted him to understand the responsibility of still having to participate in the bedtime routine, even though I knew he couldn't do it. I was cross that his cancer always gave him a way out, I was mad that he didn't have to worry about how he would keep on keeping on. I selfishly wanted him to experience some of what I felt and I desperately wanted him to be helpless enough to ask others to support him. The life that we had found ourselves living was now so messed up in so many ways and I wanted to hear him say it. I wanted him to acknowledge and recognise what this disease was doing to us all. I didn't want him to try and shrug it off. I definitely didn't want to look for the positive any longer and I wanted him to be so scared that I could see and taste his fear.

I have to add that I now know that George would have felt all of these things. What I also know is that he dealt with his emotions so differently to the way I did. His personality meant that he verged on being almost scientifically logical. He was a master practitioner in the art of separating his emotion from the situation in hand and just because he was *INCREDIBLE* at doing this, does not mean that I don't think he felt it.

But at this specific moment in time, his behaviour didn't show me that he felt this so I interpreted his response as a rather stubborn line in the sand. That line felt like it jarred with my heart and I was mad, I was sad and I felt alone. At that moment it felt like even my husband didn't understand my fear. I felt utterly isolated.

So I drove. I cried and I drove. I wanted to go somewhere but I had no idea where I was free-falling to. Dramatic changes in your life often have this impact on you and sometimes running away, as far and fast as you can, even if you have no idea exactly where you're headed, is the only option you feel like you have left. That night I quite literally drove around in circles. I chose country lanes where I wouldn't see any traffic. I howled. I wiped away my salty tears almost as rhythmically as my wipers scraped against the windscreen. Even the weather was in step with how I felt.

On some level, the universe was as broken as I was about George's impending death. The clouds were sullen. The rain poured down like tears. The darkness was the brokenness of my mind.

I'm not sure how long I was out of the house but it felt like forever and certainly long enough to make a statement. I was searching but I didn't know what I was even searching for.

I thought about all the people who I could drive to see. None of them felt like they fitted. I was so worried about what their emotional reaction might be and the sadness that I may or may not inflict upon them that I didn't dare to go to any of them. Despite my hysterical tears, I had the self-awareness to realise that I was desperately craving the power that comes from talking to a complete stranger. As the rain continued to pour and my headlights shone out into the night I pulled over and sat and thought about where I might find someone at this hour, on a cold, wet autumnal evening. Where could I go? Who would give me hope?

My thought patterns were irregular and randomised but I kept coming back to one image in particular: the vision of being sat in a warm church and being comforted by a friendly vicar, who would know just what to say. Some might say I've watched far too many Hollywood movies, others would say it was God who gave

89

me that image. But for whatever reason, I set off on my quest to find a kind-hearted minister to listen to my woes.

What I was imagining, was probably a little bit like Kevin, from the scene in 'Home Alone.' The one where he goes to watch his choir at a church because he misses his mum and in that moment, when he's comforted by the ethereal sounds of music he realises the man who lives across the road with the shovel, isn't really as bad as he thought. Kevin finds hope, comfort and inspiration, in amongst his desperation. He finds it in a church. I wanted to be like Kevin. It was all I could think about, so I decided to go somewhere I might get this response.

I looked down at my phone and asked Google to plot where the nearest churches were. Why this felt like the only plausible option at this specific point in time, I didn't reflect on and I'm sure if I had I would have talked myself out of it.

All I know is that I don't think it was all my idea. I mean it really can't have been. My experience of churches growing up wasn't ever that of Kevin's in Home Alone. Churches weren't places of comfort that I openly identified with. They weren't somewhere that I ever really went; except for weddings and Christmas carols and even then it was mainly for a celebratory sing-song.

So on that night when I was desperate, I listened to my heart and interpreted it absolutely literally. I had seen a church in my mind's eye so that is where I wanted to go – there was no in-between for me. So I set my purpose towards looking for a religious space that might open its doors and pour love into my heart. I thought that the people I would find there might also be the solution I needed to ease my pain.

I wove around the country lanes close to our house holding my steering wheel for dear life and crying in a way that mostly resembled a wounded animal. That night as I drove through all of the villages close to my home, I realised for the first time that there were so many churches in our area even though I had barely opened my eyes to even noticing them before. That night was the start of me opening my eyes. It was a way of looking at the world that was borne out of utter desperation.

The first church I arrived at was in the next village to my own. Despite the flurry of emotions I felt, I had the logic and wherewithal to think about the fact that this community was bigger than my own. Because it was a larger place that surely meant it would have a bigger church, this meant in my mind that it was more likely to be open. As I pulled up outside the quaint wooden gates and entrance porch I looked up towards the path to the front door. It was dark. The building looked unfamiliar and if I'm honest hugely uninviting.

I got out of my car and tried to open the gate in the rain. Between my wet hands and the stiffness of the lock, I couldn't fathom a way to open it. I stood and looked at the church spire. It was so distinctly unique. I'd never been a person of faith or religion but at that moment I felt hugely aware of the symbolism that stood in front of me. A spire rising into the night showing the faith that once was and the belief that generations before us had carried. The majestic stature in front of me felt so at odds with my emotions. I didn't believe in a God, I could barely bring myself to believe in any type of hope now George was so sick. But I focussed on the spire as I continued to force the gate. Eventually, it opened and I walked up to the front door.

The harsh reality about churches in this day and age is that lots of them are closed. They are dutifully run by those whose hearts still care for the community they represent. The church in the village next to my house that evening definitely wasn't like the one Kevin found in Home Alone. There was no light, no sign of life, no one to give me a huge hug, a cup of tea and soothe my broken heart. There wasn't even a warm porch that I could sit in to shelter from the rain. It felt bleak. It felt isolating. It felt totally and utterly hopeless.

The rage I had felt just an hour or so before began to resurface. I was outraged. The one time I'd decided to go and look for God I felt like he couldn't even be bothered to show up. I was utterly appalled. Disgusted in fact. How could it be that even when I'd tried to turn to something religious, it wasn't even there for me in the way I'd imagined it should be? What the fuck was this God doing? This was my hour of need. It had been our absolute year of need and I'd never once felt him. I hadn't seen him in the way I thought that I should. I was livid.

As I marched back to the car in the pouring rain, I started ranting out loud whilst crying.

'Stupid, bloody idiot, absolute ridiculous fucking churches.'

I got back in the car again and started driving. But was still so uneasy. I knew I was looking for something. My spirit knew that

I needed to be headed somewhere but I simply didn't know where I was going. It was so unclear. It all just felt so hard. What was I supposed to do now? I didn't know the way. I was depleted. I'd been an awful wife and abandoned my dying husband at home with our kids. I didn't know how I was supposed to cope with everything that was being put on my plate. I felt so angry. So lost, so broken, so alone.

Then it happened.

I was so upset that I had started to drive again and was crying so much that I couldn't see the road for my tears. I was hysterical and was making a whooping sort of sound, where you cough and cry simultaneously absolutely overwhelmed. I pulled over into a passing place on the narrow country lane. I had no idea what I was doing. I got out of the car and stood in front of it. It was dark now. There was no one around. I wasn't wearing a coat either and I was cold.

So I looked up at the sky and I roared. I roared with all of my heart and every single fibre of my being. It was a roar of pain, a roar of heartbreak, a roar of brokenness and hurt.

It was the roar of someone who wasn't willing to give up on hope. It was me versus the universe. It was now or never.

I could hear the hum of my engine, I could see the ethereal beam of my headlights into the night, the rain dancing in the beams like sparkles. I observed this and looked around to check I was on my own, just before I shouted as loud as I possibly could;

'GOD!!'

I was one huge mess.

'If you are real.' I roared, 'If you are as good as everyone says you are, then the time has come. You HAVE to fucking show me!! Show me you're real! SHOW MEEEEE!!"

I screamed into the night. I screamed so much the back of my throat felt strained.

'Enough is enough. This ends NOW. Where the actual fuck are you God? SHOW ME. You have to SHOW ME WHERE YOU ARE?! I NEED YOU. George needs you. WE NEED YOUR HELP!!'

I got back in my car. I felt better like I'd offloaded. Shouting into the night sky and letting the pain and the hurt out most definitely made my chest feel less heavy. I sat and waited. I looked up at the night sky as the rain continued to pour. I looked at my phone and there were three missed calls from George. He'd also sent one ridiculously kind text. Even though he was dying he was still so lovely. He always thought about me. The message immediately jolted me back to reality. His text simply said,

'Come Home. I'm worried. I'm not planning on dying anytime soon. I love you x'

So that's exactly what I did, I went home. I cried to my husband whilst the kids watched some cartoons. I told him I was sorry and we made up. I put the boys to bed whilst George lay and rested on our bed and then we both went downstairs and lay on the sofa. By this point his body hurt too much for me to nestle into his chest in the way I always used to. So we just sat next to each other. Holding hands. The calmness after my night-time drive about felt nice, the chaos of bedtime and the huge row we'd had felt distant already. So we went to one of our default ways of coping with adversity, escapism. As he flicked the TV on to watch an episode of 'Game of Thrones,' we suffocated the thoughts we were feeling inside. Just like the brutal show, we knew it was still going to have to get a whole lot worse before it could ever get any better. We sat in silence as the credits started rolling and the music blared. How had this become our life?

There was no 'hallelujah' moment for me that night. I didn't even want to cast my mind back to what I'd just done. I felt so ashamed that I'd run out on my husband and gone behind his back. But I couldn't help but wonder and there was still a little voice inside me that I simply couldn't silence.

What if God was ready to show me he was real? What if his greatest wish was for George and me to ask him to show us his existence? I felt scared about what I'd just done and buried these thoughts. As Daenerys Targaryen paraded around with her dragons I tried not to think about it because it felt like a guilty secret. I didn't tell George what I'd done that night, in fact, I never told him, but yet I know now that he knows. Everybody does.

All I knew was that night I had meant everything I said. I meant every last word that I'd shouted and every last ounce of emotion that I'd shown. As I went to bed alone, I thought about it again. I wanted God to show himself just as much as I had wanted to marry George. I wanted him to show up, just as much as I didn't want George to die. The roar of my heart was real. As I turned over in my bed trying to make myself comfortable in a desperately uncomfortable situation, it felt like I had been backed into a dark corner. Was the big guy the only way out for both of us? Was I only willing to find him because I genuinely thought he was the last chance I had of saving the man I loved?

As I turned on my back and looked towards the ceiling I knew that the answer was an overwhelming yes. My head was increasingly telling me there was no other logical way out of the sorry situation we were in. I tossed and turned into the right position and nestled into the duvet. If I positioned the covers in the right way it felt like George was hugging me, not writhing around in pain in our spare room. I used the meditation techniques I'd taught myself and drifted off into a fitful sleep.

What I didn't know that night was that there were plans for us both. That's because, after this evening and the crazy cry that I'd shouted out to the world, it all started to get even more supernatural than I ever even realised was possible.

What slowly started to happen and then BLEW up in my face was incredible, miraculous and filled with perfection of timing and beautiful glory that I couldn't have even scripted. All of the synchronicity and coincidence that I'd sometimes noticed in my life up until that point, seemed so insignificant compared to what would unfold next. That night, I could never have foreseen that we would both look at death in the eye and still be able to live. Still be able to hope. That's because I had no idea about the force that was coming.

It's not a Coincidence

The next morning, I got up and forced myself to carry on with what had become our routine. George's symptoms continued to develop at an alarmingly fast pace. The human spirit is founded on so much positivity that we naturally don't want to hear about how death creeps into a body. But understanding pain gifts you a fuller perspective.

We already knew that death was looming; before my drive around the local countryside the night before, it had already started and begun most notably with eating. George was an amazing eater, he had been raised by foodies and was passionate about every meal he ate – believe me, this was as amazing as it was infuriating. This passion became his purpose in both his career and our home life together. But by now George had started not being able to eat properly and for him this was torture. Eating was one of the things he loved most about being human and to have this privilege taken away from him, on top of knowing he was going to die, felt bitterly brutal. Fairly rapidly eating anything more than a really watery soup gave him painful digestive issues and an immense amount of reflux. Soon this acid turned into sickness, but the sick wasn't the kind of vomit the kids spew up, nor the sort where you can vaguely identify what has been eaten. The sick was dark brown, almost black. It looked evil.

Then there was the pain. I obviously didn't experience this first-hand, but George complained of an immense amount of back, neck and shoulder pain. We later found out that when tumours grow, they cause other parts of your normally functioning body to move out of place. This hurt him. A lot. I remember musing one morning as he complained of the pain and his enlarged stomach that it was almost like he was pregnant. The irony was he wasn't growing life, he was growing death. The back pain proceeded to get so bad that it impacted George's sleep. He was prescribed morphine to help and we both decided he should continue to sleep in the spare room, just as we had done during chemo treatment cycles to give him more space to writhe around in pain.

As the days after that night slowly unfolded, the morphine helped, but then the night sweats started. This wasn't waking up with a sweaty forehead and a clammy pair of pyjamas. It was full-blown saturation. It was the loss of so much water that it seemed like he'd slept on a waterbed that had silently pierced and leaked overnight; it was changing-the-sheets-in-the-middle-of-the-night-awful and was utterly disgusting for everyone involved. The symptoms continued to accrue until we reached a crescendo point and a couple of days after my cry for help we arrived in the hospital for his last-ditch keeping-the-cancer-at-bay treatment. He was a mess.

George could barely eat. Drinking was also a struggle. It was unbearable to watch. A few hours previously I had called the hospital to let them know we were on our way. As I dialled the number I felt like I was going behind his back all over again. After being put through to the chemo ward I asked for our favourite nurse Rachel. George had a real connection with her and she was the one who always made us feel safe and had this awesome sixth sense of knowing what to do even when everything else felt helpless. I could hear the bustle of the ward in the background, as she came to pick up the receiver.

'Hello,' she cheerily said; even the tone of her voice was soothing.

'It's Louise,' I said, 'we're about to come in,' I breathed back the pain. 'You need to know something though. He's really not good. Not good at all.'

I held back the tears and swallowed the almighty rocks that felt like they were growing in the back of my throat as I found the courage to finish my sentence.

'He is *really* scared.'

These four words were the equivalent of an SOS distress call because Rachel knew, as much as I, that George *never* said that. He was brave even in the hardest of situations and even on the day he found out he was dying he didn't tell me he was afraid. His outlook was logically pragmatic.

'I don't want to die,' was all he had said, 'there's just so much to live for.'

Not once did he show an ounce of fear or dread. He just showed disappointment. Telling Rachel he was scared signalled that we were both desperate. She knew this and was waiting for us with encouragement and hugs as soon as we arrived in the car park at the hospital, carrying sick bowls from the journey.

George just about managed to walk from the car park to the ward to get himself hooked into his marvellous medicine. The irony was very deliberate about our turn of phrase; even though the potential impact of the medicine was marvellous, its short term benefits couldn't have been further removed.

It's utterly hideous to think of what he put himself through to buy himself a few more days in his human body. But this is the reality of what you'll do if you really don't want to die. You'll do anything it takes. Even if that means making yourself feel worse when you already, quite literally, feel like death.

As the day went by, George went from bad to worse. His symptoms were horrific; his already-weakened body was struggling. This combined with the brutality of the poison that was now being pumped into his veins was not in the short term making life any better. As the day unfolded I knew that George wouldn't be coming home that night and would need to be admitted into hospital. He was so weak, a shell of his former self. It was soul-destroying to observe and hideous for him to live through. He didn't even have the energy to feel what he needed. He was simply too exhausted.

George's chemo infusions were always all-dayers. In the early days of treatment, we'd joked about how the word we'd used in our twenties, to describe a debauched day and night out, became the turn of phrase we used for cancer treatment. That night, after George had finished his chemo, he was wheeled up to the hospital ward. He was too far gone into a chemo daze and his fragile body was utterly incapable of even enduring the thirty-minute car journey home. All he had was our angel nurse Rachel, his mum who had made a dramatic dash back to be with us and a sick bowl for support. He was desperately uncomfortable; you could see the agony etched all over his face.

As we got to his room on the ward and George was awkwardly lifted into a bed, he began to cry. He was weak, He was vulnerable. He no longer had the strength in his body or mind to positively re-frame how he was feeling. He had finally reached the end of the line and the sobs that came from his infirm body were enough to break anyone's heart. He was scared and his fear and distress were utterly harrowing for us all.

As we gathered around his bed, all feeling desperately helpless, more nurses arrived to try and help him. In the end, we had a small team who helped tuck George into bed that night. But there was one who stood out more than any others; she was someone I didn't recognise and who we hadn't ever seen before. You could see how much she cared and how much she wanted to help in the way she moved her body around the room, it was as if her eyes were pouring love into him. She excused herself and came back promptly with what seemed like five pillows. All she wanted to do was make George feel more comfortable, but the sad thing was that not even fifty-five pillows could have eased the pain that night, although her intent that evening went some way to ease the worry in my heart.

George was fighting to stay alive and it was utterly amazing that in these moments of pure pain his spirit remained utterly unaltered. He was still the same cheeky boy I'd fallen in love with and felt lucky to be married to. After the nurses had made him as comfortable as they could and George's mum had gone off in search of coffee, I sat by his bedside and held his hand. We were alone and none of it felt real. It's strange how things hit you and how your mind whirs when you find yourself in these moments. As I sat there holding his hand in silence and gently massaging the soft section of skin between his thumb and index finger, my mind couldn't help but wander back to our wedding day. I'd felt so happy back then. I smiled so much before I walked into the church to become his wife. Now, I gripped his hand tighter and closed my eyes willing my mind to replay that beautiful moment and be in that moment rather than the hideous hospital room.

Would I still remember our wedding day with such clarity when he was gone, I wondered? The machines beeped and I tried to block them out, choosing to hear instead the beautiful music I'd walked down the aisle to. I smiled as I recalled how he'd looked at me, how he'd also looked so scared. As we'd stood there that day saying our vows he was anxious. It was the first moment in our lives together that I'd seen him really nervous about anything. I'd felt no nerves whatsoever that day because I knew I was doing the right thing. Despite the anxiety visibly etched across his face, I knew he wasn't scared because he was marrying me. I knew he was scared because he loved me so much. That was exactly how I felt then and how I felt now.

I opened my eyes to take in the boy in the red tie laid out in front of me. Where was he? When I'd said my vows on that beautiful day five years earlier and uttered the words 'in sickness and in health,' I had never in a thousand years thought death would come quite so soon. On such a joyous day it was totally incomprehensible and utterly impossible to even begin to imagine. But looking at him now and surveying the sights, sounds and horror in front of me, I was looking at my wedding vows.

It was like I was wearing my wedding dress, except it wasn't the corset top restricting my breathing, it was anxiety. This was my gorgeous Georgie in sickness. His cheeks had started to look concave, his eyes were sunken, his hands were bony. He looked like death. He really didn't look at all like himself until he smiled or cracked a joke. And it was in those moments I could grasp and catch hold of his beautiful spirit which in spite of everything was still very much alive. That night athough that part of his spirit had evaporated and even though no one said it to us in tangible terms, I knew the death train was going to arrive sooner than we'd anticipated. I could see it hurtling towards us every time I looked into his eyes.

When George's mum returned from her coffee expedition, I took a moment to excuse myself and find Rachel. She was outside at the nurse's station and saw me coming immediately. She walked straight over.

'Is this it?' I asked her.

She looked a little confused about what I was asking. 'I know he's going to die,' I said, 'but is this it? Is it going to be tonight? Or do we have more time? I need to know if this is Doomsday. Is Doomsday tonight or do I have longer to prepare?'

Never in my life did I think that I would have asked such a direct question about death, but I was so exhausted that I couldn't think of another way to wrap up the huge elephant that was obviously in his hospital room. She stood squarely towards me, with her head held high and her shoulders back.

'No. It won't be tonight,' she said.

Looking back, I don't know how she knew so definitely that it wouldn't be that evening. On a medical level, she couldn't have ever possibly known this. But what I'm learning about life is that sometimes you do just know the answers. There are moments in life when direction, instruction, responses or wisdom are just so clear and feel so right, that maybe they come from somewhere else.

I'm sure that to some degree Rachel's answer was based upon a mixture of experience and intuition. Arguably, she was a cancer nurse so very well versed in end-of-life care. But no one ever really knows exactly when death will happen, or do they?

That night it was more than just her I was talking to although I didn't see it like that at the time. I knew that she was convinced George's death wouldn't be that evening. It meant I could only hope that although the end was now very much in sight, there was still time for something to happen. For George to feel less pain, for him to feel more at ease and for me to make peace with the fact that I would have to live my life and raise our boys without him.

It's funny how you can recognise the forces of the universe even when you don't think you know them and aren't familiar with their ways of showing up. What else could still make you feel so certain of hope, when you're quite literally walking through the valley of the shadow of death. I certainly didn't have the words to explain this back then.

That first night in hospital was rough. George was so frightened that his mum stayed with him. He had become a little boy who needed the comfort of his mum's arms. I needed my boys at this time just as much as they needed me. Just as much as George needed his mum and she needed him too. So once George was uncomfortably installed and hooked up to monitors and his mum had found a way to fashion a duvet out of a coat, I went home.

I have no recollection of how I got there. I'm not sure if I even drove myself. It's strange how the mundane fell into insignificance yet I remember every detail of the hospital room and all of the staff that were there with laser-sharp clarity. I don't think I slept that much once I got home, I remember just crying and forcing myself to carry on. At this point, I was still on my own in the house with the children and our nanny left for the night once I got home. It was the next day that all of the close family started to arrive as we all realised it was time to maybe say goodbye.

The symptoms of chemo mixed with a body already ravaged by cancer were shocking for us all. None of us were really prepared for the speed of his decline. Our family and friends were as distraught as we were, everything just felt so hard and each day so full of pain. We were cloaked in a place of fear that somehow felt so much darker than anywhere else we'd previously inhabited. The passage of time moved incredibly slowly and the days in the hospital by his bedside felt like decades. Lots of our broader network of friends and family were also getting in touch as news of George's rapid decline reached them. Everyone wanted to offer help and support, but it was completely overwhelming. I didn't know what to do, or how to respond, it all just felt too much.

Two days later and it was Sunday evening. I was at home and in Charlie's bedroom getting his clothes ready for nursery the next day. It was in this moment as the bustle of bedtime unfolded with my mum for moral support in the bathroom that I got the text message that would be the start of flipping our world upside down. Even when I read this text for the first time, I didn't realise that this is what it would do. I thought it was just another message from a kind friend who wanted to help us. I couldn't possibly have joined the dots and seen the coincidence that night, that was because, in the fear that was surrounding my heart, as well as the hum of the house at bedtime, I'd already forgotten that I'd asked God to show me he was there just a few nights earlier.

The pressure of having to keep in touch with all of our friends and family, coupled with keeping the show on the road for the boys, figuring out a plan for George and trying to find the space to get my head around what was going to happen, was utterly exhausting. It was all-consuming. That's why when I read this message I didn't think anything of it. I didn't have the headspace to wonder if it was a little bit odd and not a coincidence. On the surface it seemed to be so much like the twenty or so other messages that my phone had received that day. I didn't read it and think anything otherwise.

The message was from one of my closest family friends. The kind of people you grow up with. I had always called her mum 'Aunty' although she wasn't related to us at all. Her daughters had grown up like cousins to me and I'd known the girl who was texting since she was a baby. She was one of those people who didn't necessarily know everything about my daily life, but if I ever needed anything, I only had to ask. She would always be there in a heartbeat, she could be counted on, probably with an immense supply of cakes and chocolates from her mum too, just to keep us going.

I've thought a lot about the people who have been positioned around me in my life since that night. What's interesting is that it was this family who brought me the connection I would get next. A family who I have always loved, looked up to and trusted implicitly. A group of people who know my parents as well as me. A family who aren't especially religious but do believe in God. Is it because they had faith that they were chosen to connect me?

107

I'm really not sure and will never know but I have thought about it and wondered if I would have pursued the message in the same way, if it had come from anyone else. But I will never know what I may or may not have done. Either way I'm utterly convinced it was meant to be Kate that connected us.

The text was long and I read it in a rush. I was coming down from a painful day at the hospital, whilst also feeling guilty about leaving my dying husband so I could be with our boys. All of this was buzzing around in my mind whilst also trying to organise the nursery bag for the following day. It was 'mum-guilt' on steroids. My head was full.

Hi Louise. How are you? I was at Andy and Steph's wedding yesterday and just after the ceremony, but before the meal, this random lady came over to me and started chatting. I'd never met her before and thought it was really bizarre that she'd even come over. We got talking and somehow, we started talking about God and her faith, I'm still not really sure how that happened! I then asked her to pray for you and George and it turned out she was associated with a healing group. I'm not really sure what this is but she gave me the details to pass on, in case you were interested? Sorry, I know this text has come out of the blue and this summary is a really condensed version of what actually happened, but she said that God had told her she was going to meet somebody! I just thought it was really bizarre that she came over to me just after I'd found out about George from my mum. To be clear, she wasn't going around preaching or anything, but our conversation really didn't feel like a coincidence. Something made her talk to me and something made me ask her to pray even though I don't usually do that! The healing group she is part of is free of charge, it's in America, but they also meet with people over skype.

I can WhatsApp you the details if you're interested? Obviously, if you're not, that's absolutely fine too, I just wanted to tell you what happened in a short way, as this felt too important not to share. Thinking of you all. Lots of love, Kate x'

All I remember thinking was, Yes. Yes, I'm interested.

I sent a speedy response saying just that and let Kate know that I'd be in touch once the kids were down for the night. I didn't start to put the puzzle pieces together then. It wasn't that obvious, despite the fact that Kate had pointed out the coincidence. I've since had lots of time to ponder this seemingly chance meeting. The wedding where this conversation happened was in fact, the nuptials of two people I know. Andy was someone I'd grown up with and I'd also had the pleasure of meeting his future wife Steph. I now know that the girl Kate met is called Brianna and that Brianna is a close friend of Andy's wife Steph.

It's wonderful how the strings of connection and friendship weave to bind us in ways that even we don't realise. It's such an intricate medley of chemistry, connection and bonds that can leave us feeling so connected and disconnected all at the same time. That wedding day, when George was laid out in the hospital, it was almost like the electric sparks of connectivity randomly linked us all at super-charged voltage speeds. It's now also so incredible to know that someone who was a friend from the past, reconnected to serve such a profound purpose in terms of linking me to my future. It feels surreal that this even happened.

But I've also come to realise that these moments of 'chance,' are not on any level coincidental. This meeting was just like the 'chance' meeting I'd had with the receptionist on the night when I wasn't playing to the three-point plan. It was exactly the same way I had been positioned to meet George all those years ago and failed first-time around to get the job I so desperately wanted. Synchronicity, coincidence, fate, or God. People call it different things, but the more I unravel, the more it seems that when you are living your existence on the right path and being obedient to the messages and guidance that you are being given, the power of seemingly 'chance,' moments can often be dynamite.

The other part of this 'coincidental' meeting that I now know is true is that Brianna asked for it. She's told me since that the morning of the wedding just like every other, she prayed. That day she prayed over the marriage of her good friends, but also prayed that God would lead her to the people she should talk to. Was it this mysterious mix of Brianna willing it and Kate's heart being open that made this conversation even happen, or was it because I had asked God where he was just a few days earlier? I will never know for certain, but this 'heavy' chat in the corner of a wedding reception in London was the start of God's intricate plan being stitched into place for George and myself.

It's strange how acting in a specific moment can be linked to something so much bigger than maybe any of us can ever realise or comprehend. It's amazing that Kate had this conversation, but then sat on it overnight. That for whatever reason she didn't pick up the phone right there and then. There was something inside her that made her wait. Something that made her tell her mum about what happened, who in turn told my dad. There were so many other people who had to say, 'yes,' before it even got to me.

But that is what is so fascinating. None of them chose to discount the value of this conversation. They were all open to the fact that the healing prayers Brianna had mentioned and the divine relationship she spoke of might be helpful. Maybe it was because everyone was so desperate to help George? Maybe it was because they hurt so much for me, they wanted to come forward with a practical solution? Maybe it was just all meant to be? Or maybe, they could all hear God, but didn't realise that this was the force guiding them?

It wasn't a coincidence that Kate met Brianna. Neither of them had any way of knowing that I'd been out a few days before and asked God to reveal himself. It was only George who was aware that I'd been out of the house and even he didn't know that I'd committed something as crazy and out of character as screaming and swearing up at the sky. I'd actually already almost forgotten about it myself; it all just felt so not me. I'd put my behaviour down to a hysterical outburst.

But God it seemed hadn't. He had well and truly heard me. He then uniquely positioned a series of events so he could show himself in a way that would seem so consequential. On the evening when I got that text I remember feeling deeply unsettled. I was exhausted. My mind was alive with many so many questions and so much fear. I was totally bewildered by the situation unravelling in front of me. I didn't know which way to turn but for whatever reason truly felt that there must be a direction I could take. I knew I couldn't possibly be the first or the last person going through what was happening to us now. I also knew that other people had to go through what we were experiencing with a lot less support and love. After much wrangling, I decided at that moment, rather impetuously, that I could only let George die if I knew in my heart that I had tried everything to help him. That I had left absolutely no stone unturned. This meant I would try anything. Even pursuing Brianna, a woman who I had never met before and who claimed to have a direct link to God.

Hoping

That night as I lay in bed the seed of hope was very much starting to germinate. I read and re-read the message from Kate and as I tossed and turned was unsure of what I was supposed to do. Should I contact this woman called Brianna from America? She was a total stranger and who on earth introduced themselves as someone who had a direct line to God? I couldn't help but be desperately intrigued by her. After all, if there was someone out there who knew God in this way, could they help us? I wasn't sure but couldn't stop thinking about it. The thought of this mystical woman meeting Kate at a wedding had taken up residence in my mind.

One of the ways I'd learnt to deal with the crippling anxiety and trauma I'd found myself in was to feel love from other people who cared for me. That night even though part of me wanted to, I decided I wasn't ready to send a text to an American woman I didn't know. Instead, I crept out of bed and down the hallway to our sleeping boys as I knew that their sleeping souls could soothe mine. I crept into Charlie's bed and wrapped my arms around him, nuzzling my face into his neck. Being with him grounded me. He made me feel safe and free as I listened to his breathing. As I wrapped my arms around him it made me remember I still had a purpose. It made me certain that there was love to be found beyond George's heart-beat as well as an overwhelming sense of responsibility and direction. As I lay there breathing in my son's smell I thought about what George would do if I was the one who was dying in hospital. Would he keep looking for answers or would he give up? I knew in an instant what he'd choose. The jolt of my resolve almost woke Charlie as he turned over and I tiptoed away from his bed.

I crept back down the corridor to my bedroom. My bed felt soft and warm but wasn't as peaceful as I hoped. I looked over to the pillows where George's head should have been. The space was pristine, untouched and made me feel sad but also raised a smile as I thought about all of the times I'd asked him to puff his pillows and make the bed straight in the morning. All of those mornings of everyday life which now seemed like a distant haze.

'We don't live in a hotel,' he'd always say, mocking my tone and deliberately parading around in his underpants. 'But yes, I will arrange your bed and your pillows with display cushions, if it makes you happy Louise!'

He could always make me smile even when I was mad at him. I thought about his resolve and realised that's what I had to do now. I had to step up, I had to step in, I had to live out some of what he had taught me and find my resolve. I had to find a way to make him smile in these last moments.

I looked again towards the vast expanse and emptiness of his side of the bed. My life was rapidly looking like the huge void but it was still my bed to lie in and I needed to find a way to be in it without him. I knew that he didn't have the energy to help me work through the situation in the way he had always done before. I knew there and then that somehow, I had to find a way to take his space, even if that meant being more courageous than I'd ever been before.

I lay back in my bed like a star deliberately trying to take up as much of the king-size arena as I could. I'd already switched my bedroom light on for company so I could set my mind to the crazy task in hand of what leaving no stone unturned looked like. As I stretched out I tried to think like George but felt like there wasn't much to play with, I knew in my heart though that he would have found some options, some way of getting through this. He always did; that's how he was wired.

My mind hurt as I thought about what I could actually do to help him? It had been so hideous the last few days watching him writhe around in pain I couldn't bear it any longer. A few hours earlier as I'd sat holding his hand at his bedside I had even found myself thinking that if he was a dog, he would have been put down by now. I tried desperately to think of what I could do and my corporate geek quickly grouped the options that I had thought up into three buckets. I laid there with an imaginary spreadsheet open in my head and even colour coded the three columns; spirituality, medical trials and euthanasia. It felt so final to see these choices in my mind's eye.

Given that the last option hadn't been legalised in our country I wasn't really convinced it was a goer, but I also couldn't help but wonder if the pain was still going to get worse. The thought of this made me feel sick and so I forced myself to include this option on the imaginary list I had created. I even thought about the logistics of getting George out of the hospital and across the channel to Switzerland. It would be hard, pretty much impossible in the state he was in, but I would do it if it meant an end to the unspeakable pain he was in at that moment. I grabbed my phone on the bedside table and quickly asked Google about the clinic where you could do it. Where you could ask for a human being to be put down. The web page felt alien, uncomfortable and made my stomach flip. I closed my phone immediately because it didn't feel right, I knew in an instant I couldn't take him there.

Then I found myself wondering the most hideous of thoughts. Could I do it? Could I put him down? Could I kill him and put him out of his misery? I then spent some time considering how I'd do it. We didn't own any weapons, only kitchen knives. The only drugs I had in the house were for headaches and he couldn't really swallow anymore either. My mind went back to the knives and I thought about stabbing him in the chest, could I do that? Could I take a knife into his room and just get him to put it into his heart? The thought made me shudder. There's no way I could kill someone I loved as much as him, however desperate I felt. I was alarmed by my own thought processes and I found my mind drifting to all of those who had committed crimes of passion. Did they feel this desperate? Did they really think that death was the only way out? I wiped away the tears, I wasn't just sad, I was ashamed. I recognised that I was being frantic and I didn't like it. In my heart I knew I wasn't going to commit a serious crime or try and attempt a cross channel journey with a very sick husband. It all just felt so hopeless so I forced myself to think about the two options I had left.

Next up were the medical trials. Was there really nothing else that could be done? What about treatments in Europe or going to America? Was it worth us emptying our bank account to pay for experimental drugs, or was there something on offer in our own country that no one had yet realised? I thought about all of the potential research we would need to do. Where would I even start, did we even have enough time, how could I get around this?

My commercial training had always taught me to outsource the tasks that I knew someone else could get done better. This way of thinking kicked in and as I carried on lying there, thinking of who I could ask to help, I wondered who I trusted to take on this mantel, who did I know? Who was bright enough to look pragmatically at scientific research, as well as look into what medical trials may or may not be available? I went over my friends and our network in my head. It was almost like I was doing an interview and scanning their life experiences as if I was recruiting for the most absurd job-role ever. Then I landed on it. Sarah!

She had been my bridesmaid when we got married and we had studied together at university. We were great friends but most importantly I trusted her implicitly. I also knew how bright she was because I'd sat next to her in seminar groups and seen the way she operated. Her intellectual capability was always so humbling and she was one of those unassuming, super-bright types who could always just do everything. She was perfect! I reached over to grab my phone and looked at the time. It was already approaching midnight so I knew I couldn't ring her now. Instead, I texted her replying to the message she'd already sent earlier in the day asking if there was anything I needed or how she could help. I punched out the words quickly knowing that she would understand and be able to act on them.

'Hey my love, that offer of doing something. Could I ask a huge favour? We have never looked into medical trials in this country or abroad before. George is now so sick that I'm getting desperate. Can I ask you to research if there are any treatment options left for him, here or abroad.? I'll email you a file with his medical notes tomorrow so you have it. Love you, L x'

I felt a weight lift as soon as I saw the message had been delivered to her phone and it felt good. That left spirituality still open and I knew before I even thought about it that this had to be me. It was such a personal thing that it couldn't really be anyone else. But I knew nothing about this type or way of living and didn't have any friends who knew much about it either.

The reality is as humans we are all so different in our belief systems but are also so very similar at-the-same-time. Did I know anyone who could help? As I lay there snuggled up with only my teddy-bear for company, I wondered if it was God who had made us as Adam and Eve and if it really all had multiplied from there?

118

But was I even like Eve? Who was she? I didn't know her! I really didn't think the world had begun with an energy like God. I mean how could it, I liked science too much and knew that the big bang theory was entirely plausible. But what about God, was he really the force that had started all of this, was he even real and if he was why wasn't he already here? I lay back in my bed and thought again about the night when I'd gone out looking for him. It wasn't even a week ago, but it felt like a lifetime. Did I really think he was actually going to show up and save us? And who on earth was this Brianna woman?

I switched the light off and tried to meditate myself to sleep but just couldn't. All I could hear was my small clock ticking gently on the bedside table next to me. There was a huge question on my mind now that I just couldn't answer, was he real, did the man in the clouds actually exist? As I lay there desperately trying to tune into the sounds of the clock, I found myself thinking back to my childhood. I'd learnt that taking my mind back into seasons of happiness was a good way of drifting into sleep but it was just so hard to find memories that weren't full of George.

One leapt out at me and the memory I found that night was me as a young girl. I was in my bedroom just like I was now, but in that moment I was at my parents' house and was perched on the end of the bed, rather than lying down. I was looking out of my childhood bedroom window because the view reassured and grounded me. It was nice looking at the other houses back then and wondering. In my mind's eye, I tried to peer through my six-year-old self to see if I could look into anyone else's homes and catch a glimpse of their lives. Even back then I remember wondering if they were like me and if we were connected?

In my memory I can hear the noise coming from downstairs, it distracts me from the ticking clock in this reality. My parents are with my brother in the kitchen and I remember the feeling that I sometimes used to like being on my own back then, it was nice and didn't happen all that often. I try and swallow up that feeling now as I lay alone in my marital bed. I look out of the window hoping to see something or someone but all I see is the fading light. I keep looking but there's nothing. So I turn my attention to my bedroom and fix my eyes on my jewellery box. As I lie in my bed as an adult I smile. I loved that jewellery box and remember how I used to stand on my bed and reach it down from the shelves. At the time I knew I wasn't supposed to climb up and yet took so much pleasure from being free back then, I needed to remember this now. It was almost as if I was back there and holding the box in my hands, feeling the patterns that were so smooth and special on my palms. Gently, I place the closed box on the window ledge and stare. I put my fingers on the metal clasp and pull it upwards, making sure I feel all of the detailed edges before I lift the lid. As soon as the box opens the ballerina starts to spin and the music starts too. It's old-fashioned and I watch the dancing-girl twirling in front of my eyes. Her tutu is a bit wonky. I smile replaying this memory, she looks a little like me when she dances.

I close my eyes and try to hear that music again. And then I remember what I used to do next; it's a part of the memory I've not revisited before. I remember that I was scared that day. I loved dancing, it made me feel happy but I often felt like I wasn't good enough; that I didn't quite look right because my arms felt wrong and my toes were never quite pointy enough.

Then I remember. I used to clench my eyes shut and whisper back then but I'm not sure who exactly I was whispering too.

'Help me. Help me. Help me with my dancing,' I would say, I remember that I would sometimes open my eyes to check no one was with me. Sometimes it felt like there was.

I jolted myself back into reality and looked at the clock on my bedside table. It was approaching 1 am. What was I supposed to do now, the thought of George in the hospital felt so desperate but I knew I shouldn't be working out how I was going to help him so late into the night but really couldn't help myself. It's like that when you love someone so much it physically hurts. So I tried to think of all of the people I knew who were religious.

There were a couple of people from work that I'd been in teams with who had always prayed. At the time I'd often looked enviously at their faith-filled lives but yet the logical part of my brain just couldn't understand how they believed in something I couldn't see? How were they basing their lives and beliefs on something that I didn't understand? I didn't get it. I sighed. It was worthless trying to do this thinking now. I needed to detach and switch my brain off. Somehow that night after all of that thinking and walking around old memories I fell asleep. The rest wasn't quick to arrive and it felt hideous when I was awakened by the cries of Jamie at 6 am.

The next morning I carried out the usual drills: nappy changing, breakfast eating, dressing. Somehow these mundane tasks had become therapy. Before I knew it, I was kissing the boys on their heads as our nanny came to take over from me and I was in my car again, driving to the hospital. It was in that moment that I came back to Kate's message.

I didn't know where on earth I was supposed to start with something as big as spirituality, but maybe her text about this woman Brianna was the answer? By the time I got to the hospital and I had resumed my position next to George's bed, I was ready to text Kate, I thought it was best to keep it brief so I simply said,

'I'd really like the details of those healing rooms please. x'

Understandably George wasn't much company at the hospital. I would arrive around 10 am and 'tag out' with his mum who had done the night-shift, holding his hand for comfort so he could rest. George would try and pretend he was OK even though by this point he had a tube inserted down his nose in an attempt to alleviate the pain in the back of his throat from the permanent bile he was regurgitating. Cancer had taken hold of his liver so much that it was squashing his stomach. It was disgustingly repugnant to observe and there wasn't much that could be done to help, George was exhausted.

On top of these symptoms, he was also a few days into chemo side effects. These were bad enough when he was feeling relatively well, so by adding dying, as well as not being able to eat or drink into the mix, multiplied by the hideous sick feeling only chemo can make you feel, it equated to a totally brutal experience. An experience which was utterly inhumane to observe.

I spent that day at the hospital on my laptop and walking to and from the coffee machine rather than talking. I kept my friends updated on text. I checked in with Sarah who had received my late-night plea for help and had already started her scientific research. I looked at the blank search engine open in front of me on my web browser. Where would I start with looking into spiritual healing? What even was that anyway, was it religious, was it a tie-dye wearing thing? I had no clue. Cautiously, I typed into the search bar, 'Spiritual healing techniques for cancer.' I was amazed by what came back.

I spent my morning on Google looking at different types of spiritual practices. There were so many people all over the world claiming that they had the magical cure I was looking for. There were a few websites that caught my eye and some even had prayer groups and healing circles I could request for George to be part of. If they had healing in the title, I assumed they had to be positive. From the anonymity of my email address and social media accounts, I contacted reiki, crystal and acupuncture therapists. I also spoke to reflexologists and healers. It felt good to be doing something as I had promised myself to leave no stone unturned.

Shortly after lunch, I didn't know what to do. I was still waiting for Kate to get back to me with information from Brianna and I kept looking at my phone willing something to happen and someone to save us. George was restless and falling in and out of sleep and after sitting in silence for what felt like forever with only the sound of the hospital monitors for company, I decided I needed to get help to process my thoughts.

The week before when our life had so rapidly spiralled, my psychologist Patricia had told me at one of our regular appointments that I could text her if I felt off balance. I sent her a message telling her what was going on and her response was almost immediate. I ended up stepping out of George's room and speaking to her briefly on the phone whilst huddled around the water-cooler, so the whole hospital didn't hear my sobs.

'There's just so much I want to tell him but don't know how,' I cried over the phone-line.

'Are you able to write?' She asked

'Yes,' I said through the tears.

'Then write! Write it all down,' she implored.

Her response was all the encouragement I needed so dutifully I went back to his bedside, pushed my legs up against the metal radiator underneath the window to keep warm and furiously typed on my phone. It felt better to write there, rather than on my laptop. That way it felt like I was sending him a message.

Monday 7th November

Dearest Georgie,

There is so much I want to say and as I sit here listening to the comforting sound of your sleepy breaths, I feel like I don't know where to begin. Thank you seems right. Thank you for making me believe in true love and fairy tales.

I never thought I could meet someone, who could understand me better than myself. In you though, that's what I have.

Thank you for loving every single part of me. Your love has truly helped me grow and change as a person. You've helped me see things in a way that I never could before and you've helped me achieve things that I never in my wildest dreams thought were possible.

Thank you for pushing and driving me to do things in life that I would never have previously even thought about. Thank you for all of the beautiful memories we have created as soul mates and as a family. I'm so desperate not to forget all of the small things, like our happy dance, like our cuddles, like our ability to know what the other person is thinking before we've even said it. So as I sit here holding your hand listening to you breathe and waiting to see which side the coin flips for us on this occasion, I can't help but feel thankful. Yes, I feel scared, for me, for you, for our boys, for all of us. But you have my promise that I will make whatever happens next, as bearable and comfortable for you as I possibly can. I feel frightened about what the next few days, weeks and maybe even months might have in store. I feel worried about how everyone will cope. What will happen when you're not at the centre of things to push us all on?

However, overwhelmingly I feel thankful. Thankful, that I have been blessed enough to call the greatest man I have ever met my husband. Thankful that you are the father to our two beautiful children, thankful that I was lucky enough to fall in love with you and be your wife. I have given up thinking about our situation as painful and unfair. Despite the pain, anguish, jealousy and all of the other hateful emotions, that I have felt over the past months. It is your strength, your fire, your positivity and your self-belief that have always kept me going. I now truly believe that whatever the outcome I have to take this strength and self-belief that you have so selflessly given me and use it wisely.

It brings a coy smile to my eyes to think about how you truly are Superman. It makes me sad to think, that maybe we've now found your kryptonite. I do however refuse to let this difficult chapter, mean a life of anything but happiness for your beautiful children and me. My soul loves your soul forever, L x'

Later that afternoon when George came around I told him about this letter. I even read him some parts but I never got the chance to read him the whole thing he was just too tired. Before I knew it his mum had returned for the nightshift and I was kissing my frail boy on the head saying goodbye and returning home to my other boys who were lovingly waiting for me there. Our nanny ushered me through the door when I got back weary and emotional. She hugged me before I reverted into mum-mode and stories.

That night after the bath and bedtime routine I fell into my bed. I tried to make a tent like we'd done in the old days but it was useless as even that didn't make me feel safe anymore. I looked at my phone and saw that in the rush of putting the boys to bed, I'd missed that Kate had finally got back to me with more details on Brianna and the healing circles she was linked to. The text gave me some key contact information for a church based in California that she was somehow linked to. The thought of that church couldn't have felt further removed from gloomy Nottinghamshire that night. Kate had also sent the links to their website and some helpful tips from Brianna about how I could get in touch with them for prayer.

Once I knew the boys were asleep I got into my pyjamas and then into bed. I pulled out my laptop from the bag thrown down on the floor by my bedside table and logged into the church website. Just a few clicks later I'd found the healing prayer request form. The web-page told me that I had to download a Microsoft Word document. I was annoyed,

'Really?' I thought, 'is this how people actually pray? They use MS Word?!' I wasn't sure what I'd been expecting but it felt so corporate and so alien. I studied the questions that followed and came to the conclusion that it was almost like a request for feedback form that I had filled in multiple times at work. I definitely wasn't vibing this approach as it wasn't at all how I'd imagined this healing-prayer process to be.

'Was it even a process?' I wondered out loud. I couldn't get my head around it. I stared at the questions on my screen for a little while and even attempted to type some responses. I soon realised that I had to ditch the form because it wasn't working for me so I clicked out of the screen and looked back at the website to see if there was a phone number I could call. I looked at my phone, it was getting late in the UK, so jumped across the screens to clocks. I was quickly informed that it was still only morning in California so took a deep breath and punched the number into the screen.

I got the ring tone almost immediately. It took me back to the moment in time when my older brother and I used to get up early on Saturday mornings and desperately ring kids' TV shows. We were obsessed with trying to get a mention back then. We used to feel so much hope on those dark mornings, so much excitement. I felt that hope bubble up in me once again as I was so expectant this might be it. Could this be the salvation connection I'd been hoping to make on that wet rainy evening just a few days ago? The phone kept on ringing. I waited.

'Come on,' I said out loud, 'pick up. Pick up!'

After an epic amount of ringing, I got through to the answerphone. The voice was classically charming, in the way that only the Americans can be. It was very 'hospitality.' But the last part of the recording took me aback. Rather than hearing,

'Please leave a message after the beep,' I was shocked to be told, 'you are loved.' I was taken aback by the intimacy.

Here I was on my bed in Nottinghamshire phoning a church in California I had never even heard of but taking so much hope from such a simple phrase. I knew I was desperate but this message had struck a chord in my heart somewhere. It was inexplicable, so beautiful and exactly what I needed to hear. At that moment I'd even go as far as saying it imprinted a little bit of sparkle, hope and wonder into my heart. I didn't leave a message; I wasn't really sure what to say. But even though it was the US and call charges were extortionate, I called back another two or three times just to hear that I was loved again. It soothed my soul. It re-balanced me.

In many ways, I recognised that I was off-balance but those three words gifted me rest and sleep. They allowed me to recalibrate before the day started again and I had to start the relentless whir of getting the kids up and dressed, handing them over to our nanny before driving across Nottinghamshire to go and sit next to George as he died.

So another day rolled around. But on this day by the time I had myself installed at George's bedside I was deeply intrigued. The answerphone experience the night before had led me to want to understand what these 'healers,' actually did and who they were. So I sent another message to Kate asking if there was any other way of getting in touch with them.

The texts flew around the globe like wildfire that morning. Kate contacted Brianna and I was also sent her number so I could contact her directly. Brianna had, in turn, reached out to someone in her network called Emma. Emma attended the church in California and often worked in the healing rooms there. Brianna seemed to think that going through her might be a better way of us getting in touch for prayer.

As I sat by the bedside again and waited, twiddling my thumbs and watching pain creep into George's body, I felt in my heart that I was circling something. I couldn't quite put my finger on what it was though. Was it the connection between me and these women from America, was this God's doing, is that how he worked? I really didn't understand what he could and couldn't do. I didn't even think he was real but what I did understand were words like 'fate,' and 'it's meant to be.' I also knew that I loved George more than I could even articulate and truly believed that the connection between us was powerful. As I sat there holding his hand I wondered if my love was enough to save him and could feel my own mind jostling.

'Did I really just want a miracle?' I thought. 'Was I searching for George to be healed, like the woman the doctor had told us about, all those months ago?' Then the thought was clear. 'Yes. Yes, I did. I wanted a miracle, I wanted anything I could get my hands on that might help but I didn't know how to get it, how to believe God was true and could save. All I knew was that I loved so hard and fiercely that I wanted it to save him. I didn't know what else to do other than pour this love into words.

Tuesday 8th November

Dearest Georgie,

Today my letter is about fate. I'm not sure why we're in this pickle and why destiny means that this is happening to us, but sadly, it is. I keep hearing your voice in my head and reminding myself that I have two choices, happiness or unhappiness. I'm determined to choose happiness but am scared about the amount of unhappiness that we both might be forced to experience along the way! You have my word, that I will keep my head, whilst those around me maybe lose theirs. But at the moment it's hard. It's bloody hard. I need you. I don't know how to do this on my own! I have waves of feeling like I'm invincible and I can help you, our boys and our families through this. But then they're swiftly followed by waves of pure emptiness, devastation and uncontrollable grief. Grief for a loss that has not yet even been realised. This unhappiness is cruel and all-encompassing- it's unbearable. This is why I can only look to the light. I have to choose happiness and believe in fate, believe in something bigger than us all even though I don't know what this is.

There have been so many strange twists of 'fate' in our story together. The fact that I wasn't accepted into the chocolate factory first-time round felt like such a hard blow at the time. I now truly believe that this was down to the fact that the stars aligned ahead of us so I could meet you when you were wearing your red tie and reading the paper the first day.

The fact that I've already had to nurse you through sickness; your stints in hospital for various hip and collar bone replacements mean I'm already used to all of this; the mother of all hospital stays. The fact that you drove us to relocate our life to my hometown just before you were diagnosed. The fact that certain people have come into our lives and those that were distant lights before, now burn so much more brightly now we need them most.

Fate is a beautiful, illogical destiny that we have no power over. It is this sense of powerlessness that I'm finding remarkably comforting. Knowing that I can only do what I'm doing today. Knowing that I can only keep putting one foot in front of the other, trusting and hoping that I will understand the reason soon as to why all of this has happened and come to know if some divine force or your Superman body can help us find a way through?.

I don't think this has really happened for any kind of reason, you definitely don't deserve it and I don't think we need to be taught any lessons. I can't help but wonder though what small positives I can take from this desperately bleak situation? Is all of this going to make me be a better Mum? Is it going to make me a nicer person? I really don't know! And then, it all just seems so brutal, that the person who I love most dearly has to go through all of this to teach me something! Or am I just missing the point entirely? Maybe that's just it? There is no point? It's all just the existentialist passing of time?

I'm sorry my love. I'm so sorry that this is the hand you have been dealt. I wish I could take your place. I just hope my love can give you wings and strength to fly through this in a way I don't know or see yet. I don't know why, but there IS a reason that I'm here helping you through this. The only reason I can find for now is that my soul feels at peace near yours. It will love you always and forever. Part of me will always be yours. Whatever happens next, I'm with you, always. I love you, Lx'

That afternoon was the first time I opened my heart to the fact that there was something bigger going on. It was the first time I allowed myself to believe that Kate's text wasn't just a coincidence. I also knew I wasn't going mad and my regular check-ins with Patricia the psychologist confirmed this.

Yes, I was looking for a reason and wanted to attempt to rationalize what was happening but was that a bad thing? All I wanted was some comfort and I had always seen some of that in people I knew who believed in God. I could see their passion and their purpose but couldn't understand how they believed in something they couldn't actually see. I was starting to see some of the seemingly consequential connections that had been buzzing around us in our lives together though. They were increasingly becoming more and more obvious. Was I only now attempting to piece them together and make sense because he was dying? As the day continued to tick on and in spite of some of the connections I had made, there was only a negative change in George. It was disgusting and all that was visibly happening was him falling further down into darkness.

Later that night I was so exhausted that Mum came and slept

with me in my bed. She held me close as I cried myself to sleep and hugged me in the same way I hugged the boys. When the sun rose on Wednesday morning we were all prepared for another hard day and as I got dressed, I couldn't help but wonder if this situation could get any worse, it all just felt so black.

When I got to the hospital the medical team had made a decision overnight that it might be sensible for us to talk to a gastric specialist. George was in so much pain that they wanted us to investigate the possibility of him having surgery to alleviate the huge amount of discomfort he was in. The medics were as distressed as we were that they couldn't manage the pain. We all knew that having an operation was drastic but it felt like the only viable option that could help. It was scary too because none of us had factored in another surgery at this late stage and George was already so weak even though he was desperately trying to be strong.

That Wednesday was an incredibly difficult day. Brianna was in touch a few times over text as I kept trying and failing to get hold of her friend Emma in the States. Because of the difficulty I'd had pinning Emma down, we decided instead that Brianna would come and pray with us in person that weekend. It was every part as random as it sounds but I was getting nowhere else with any other spiritual avenues I'd been pursuing, despite the fact I was permanently wondering if there was something more.

My head was so full that I didn't process what I was organising with Brianna. In the cold light of day I was talking to a stranger and had invited her to come and pray with us, something we didn't even do, at one of the most hideously intimate moments of our lives. George had already told me very firmly that he didn't want a load of visitors streaming past his bedside.

'Family is fine,' he said, 'but everyone else is a no. I don't want anyone else to see me like this, I don't want the whole world coming to say goodbye.'

I'm still not sure why I thought it was OK to invite a complete stranger into my husband's death - at the time I didn't even give it a second thought. It was because I was so certain it was something I needed to do.

George was in the most pain he'd been in since the beginning and I passionately believed that this couldn't be what his death was supposed to be. That the end of his beautiful life could be as miserable as what I was seeing in front of my eyes.

All of the training I'd undertaken in the corporate world always informed me I was positive. But the positivity I was feeling now was something else, it was like I was channelling it from an unknown source.

It was completely at odds with the situation I was in. Even I couldn't explain how the love of my life was lying in bed next to me, writhing around in agony and I still felt sort of positive that something would happen. That it might all be OK. I was so expectant of salvation and believed that there just had to be another way out.

I knew it couldn't just end like this; it was too hideous for such a magnificent human to leave the world in this way.

So I kept writing in an attempt to figure it all out.

Dearest Georgie,

Today I feel frightened. It's scary that we're having to accept the reality of what might be happening. I've got so many questions I want to ask you about how you want things to turn out for the boys? What kind of funeral you would like? If there is anything you want me to do? If there is something you need to tell me so your mind can be at peace? I can see your mind whirring. The wheels are spinning inside thinking about the boys, wondering if you will see them again, wondering if you'll get to come home. I can see you soaking in my face as you tell me how much you love me.

I'm oscillating between extreme fear and extreme hope. I can't explain it! It's the hope that is propelling me on. I want to look past the bleakness of your diagnosis, the concave nature of your cheeks and the anguished look in your eyes. I want to help you believe that it will be OK, because I love you. I believe in you, your body, your strength and your soul. It's so hard to sit here imagining the scenarios in my mind.

What if this is it? What if this isn't it and it's going to get a whole load worse? What if we can still make a come-back? What if we can defy the odds and make miracles happen? Some people do and if anyone can I sincerely believe it's you.

Willing a miracle is what's driving me on. I accept the flip side of this situation and what it means - I've spent so many hours these last few days, thinking about how my life will be without you. How we will never ever forget you and how we will celebrate the fact that we were lucky enough to love you. It pains me to say that I've already started to mourn you even though you're here! I'd be lying if I said I hadn't thought about if today will be the last time I'll see you?! I've given up trying to prepare myself for the utter devastation that I know I will feel when the time comes. I can't even bring myself to think about it.

But there's only so long I can think about such grief and pain and the gigantic unknown it all is. What makes me smile and gives me wind in my sails is to think about our boys and to think about miracles. You told me today that the boys will look after me. I know they will. In Charlie and Jamie, I have got the greatest gift anyone could ever give- unconditional love. I also have part of you that will forever be mine.

So that brings me to you my love. You're such a fascinating mix of science and spirituality. I can see your head struggling to make sense of the scientific warfare going on in your body but I can also see your soul looking for peace. That peace is what gives me strength and is what is helping me believe in miracles. The miracle of healing, the miracle that some divine power somewhere will help your body work this through. Don't give up yet my love, it doesn't feel like it's time. Hope is coming, I love you and your soul forever, L x'

George never heard the highlight reel of this letter. He was too ill and I didn't get the chance to talk to him about where he was finding the moments of peace I could so visibly see either. I'd always known that he was spiritual, he had always had it in him to look at the world through this lens, but he wasn't a follower of God. It also felt hideously inappropriate to tell him I believed it was going to be OK even though I could clearly see how much pain he was living through. So the day continued and we waited until the early hours of the evening to see the gastric surgeon who we would then have the most unbearable chat with. We were forced to discuss the possibility of signing up to the risky procedure of a bypass; an operation that could kill George as he was already so weak. We were desperate to try though and do anything that might reduce the pain.

The evening meal trolley came around and as usual, George didn't take anything but instead sucked on ice cubes from the 'bar' that we had fashioned in his bathtub. That week I took drink requests from him like I was a Las Vegas bartender. Everyone wanted to find something that might ease the pain so no request from him was too out there. Flat cherry coke, yep, I made that happen. I still remember the bizarre looks I got, as I stood outside his room, beating coke inside a jug with an egg whisk, to try and get the bubbles out.

'I'm just making it flat,' I shouted as I smiled.

When the surgeon came that evening, we were both sucking on ice lollies; they had been the request from the bar that day and I'd dutifully made it happen. As we sat there earnestly moving the ice lollies around our mouths we looked like kids. The chat soon took on a heavy and serious tone. The man before us was a new guy and he looked a little old school in his suit. He took charge of the conversation and told us rather gruesomely what it would take for him to operate. He looked George in the eye and boldly said.

'There's a strong chance you could die on my operating table, you need to know this before you sign the forms.'

Even though we'd already been told this information by the nurses it somehow felt different now we were sitting in front of the man who would wield the scalpel. It was an awful lot to take on board whilst also knowing that this would not be the miraculous cure we both so desperately wanted. We looked at each other and looked back to him.

'Where's the form?' George said passing his ice lolly to me. 'I want to sign it.'

After the surgeon left, our heads were in a horrid place. Rachel came up to see us from the chemo ward and I told her that we felt backed into a corner. She comforted us with her kind words and after I'd made sure George was alright with his mum I drove myself back home. As I navigated the country lanes and reflected on the day, I knew that George had effectively signed his death-warrant for Saturday. The three options I'd come up with only two days earlier were rapidly failing us. All it seemed we had left was this brutal choice of surgery and it felt like George was being forced to run uphill towards the end of life.

My musings were rapidly interrupted by the loud ringing of my phone through my car speakers. It was Emma who was Facetime calling me from America.

'I can't pray now,' was all I said when I answered, 'I'm driving.' It was never a sentence I had ever expected to utter, but somehow, I just had. In the crazy world I was now inhabiting, it was somehow normal to sign up for surgery in one hour and then tell a complete stranger, on the other side of the world, I couldn't pray, in the next. Even though I wasn't entirely sure what praying even was.

When I got home Mum and George's sister were waiting for me with a warm dinner and hugs whilst our nanny put the boys in the bath. As we gathered around the table for dinner I filled them in on the big decision we had made that day. Nobody in the world knew about what we'd decided apart from myself, George and his mum. We were the only three people outside of the hospital team that were aware. As I relayed what would happen it was an emotional moment for Mum and George's sister as we all knew what this surgery might mean. As we sat huddled at the end of the dining table we all agreed that as long as George wanted the operation then it was the right decision to make.

As we were finishing up our meal my phone rang. I looked down hoping it wasn't the hospital with bad news. To my surprise, it was Brianna who was calling me. Up until this point we hadn't spoken on the phone, we'd only texted a few times and I knew this was a call I had to answer. It felt like my soul knew there was a message for me which is why I think my stomach flipped as I picked up. I had no idea what this woman who could talk to God was going to say. I excused myself from the table and walked into the other room so I could answer.

'Hi Brianna,' I said, trying to sound together.

'Hey Louise,' came this lovely American accent from the end of the phone. It was strange. Kate had told me that Brianna was American but I was still shocked to hear her voice. It was so different from all of the other voices I'd spoken to that day, so at odds. Immediately it took me right back to the answerphone message from the American church I had listened to a few nights ago. It also conjured up images of out there, over-the-top Christians I must have seen somewhere on TV. I always thought they were a bit weird maybe even brainwashed.

'So,' said the American drawl, 'how are you guys?'

I was taken aback by the simplicity of her tone and the authenticity of her line of questioning. It was so lovely, but felt so alien given that she was a stranger and I was suddenly reminded that I didn't know her at all. I felt myself stumbling for my words and kept moving my mouth until eventually something came out.

'Well, erm, things aren't great,' I started, 'well actually, things really aren't that good at all. He's very, very sick.'

I didn't know what else to say, how could I even start to describe how bad it had really got? It hurt my heart and my head to have to even describe it. As I stood there, thinking about what to say next, she spoke for me.

'I see,' she responded. 'Louise, I'm just so very sorry.'

It was odd, so many people had said this to us since George had been diagnosed; this type of phrase had become part of the rhythm of our conversation, but somehow her response was different, I could just tell that she just got it. I couldn't put my finger on how I was so certain of this but I felt that she understood the pain in my heart there was something in her tone that genuinely was really sorry. She meant that she was sorry in a way unlike I'd heard from other people before. Usually I just sensed that they were relieved this nightmare wasn't happening in their lives, but her tone and her grasp of the situation unnerved me.

'I've been praying tonight over George,' she went on.

I just stood in disbelief, rooted to the floor as my mum looked on. Who was this woman? She seemed so nice and yet didn't even know us. She knew nothing about us other than what Kate had told her at the wedding. I was shocked to hear she had been praying for us, I didn't know people even did that and definitely didn't know anyone else quite like her. It all felt so kind and I felt humbled.

'The thing is,' she went on, 'I'm not going to be able to make it this Sunday. A few things have come up and I'm going to need to come on Friday?'

By this point, I'd turned a little cold and was looking with my eyes wide open at Mum. She mouthed to ask me if I was alright.

'So, can I come and pray on Friday?' She was cheery now. 'I've actually got loads of work to do but I still really want to come.'

I couldn't think of how to reply and was in shock. How did this girl who I'd never met but had spoken to my friend about God at a wedding and then asked to pray for us, even though she'd never met us, know on some seemingly bizarre and apparently inconsequential level, that Sunday might be too late? For whatever reason she couldn't make it. But how could she know we'd just potentially signed off George's death? Did she even know, did she even realise the ramification of her re-organising the day she would visit?

I felt sweaty. This was scary and I was completely freaked out. I can't remember what I mumbled about the fact that George was going to have an operation. She once again kindly continued, to hold the space for me to process what was happening; the enormity of every last part. Even though I wasn't actually sure if she was even aware herself? It seemed she knew but didn't know.

My mind was racing. Who was she? I began to wonder if maybe she was a psychic medium, I'd never believed in anything like that up until this point, but this seemed to be too on the money. Too accurate.

'So, do you know if the hospital has Wi-Fi?' she asked, continuing to fill the gaps, as I grappled for words.

'Yes,' I said, 'there's definitely an internet connection available.'

We finished up the conversation, by re-organising for her to come that Friday. I thanked her profusely and said goodbye.

I didn't know what do to next so simply went and sat down at my dining room table and put my head in my hands. I was so shocked.

Mum and George's sister had been clearing up the dishes whilst I'd taken the call.

'What's going on, love?' Mum asked.

By this point I was numb. I didn't know what to feel.

'I don't know,' I said, 'it's something really weird though. You know how I just told you about the operation? Well nobody knows. It's literally you guys, George, the medics and George's mum. I don't know how, but I think she knows. I think she knows, but, doesn't even realise that she knows. I think Brianna knows that George might die on Saturday! She's just changed the day that she's going to come and pray. She's coming on Friday instead. I just don't think it's a coincidence. It can't be.'

Mum looked at me, her eyes wide and her mouth tight.

'Right,' she said, 'Well, we'll have to see what happens then.'

Praying part I

After dinner, I was forced into fast-tracking Charlie's understanding of death. I didn't think it was worth trying to explain to Jamie in the same way because he'd only turned one a few months earlier. As we sat and read books together at bedtime, our bodies snuggled tightly together, I knew I had to find the words to let him know what was happening around in. I held on to him super tight and said, 'Daddy is so very poorly Charlie. He's not going to come home. The doctors have said he's going to die.' I watched his little face look at me, baffled and confused. I knew at that moment he really had no understanding of the weight of the words he was hearing.

'All of our bodies break at some point you know, they stop working, like old cars,' he looked at me and smiled,

'Car, car?' These were his favourite toys.

'Bodies will always break,' I went on, trusting my heart to know the way and find the words, 'and then, well, we die.'

I sat and held him close, breathing in the smell of his hair. He didn't say anything back, but simply gave me the bear named Hereford that belonged to George as a child and was now Charlie's firm favourite.

'Hereford cuddle?' was all he said.

He didn't understand the gravity behind what I was saying but could easily navigate the sadness all over my heart. Children, I was learning, could read and often respond to emotion better than most grown-ups.

I went to bed that night with my mind filled with so many things but found enough peace to rest just a little. Mum came and lay next to me in my bed again. Her presence was soothing, she wanted to take away the hurt, show me that she was there and being close to her relaxed me in the same way it had done as a child. But we both knew, that however much she lay on George's side of the bed, it wouldn't take away the pain. She couldn't ever fill the place he occupied in my heart, not even with all the love in the world.

How had it got to this point? How was I thirty-three years old and sleeping with my mum because I was scared? I had to force myself to block out the fear and not see the image of George lying in his death-bed several miles away. In order to sleep I had to make myself detach and focus on what I still had and all of the other love that surrounded me. I snuggled into my mum's chest just as I'd done as a child and could hear her heartbeat and love. Somehow that protective force-field lessened the pain and bound protective energy around me as I slept that night.

Thursday morning came around fast. I had decided with Mum the night before to see Patricia my psychologist before going over to the hospital. I had found her advice on writing letters to George so helpful that I was keen to see her face to face to understand if she had any more wisdom that may soothe my soul; particularly because I had this whole situation with Brianna brewing. As I knocked on her red front door, feeling the brass knocker between my fingers, I felt expectant and hopeful that she was going to offer some hope as to how to navigate the storm. I sat down on her comfortable sofa and explained how very sick George had become since we'd last met face to face. I didn't cry simply because there were no tears left that morning. I carefully told her about the letters I'd been writing and we talked a little about their content and how it felt to get the feelings out of my soul and on to my phone. I then went on to explain that my family friend Kate had connected me to an American called Brianna. A woman who claimed to be connected to God and who Kate had found peacefully disarming with her empathy for our circumstances at a mutual friend's wedding.

'It's strange,' I began, 'I did something drastically out of character just a few days before I was connected to Brianna.' I felt almost ashamed as the words tumbled out of my mouth,

'Before George went into the hospital, we had a big falling out. I was so mad with him that I took myself off in the car, searching for something, I'm not sure what.'

I was looking at her directly into her eyes now searching to see if she would show a flicker of judgement that I had left my sick husband at home alone.

'I cried out to God,' I blurted, 'I'm not really sure why I did it, but I asked him to help me. I think it's because this all just feels so desperate like there's no way out. No hope'

It felt strange to admit this to another human and share the secret of what I'd done. She continued to look at me straight in the eye, gently nodding and willing me to continue.

Patricia had seen me in more 'normal' life circumstances, grappling with the baggage George's disease had brought, as well as everyday life. In our previous session, I had navigated and talked through the scenario of what George's death might be like for me and him. Now I was actually living this scenario it was most unlike what we'd spoken about and worked through. He was in so much more pain than I'd ever believed possible and I was feeling so much more desperate than I couldn't have even imagined. But Patricia had the measure of my way of thinking and my view of the world. She knew my likes and dislikes and spiritual views had never really been up for debate before. They weren't something I ever thought I had yet alone put on the table for discussion.

'I was so desperate,' I said, 'that I didn't know what else to do.' I waited to see if she'd fill the silence but there was still quiet.

'I'm not sure if it's one big coincidence or not, that this American woman has got in touch with me.' I paused, took a deep breath and then said what I was holding back.

'And that she's told Kate that she has this connection with God.' I paused and Patricia gently nodded again.

'Whenever I talk about her though, it's really odd. She seems to crop up, it's like the universe is bouncing her at me even though I've only known her a few days,' I trailed off realizing that I sounded almost delusional.

'She called last night for the first time,' I looked across distantly at the greeting cards displayed on the mantelpiece, almost not daring to say out loud the words that came next.

'I can't explain it Patricia, I feel like we're connected. There's something about her, it's like she knows what is going on! We seem to have this strange, almost out of this world connection that I can't quite put my finger on.'

I stared at the artwork on the walls feeling almost ashamed to admit my thought process out loud. And then, at that moment, the precise moment I told Patricia Brianna and I seemed to be connected, my phone pinged. The jolt of the sound unnerved me and brought me back to reality.

'Let me check this,' I said, 'It could be George's mum asking for me to bring something to the hospital.' I looked down at my phone screen and then back up with my mouth wide open in utter disbelief.

'It's her,' I said, 'she just texted me, I don't believe it.' I was shaken to my core.

Patricia sat back in her chair and looked at me over the top of her glasses. She breathed in gently before asking,

'Is the message anything of significance?'

I looked down at my phone and scanned over the words, the message was simply about train times for the next day. Was I going mad, was I just reading too much into all of this because George was so ill? Patricia broke my pensive silence with her soothing voice.

'It does appear that there maybe is a connection between the two of you,' she was validating what I was seeing to pull me back into the conversation but then said,

'Do you think she might harm you in any way?'

I was alarmed by the direct line of her questioning. We'd never had a conversation quite like this before and even I hadn't seriously considered that this might be the case. I felt scared.

'You're most certainly incredibly vulnerable at the moment. Do you think this lady might want to take advantage of you or George or hurt you in anyway?'

I was shocked by what I was hearing.

'No,' I said genuinely believing that this was the case, 'but there's definitely something about her, she's not dangerous though, she knows people I know, they can vouch for her. She's friends with my friends but I also feel like she knows stuff. It's all so odd.' I trailed off once more.

'Who do you think she is?' Patricia probed, 'what do you think she stands for?'

I sat reflecting; it was a really big question.

'I really don't know,' I thought out loud, 'but something inside me tells me I have to find out.'

The conversation proceeded to wrap up quickly after this as I was needed back at the hospital. Patricia hugged me and watched as I stepped out of her house and into my car waving me off like a protective Aunt. Our session had unsettled me more than I'd anticipated but I forced my mind back to George and back to the day in hand.

There were no crazy drink requests that morning so it was a straightforward drive over to the hospital. George had rallied ever so slightly overnight, as a couple of days previously, I'd insisted the hospital give him intravenous food to complement the saline he was being given.

'He's already in so much pain,' I'd argued with one of his doctors, 'let's not starve him too.'

When I arrived he was as I'd left him, hooked up to so many machines, eyes wincing in pain and his face looking paler by the hour. It was just like all the other days that had gone before and so I sat and we waited.

We were wearing our Invictus T-shirts that day. In the summer between radiotherapy and liver surgery, when George had cycled one-hundred miles around London for charity, his friends had gifted him an Iron-Man comic-book-style print at the end of the race. Out of the speech bubbles were the words from the Invictus poem. When our friends had found out that George was dying our post box had suddenly become inundated with gifts of encouragement. There was one stand out present though and it came from the group of friends that George had cycled with. They had sent us the same Invictus 'Iron Man,' but this time it was printed on his and hers T-shirts. It was totally cheesy almost a little cringe but we loved them.

On that Thursday morning the only request I'd had from

George, via his mum was,

'Bring the Invictus T-shirt.'

Dutifully that's what I did. As soon as I arrived we put our matching T-shirts and game faces on so we could sit and wait together, watch another day roll around and anticipate death. Being sat next to a terminally ill patient was upsetting, but if I'm honest it was also at times pretty boring. We were in a holding area waiting for this big and scary life-event to happen, but there were also long periods of time when nothing at all happened. In these moments I'd gently hold George's hand, clock watch, quietly respond to the messages that were coming in on my phone or simply just sit and write. I'd also spend time just looking at George. Soaking in his body and wondering if I'd still remember what he looked like as I grew older and the number of years we would be apart expanded through time.

The moment of the day that I would always anticipate would be when one of the doctors appeared. This wasn't because it was exciting. Most of the time it was just more bad news, sprinkled with words of encouragement. But at the same time, it was still a moment in the day to wait for and anchor around. We were utterly at the mercy of their schedules which could vary from first thing in the morning to fairly late at night. So I would sit and see if I could predict when someone important might arrive. It was a weird game I played with myself.

That day the doctor didn't make her rounds until much later. I felt relieved when she arrived because I knew that once we'd spoken, I could go back home and see our boys.

'How are you feeling today George?' she said, 'let's take a look at what's going on, shall we?'

The start of these chats had almost become like wallpaper to me. I listened but didn't concentrate as the doctor and nurse discussed whether any of the prescribed medication was helping to ease the pain. It was only when she started to ask about the operation that things got a little more interesting and I sat up in my chair.

'Are you really sure you want to do it?' she asked, looking at George directly in the eyes and completely by-passing me.

'Well, what else do you think he's supposed to do?' I interrupted, realising that I looked ever so slightly ridiculous wearing the same T-shirt as my husband.

'There's not really any other choice,' I said, 'we're totally backed into a corner here.'

'There are always choices,' she said as she looked squarely at me, 'You could quite simply do nothing.'

Doing nothing wasn't in our DNA, did this woman not know us well enough by now to realise this? I was so mad with her response but before I had the chance to think of something restrained to say, George quietly answered in my place.

'I don't want to do it,' he said starting to cry, 'I just can't.'

I was stunned by what came out of his mouth and I didn't even give the medics time to reply,

'Oh, my love,' I said gripping his hand, 'then you don't have to! Remember what we said, we always said that when it was time we would know.'

By that point, the fact that two other people were standing in the room with us had completely gone out of my mind.

'You are the master of your fate. You are the captain of your soul,' I forcefully quoted at him. The words of the Invictus poem flying off my lips as I jumped on to the bed and threw my arms around his neck to protect him. He was still crying and I wiped away his tears with my fingers as he said,

'I just can't do this anymore. Any of it.'

It was all I needed to hear to put the brakes on. He was broken. Quietly, inside another piece of my heart was breaking too. When someone you love tells you they've had enough of dying, even though they're not even dead, it's all so very hard. The hope I had fleetingly been feeling felt far away and it rapidly seemed that there wasn't going to be an easy way out of this mess. George had been so brave and while there had been several moments of fear and weakness, there had never been anything like this.

The bright lights of the hospital always had a harsh way of bringing you back into focus. There was still the business of decisions that needed to be made and my gorgeous George lay there weeping, looking so helpless and holding my hand. I looked towards the doctor and the nurse.

'So, what do we do now?' I asked.

'Well we just wait,' said the nurse. What she meant was that we sit it out, we wait for nature to take its course and watch whilst George's body ravages him from the inside out until he dies.

Even though I didn't want to wait I respected that would be

what would happen because George had chosen this route. I didn't show him how upset I was because he already knew I wasn't a fan of waiting; that was why he'd agreed to have the operation in the first place. He wanted to be a hero, he wanted his body to get better as much as I did. But it was rapidly becoming apparent that this was never going to happen. Nothing was coming through for us. The corner we had been backed into was getting darker and darker, further away from the light. In these moments of despair, it's often when you learn the most about yourself and your relationships with others. I learnt a lot about my marriage even in those last few days.

Our relationship wasn't just about romantic love. It was also about wanting what the other person wanted and above all wanting to shoulder the burden of some of their pain and hurt. All I had ever wanted was to help George. To shower him with my love. I never wanted him to be forced into doing something with his own body that he wasn't completely happy with. That wasn't what I'd ever signed up for as his wife. The decision to have drastic surgery and 'die trying,' as I had so crudely called it, was completely stopped in that instant. If George didn't want to have the operation then I didn't want it either. I knew I was on his side with this. It was what we did, we looked out for each other. Till death us do part.

What happened next was a haze. There was lots of chat about carrying on with the various treatments that weren't working. Then there was the daily debate which tried to ascertain George's specific symptoms and if there was anything else the medics could prescribe to help him feel more comfortable. We vaguely talked about hospices and if we should move him somewhere else. We covered what would happen now, how George might die. At some point in the conversation, it was suggested it might be sensible for George to see a hospital psychologist. A couple of hours later an unfamiliar figure appeared. She wore a black city-style suit and carried a briefcase and looked entirely different from Patricia. Her professionalism frightened me. I was asked to step outside and respect George's privacy whilst they spoke. I never did find out what they talked about that evening. It wasn't for me to know.

As I sat outside by the coffee machine for what felt like weeks a nurse returned and I was invited back into the room. The lady in the suit politely asked if I could go and buy polo mints from the vending machine. I was bemused but dutifully did what I had been asked. It turns out these were for a mindfulness exercise she had taught him. We were told to get the mint and suck it for as long as we could. Feel it in our mouth; the texture on the teeth, the saliva around the edges, the minty freshness in the space in between. We spent a long time, sitting alongside one another, wearing matching T-shirts, holding hands and knowing there was nothing else left for either of us that night. Both of us forced ourselves to be present with our polo mints. I haven't sucked one since.

The evening felt desperately flat. George requested to be left on his own and it was the first time that his mum didn't stay over with him. As I drove home I found myself pondering that death couldn't be this brutal and wondering if there was something more that could still help us. Surely there had to be. The polos helped a little on my drive but after half an hour or so I realised my soul wasn't soothed. George had decided to die but the apparent course his body was taking him on was ridiculously harsh. When I'd imagined a cancer death, in all of the scenarios I'd talked through with Patricia, I'd never believed it to be this bad. I naively thought that he would be medicated through it, knocked out by opiate-based drugs taking him to a place of serenity before his body was done. I couldn't bring myself to think about it getting any worse for him than it already was. It was like I was watching him being tortured.

It turns out though that hope was coming. I still hadn't realised that Brianna was the key to what I'd asked to be shown. At this point, it seemed impossible to fathom that someone coming to pray would even help. After all, nothing had helped us so far.

I went home that night and barely slept. I awoke to Friday morning before the sun had even risen. It was a big day not just because I knew I had a stranger coming to pray with us – I mean yes, that was nerve-wracking, because I didn't pray. But the fact George had just decided he wanted to die sooner rather than later, was much more pressing on my mind. I was living out an extreme version of don't sweat the small stuff.

If I'd signed up to pray in any other set of circumstances I'm certain I would have talked myself out of it. I would have worried and thought too much about what other people might think. I would have told myself prayer wasn't real and I was being ridiculous. I would have convinced myself that it was a bad choice and be afraid that I'd get brain-washed into believing something that I thought was there to placate others and make them feel better about the brokenness of their lives. I most definitely wasn't glad that George was dying. But what I am amazed and utterly grateful for was how I didn't have a moment to think about what I was about to do next. The timing was impeccable and not a coincidence.

When I arrived at the hospital the reality was there had been no change in George overnight. He was still in so much pain and the only change had been a mental one. Browbeaten into a corner he'd decided it was now on his terms as to when he would die, but just because he had decided this, it didn't change any of his painful symptoms. He was still hideously uncomfortable, arguably even more upset and was in a huge amount of discomfort.

Despite the fact I was desperately intrigued to find out who Brianna was I wasn't up to going to the train station to collect someone I'd never met before. I had wanted to spend as much time as possible with George, so Kate willingly stepped in to help. She didn't ask any questions about what we were going to do and I believe because of this, it was meant to be her who brought Brianna to us. After all, she was the one who had followed her heart and connected us in the first instance. And so it was shortly after lunch when George's room was dark to help welcome some sleep, that my phone pinged with a message from her.

'We're downstairs in the canteen. K x'

As I walked down two flights of stairs it was the first time I actually had the chance to think about what I was doing. In the short distance I walked across the hospital to meet Kate and Brianna, the saboteur's voice kicked in good and proper. I raced across the scenarios that I'd not even had any time or inclination to think about before. It was like there was a loud-speaker in my mind.

'Was I mad? Is this what losing your mind looked like? What if I had invited a stark raving loony into one of the most closed moments of my life? What will George think? What if this woman is a bit odd? What if she sees that you don't believe? C'mon Louise, you're not even a Christian, what on earth are you doing? You don't believe in God! You know he's not real!'

As I wrestled with all of these thoughts I realised it was utterly pointless. Brianna had travelled from London to come and see us and had asked for nothing in return. If I'm honest, I kept expecting her to request some type of payment but she never did. I was just so utterly dumbfounded that someone could be so kind and show such grace to a couple she'd never even met.

As I turned the corner into the canteen I saw them straight away. They were huddled around a table together and Kate was wearing her work uniform. I remember feeling relieved when the face next to her looked up and smiled.

'It's OK,' I thought, 'she looks normal.'

It's funny how we make such snap decisions based on what people look like and at that moment I've never found jeans and a Breton top more soothing. I felt instantly relieved when I saw she was wearing the same type of clothes that I would wear. She could totally pass for one of my friends which made the knot in my stomach subside. Her long-curly hair danced around her face as she looked straight into my eyes. She had perfected the art of knowing how to talk before she'd even uttered a word. Her smile showed so much compassion in one glance.

'This is going to be OK,' I thought, 'she doesn't look mad.'

I'm not sure what I did first or how I said hello. All I remember is that there was a beautiful Bible laid open on the table and the pages were lovingly underlined with handwritten notes at the side. As I soaked in this authenticity, I knew instantly that I had to be honest with her. I couldn't pretend to have a faith that I didn't have. I couldn't big-chat my way through this one to get the results I so desperately wanted. Faking it until I made it wasn't going to help me this time and I knew I had to be honest.

There was some polite chit chat about how her train journey had been and me thanking her for coming, then I took charge of the situation.

'I don't know how much you know about what's going on,' I started. 'I'm not sure what Kate has or hasn't told you about George's diagnosis. I know we spoke briefly on the phone the other night, but it's bad.'

I briefly gave her the summary of his symptoms; what we had tried, the decision to have and then not to have surgery. The fact that he was in an unbearable amount of pain. The fact that he was dying. Throughout all of this Brianna just nodded and smiled. At the time I was so wrapped up in my own story I didn't stop to think about the impact any of this may or may be having on her.

She continued to nod, listen and let me talk. It was when I'd finished giving her the medical debrief that I looked down at her Bible again and I think I was still looking down when I spoke to her. This was because I was worried she might think I had lied and got her here under false pretences.

'So look. I've just got to be honest,' I said as I was holding on to the edge of the table. There was definitely a sharp intake of breath before I found the courage to tell her what was really on my mind.

'I don't believe in God,' I blurted.

I looked up waiting for a response, but her face didn't show an ounce of shock or concern so I continued.

'I never have believed. I just don't think it can all be real.'

It felt so good to get this off my chest. I don't think I'd ever pretended to her that I did believe, but for me, she needed to know. I didn't want there to be a seed of doubt in her mind and needed her to know unequivocally that I didn't think God was actually going to help.

'I just don't really get this whole Jesus thing either,' I continued. 'I mean, I'm not saying he wasn't a real person, but I think over time, it's probably just been made up and exaggerated a little. I know that his existence was proven but I don't think he was God. I think he was probably just a great guy that did some wonderful stuff.'

I looked directly at her; I was worried that I might have just said something hugely offensive. To my relief, she continued to look as cool and calm as she'd seemed the whole way through.

159

'So, this is the thing,' I looked at her straight in the eye. 'I desperately want one of the miracles that your Bible talks about. I want a miracle SO badly. I want it more than anything I've ever wanted in my life ever! I would do anything in my power to see George heal. But I just know he isn't real. He can't be. I just wish I could sit here with you as a believer. But I'm not.'

I looked down. I sort of felt ashamed to admit that even though I wanted a miracle, I was actually also saying out loud that I didn't think God could be true. I'd got her to travel all the way from London, to come and see crazy old me and a dying young man and yet I didn't even believe.

Her response is something that will make my heart swell for all eternity. It wasn't the story from the Bible that she shared or the fact that she remained so at ease. It was that she leaned across the table, took my hand and soothingly said seven words that dissolved the worry in my heart and took away the knot in my stomach. They instantly re-lit the fire of hope that I'd felt burning inside me, as well as melting away the shame, anxiety and disbelief. She piercingly looked into my eyes, gripped my hand tightly and with a passion in her heart unlike anything I'd ever seen before, declared,

'I have enough faith for us all.'

I didn't know how to respond. I was floored. Who was she?

Praying part II

Moments later we were in his room. I had waved Kate off downstairs with a knowing glance and desperate look of thanks and hope. She had arranged that her younger sister would collect Brianna when we were finished praying. She didn't want to intrude and come with us to pray so she used her job over on the other side of the city as an excuse to leave.

'We're here,' I announced as Brianna and I walked into his room. I darted over to the side of his bed I had claimed as my own and quickly resumed my position of protectively holding his hand as tight as I could. He was awake but his eyes were closed even though he was expecting Brianna. I had confided in him when he was awake enough to hear it, that I had been wondering if spiritually this woman knew more about his death than we did. George also knew that I was in pursuit of anything that could help him and trusted me to know that I wouldn't ever put him in situations to hurt or to harm him. As I sat in my chair gently rubbing the lovely part of the skin, between his thumb and forefinger, I tried to breathe out my nervous energy. I wanted to show that I would protect him, no matter what.

Brianna set herself up at the end of George's bed. It was awkward, almost like the start of a meeting at work when you don't know the person you're sat opposite, but you both know you have some big topics to discuss. Instead of talking about the task in hand we danced around logistics, like where she should sit and if there were any plug sockets. It felt strange that this was the atmosphere I'd invited into our space. The formality of the conversation was somehow at odds with the enormity of what was going on. With George laid out in his bed, wrapped in sheets, wearing his favourite T-shirt and with tubes and machines attached to his body. She started to unpack her laptop and her Bible, alongside some Ribena, a paper bag and a tiny little glass pot that looked like it had a clear liquid inside.

'What on earth was she up to?' I quietly wondered.

Brianna interrupted my thoughts and asked if it was OK to play some music. As soon as I'd nodded my head in confirmation the music began to fill the room and Brianna started to pray. I didn't know if I should close my eyes or have them open as I watched her. I awkwardly wondered if I should have my hands clasped together in the way I'd seen people stand in church but it felt so uncomfortable. As I tried to relax into my chair desperately attempting to listen to the words but not being able to hear them, my mind was focussed entirely on George. What was he thinking and feeling? Did he actually want to pray, or was he just doing it because I'd given him no choice in the matter?

As my mind raced around I realised again that I wasn't listening to the music or the soothing words flowing from Brianna. And then I felt George move. He opened his eyes and looked up whilst speaking directly to Brianna,

'Will you come and sit beside me,' he said. 'Please, will you hold my hand?'

I was shocked, it was the first time George had invited anyone outside of his close family to sit intimately with him. Ever the charmer, he had always been so polite to the medical team who cared for him, but he had never invited any of them into his heart. This gesture made me feel so relieved that I started to cry.

The magic of the circumstance made something shift in George's heart and I saw a small glimmer of light that I'd not seen in him for weeks. It was the biggest piece of encouragement I needed to carry on with what we were doing. Brianna continued to pray and I tried my best to focus, listen and hear the words in my heart. She made us feel at ease even though what she was doing felt so alien to us both. And when I actually began to hear her words, I was astonished by what she was uttering. It was deeply personal, so beautiful and so very different from how I thought prayer went. Her words were everything I wanted to say but hadn't quite found a way of asking out loud. I desperately wanted her words to heal him and make it all go away.

Brianna got up out of her chair.

'Is it OK if I lay my hands on you?' she asked George gently. He nodded and she stepped forward with a sense of strength and power. Her tone was disarming and commanding.

'In Jesus' name, I pray that the cancer be gone. In Jesus' name, I ask that this disease leaves George's body now Lord. I ask for no more pain. No more pain now in Jesus' name.'

As she gently rested her hands on George's chest and continued to repeat these words I sobbed. It was a heavy kind of sob where my shoulders moved up and down.

This was because what she was asking for was all we had ever wanted. All we had ever desired was for this disease to go away. It was maybe so obvious to ask for it to leave but it wasn't something we'd ever done. Until that afternoon we had never actually said these words out loud before. No one had ever spoken over George in this way. No one had ever commanded that this disease stopped screwing with our lives. That it left his body and us alone.

But somehow this beautiful American woman who we'd only just met had dared to ask out loud for everything on our hearts. She found the words to say what we couldn't. She had the nerve and the know-how to ask for what we really wanted. It was incredible and once it had been said seemed so obvious that we should have asked before now. Her prayers were powerful, deeply emotional and very cathartic - healing for the soul in fact. As I continued to cry Brianna came and put her hand on my shoulder. I was a mess and I bowed my head down. Snot was mixed in with the tears and I couldn't hold my sadness in any longer. I still felt *such* a fraud.

What Brianna was doing was undeniably beautiful, but I was terrified. I was so desperate not to let go because the fear of what might happen if I did was overpowering. It was up to me to be in control, George didn't have the power to fight and protect us. I couldn't let go, that was for him to do, not me. It was my responsibility to keep him safe.

At this very moment, the pragmatist in me was stopping the peace from creeping into my body despite me wanting so desperately to feel. I could almost sense it approaching like a fuzzy magnetic feeling but was determined to hold back. Brianna was stood over me now, with her arm around my shoulders, quietly muttering words of comfort and encouragement into my ear. I began to wonder if she was deliberately stepping into our brokenness to convert us. But I could feel from her energy and sense from the tone and passion in her voice that she wanted George to be healed as much as we did. I could see that she believed the miracle was possible. The fire was evident in her eyes and I could hear it in her voice as she prayed. I couldn't explain it, but I knew deep down that what I was hearing was another heartbeat speaking to ours. I began to give in to the conclusion that maybe her intent was utterly selfless. After all, she hadn't asked us for anything and seemed to be unbelievably empathetic.

Brianna carried on praying. The ebb and flow of the genuinely meaningful words being poured over George's body were deeply healing. After a fair few minutes of battling the internal conflict, I decided that now I had to go with it. The more prayers Brianna said, the more I adjusted to the unfamiliar concept of what she was doing. I pushed down the feelings of fear and tried my best to be present, listen to the words being spoken over my husband

and will them, just like she was, to happen.

Her prayers were genuinely authentic. They spoke to my soul and George looked so peaceful. And as I sat there, still conversing with my mind over my uncertainty, Brianna stopped. When I opened my eyes I saw that she had moved back to the other side of the room. George remained in a state of peace as Brianna looked at me with a cheeky smile.

'Louise, I have something else for you. From God. He sensed you might be a tough nut to crack.'

Brianna spoke with such confidence it made me sit up in my chair. I felt like someone had run a cold hand down my back and was utterly uneasy that she appeared to be reading my thoughts. She continued with the same cheeky look,

'God sees you; he wants you to know that he is with you. So, he's asked me to write a letter to you both. A letter about who you are, how you're made. Oh, and I know what you're thinking. You think I've looked you up on Facebook or something but I can promise that I haven't. God speaks to me. He speaks to me very clearly in ways that are sometimes quite remarkable. He knows you, Louise. He knows who you are. I've got his letters. Do you want to read them?'

The way she announced that she had these letters was as if it was an everyday occurrence to get a note from God. Like it was the kind of letter she wrote most days, just as I sent emails. Even though I was petrified, I wanted to read what she had for us. I mean if someone had randomly come into your life, sat down with you and your dying husband all whilst seemingly knowing stuff about you both, in spite of the fact you'd never met before and then announce that they had a letter for you from God, I think you would probably want to read it. You'd be hoping there might be something inside that might give some answer and tell you why this was all happening. You'd want to know what the big guy had to say just as much as I did. Brianna went to give us our letters and at this point, I got up, dived across the room and almost snatched them out of her hands.

'George can't read this himself,' I said, 'he's too weak. I'll have to read it for him.'

The stealth doubter in me was on high alert. I wanted to know what was going to be in George's letter before he laid eyes on it. I wanted to protect him and wasn't prepared for him to be subjected to any more pain. Even though everything up until this point had been so beautiful, I still wasn't that trusting. I took the notes that were in crisp blue envelopes from Brianna's hand.

I now know that blue is a colour which spiritually signifies the healing power of God. It represents the sky and is also a reminder of the heavenly realm. All I knew back then though was that blue was George's favourite colour. I held the envelope and turned it around in my hand observing the crispness and beautiful handwriting. Before I opened the note I knew that the colour was significant but I just couldn't explain why.

I breathed in deeply and tore it open. It was George's letter that I read first and as my eyes quickly scanned over the words, I realised it was safe for me to read them aloud. They weren't dangerous, far from it. They were incredibly special and I'd never seen anything like this written about my husband before. It was like someone had looked inside his heart and written what was etched there. I was stunned, amazed and bewildered. Could they really be from a power that knew him as well as I did? They seemed to be and if that was the case, could this power help him? I didn't know. I was in shock, so I just gently read the words out loud to him and clutched his hand.

'George you are an overcomer. You believe the best of people. There is a joy that surrounds you. You value family and friends and they love being around you because of your lively positive nature - like the guy everyone wants at their BBQ or picnic. You have the ability to think into the future strategically- you think generations ahead. You think about legacy. You are dearly loved by God. Precious to him. He says that the weight of being brave and being an adult can come off you as you sink into his embrace. Climb up into his lap and allow the Father to hold you. He is so pleased with you. He wants to give the grace to allow you to see yourself with kindness and forgiveness. You are a man of victory, even if you interpret certain situations as a weakness. God is fierce in his claim for you. He wants to be your Father. Peace beyond understanding is available to you.'

There wasn't time to take in a reaction. To think about the enormity and trueness that was pouring out of the piece of paper in front of me. I was like a crazed animal, devouring the words like a meal I hadn't eaten for months. Selfishly I wanted to see what my note had to say. The only way I can describe it is how my boys open their presents on birthdays when they don't take the time to stop or appreciate and just dive right in. That's exactly what I did, I dived in headfirst to the next blue envelope. I didn't give George a second to respond and my envelope was already on the floor before he had even managed to speak.

'Louise, there is a warrior within you. It might not always feel this externally but there is a steely will within you that will not give up. You have a beautiful heart that nourishes others. There is a beautiful innocence within you that is like that of a little girl who isn't jaded and believes for the best, in the good, in dreams. I have the image of a little ballerina who might be timid at first, scared in fact, but then as she begins to dance, people begin to watch and are endeared to her. Your heart is endearing to God. You are absolutely precious and God wants to break the barrier for you to hear for yourself how present he is with you, with such compassion and so much encouragement. You can lean into him even more. Just as a little girl you kept a special box with those things most precious inside, you are his precious one and he keeps you close to his heart.'

I sat rooted to my chair. I felt light-headed because I'd been taken back to the bedroom in my parents' house, to the memory I'd been playing over in my mind the other night. How could this seemingly inconsequential moment from my childhood, that no one on this earth knew about, be linked to my husband's death? How could God know about this, how could he have seen me? How did he know I used to dance? How did he know I used to talk to someone, was it him I was talking to back then? Who was this force that Brianna was connecting with?! It was definitely something that was bigger than me and bigger than George. I could see that whatever it was it didn't just know us by name, it knew us by the pattern written on our hearts. It knew all of the intricate detail and stories of our lives. It also knew about the imprint we had made on the world. It knew small, deeply personal detail. It was unbelievable. It was unreal. It was insane.

But at that moment, in that second, I still couldn't bring myself to believe in a God. If he was real why wasn't he doing something and why was the man I loved, more than anything else in the world, writhing around in agony? How could he allow this to happen if he was there, with us? It didn't make sense.

After we read the letters the atmosphere in the room tangibly changed as if the energy had shifted. I no longer doubted that Brianna was connecting us to something because I could feel and read it for myself. It was like my soul was being beautifully drawn upwards and I forgot that I'd been so scared just a few moments ago. I felt peace even though I felt so angry. I just couldn't explain where it was all coming from, but it was there, it was what I felt. Extraordinary peace in a moment of heartbreak. There was a moment of silence and then Brianna edged her chair back to George's bedside. He was so happy to be close to her and I smiled, basking in this tranquillity. After a few minutes Brianna edged closer to him.

'George, what else is weighing on your heart? God is showing me that you need to give it to him?'

George held on to Brianna's hand and began to cry. He pushed away the many wires that were hanging from his body to make space for her and quietly found the strength he needed to speak.

'I'm so frightened,' he said, between tears. 'I'm so worried to go. My boys are so young. I'm so scared of what will happen to them and Louise. I'm just so scared.'

'Oh, my love,' I cried back, 'you must not stay here for us. I will find a way through this. We will live to tell this story, I promise.'

As we both cried, Brianna murmured more beautiful prayers and then asked if she could anoint George with the oil she had brought with her. After she'd gently made the mark of the cross on his head she said,

'I think we should also take Holy Communion.'

If Brianna had suggested this any sooner there is no way I would have participated. I'm sure I would have found a polite way to decline. But her prayers had taken us to a place of peace and although we were sad, we were also being powered by this incredible energy. A force that had somehow wrapped around the room and was willing us forward. So for reasons I can't explain, neither George nor I felt it was weird to participate in communion. In many ways, after hearing such deeply personal words, it felt like the most normal thing we'd done since he had been admitted.

Brianna went back over to the table and picked up the sandwich bag and Ribena she'd laid out earlier. At the time, I'd simply assumed this was her lunch, I didn't think we would ever be taking communion as well as praying that afternoon.

'I thought it would be inappropriate to bring wine,' Brianna smiled cheerily whilst holding up the Ribena. 'This will do won't it, it's still grape?'

I didn't know what to say or how to respond, this woman was

something else, so I just gently nodded my head.

'And I've got some bread here that I picked up from the canteen earlier,' she continued, 'this will work I'm sure,' she said as she gently began to break the roll whilst whispering more prayers.

'I'm not sure that George will be able to eat or drink,' I said.

'Oh, don't worry,' she smiled, 'God's got this.'

After she'd poured some Ribena into a plastic cup and broken the bread into tiny pieces she went over to his bedside. I was amazed to see George actually drink some drink and eat some food (albeit a tiny piece.) It was remarkable, he hadn't touched anything for days. I was moved to my core and rooted to the floor in utter disbelief at what was happening. I think George was too but his symptoms were still so very visible and despite feeling like we were on a cloud and the beautiful prayers that had been spoken, the pain was still etched all over his face.

The torment and exhaustion jolted us back into reality. Brianna read the signs before I needed to tell her. She packed up her things and we quietly excused ourselves as George drifted off into an uncomfortable sleep. As we walked out of the door, I felt uplifted, almost like I was walking on air. I wasn't sure how I could be feeling this even though my husband was dying and laid out in agony.

'That was amazing,' I said, 'utterly beautiful. Thank you. I'm not sure what you just did in there, but I feel like I'm up on the clouds. This is the most peace I've felt in weeks. Thank you. Thank you. Thank you, Brianna.'

She looked at me and smiled,

'Louise you can have this every day if you want it. It's yours for the taking.'

'But I don't know how you do it, if he's even real. How can he be if George is so sick? I don't know how to pray. I certainly don't know how you pray in the way you do. I can't do it. I want to, if it can bring something like peace, but I've never been taught. I'm not even sure where I start?'

'I'll teach you,' she said. 'You can do it. Everyone can. All of our hearts know, it's just that sometimes you just have to be shown the way.'

We carried on walking downstairs and back towards the reception foyer. I felt like everyone was looking at me and could see something different and wondered if it was obvious, by the way I was walking. If it looked to others that I felt like I was on clouds, even though George was dying. It was almost like the fuzzy feeling I felt after making love and then being forced to enter a room full of people shortly after. It was that same feeling of orgasmic intense pleasure gently diffusing around me. As Brianna gathered her bags together, I hugged her. We said our goodbyes as she was wrapping herself in her gorgeous cape-style coat. It was then that she dropped another bombshell.

'By the way,' I said, 'please say thank you to your friend Emma at the church you recommended in America. We've not managed to get through to each other this week, but she's been so kind.'

Up until this moment, I'd assumed that Brianna and Emma were the best of friends; they were both American after all.

'Oh, right,' said Brianna as she shrugged and smiled,

'I should probably tell you this. I don't really know her that well. She's not a close friend, not really. We met at a huge creativity conference for Christians, several years ago. She knew about the show God has commissioned me to produce and had a word for me.'

This was all becoming a bit of blur now, all I'd heard was, 'I don't really know her that well,' and was stood there wondering why on earth she'd put us in touch.

'When we met a few years back, she gave me her cell phone number. She said she was sure that at some point, there would be someone in the UK who would need to get in touch with the healing rooms at her church, but that maybe they would struggle. If they did need healing, she told me that I should tell them to contact her directly and that she would be the link. That's the only reason I have her number. I don't really know her, we're not the best of friends or anything, it was just because she thought we might need her.'

I was shocked. How could another woman I had never even met have the foresight that I would be connected to Brianna and know I would then need her phone number? That I would struggle to get hold of her church, despite the fact, I didn't even really know who her church even was? I was yet again completely dumbfounded. Was I reading too much into this? I didn't know what to say, so didn't respond but these non-coincidences were becoming too obvious now. I was being forced to sit up and start to take note.

Brianna went back to London by train that afternoon. Kate's younger sister Laura was waiting for us both as we'd arranged by the time we made our way back to the reception.

'Thank you,' was all I said as I hugged Brianna tightly, feeling as though she was some sort of real-life angel.

Laura looked at me knowingly to ask without speaking if I was OK. I gently nodded.

'Tell Kate we're so thankful for connecting us, tell her it was the right thing to do.'

Laura didn't say anything else; she knew me well enough to know it wasn't needed. Quietly she asked Brianna if she was ready to leave and squeezed her arms around me tightly. I watched the two of them walk together across the car park and felt a surge of gratitude; for them and Kate. I didn't know it then, but the next time I would see them all again in person would be four weeks later.

Back in the hospital, there was nothing left to do except resume my position next to George's bed. There was no more physical change in him that afternoon, but something had altered in my mind. George was in a deep sleep. His soul was inching towards peace and he'd finally managed to rest, despite the fact he was still in so much pain.

'Could he actually be healed?' I whispered this thought out loud to myself, not really daring to believe that it could be true.

'Was prayer the solution I'd been looking for all along?'

As I sat there pondering over this thought my phone pinged. This time it wasn't Brianna messaging but Sarah. She knew how desperate things had become and had promised to give an update on medical trials by the end of the day. I took a sharp intake of breath before I read the message. Would this be it?

'Hey lovely. I've spent hours online looking at all of the different options. I've also spoken to a wonderful lady at Cancer Research. I'm so sorry to say this on text but I don't think there is anything else you guys can try in this country. There are various treatments available in the US and in Germany, but we don't have access to them here and they cost lots with no guarantees. The woman I spoke to didn't seem to think they would be worthwhile. I'm sorry I don't have any more positive news Lou. I love you, Sarah x.'

I sat and stared at the phone screen with the tears silently splashing down my face. Despite the peace I could feel in my heart it all just felt so desperate and like there was nothing left.

The evening rolled around and we were all relieved to see George's dad make an appearance; he had been away in America on business. George and his father had always had a lovely relationship and weren't ever in each other's pockets; just very respectful of each other's wisdom and strength. Along with his mum, brother and sister I was so relieved to learn that day that he had returned home early; everyone knew things were looking desperate for George and we just wanted his close family to be together by his side.

As I ushered his father into the room, accompanied by George's brother, my gorgeous husband rallied and I left them holding hands peacefully listening to Classic FM, a radio station his dad had requested. As I let the door swing shut behind me I reflected on how thoughtful he was even in death holding hands with his family to show them he was OK. As I also heard the beautiful music wafting into the hospital corridor, I remarked that it was only the second time since we'd arrived that any music had been played. The first was that afternoon when Brianna had played her worship music and prayed for the Holy Spirit and God's heavenly kingdom to enter his bedroom. I didn't really understand what she had meant by either of these suggestions. But what I didn't know that night, was that the radio would remain switched on for the rest of what would happen in the week ahead. The classical radio station would deliver the soundtrack to accompany the glory of what would unfold and speak directly into all of our hearts.

Leaving the hospital that night I was sad and confused. I went home to the boys and was exhausted and so unsettled as I sat alone in my kitchen eating food my nanny had prepared. By this point, I'd asked for everyone other than my best friend to leave the house so I could have some space. I found the continual company of family as well as my own parents exhausting and overwhelming. But as I sat there with the baby monitors on one side and a glass of wine on the other, I couldn't stop looking at the notes Brianna had given us from God. The words described both of us so perfectly with such truth and beauty. I knew it was real that they had come from something or someone we both knew; they were too perfect not to be.

I tiptoed upstairs and hugged my sleeping boys who had been put to bed by our nanny a couple of hours earlier. I then took a shower and stood under the steaming hot water with the tears running down my face. I had never felt so broken and didn't know what to do.

'What had I started?' I wondered out loud, 'was God actually real?'

The force I'd felt in the room earlier was tangible, I mused. But why wasn't it saving us if he was there? Maybe it was because I hadn't asked and told him what I really wanted. Maybe I was supposed to get down on my knees and beg?

I got out of the shower and wrapped myself in a warm towel from the radiator. The fabric felt soft and protective around the vulnerable emotions inside my head. Should *I* pray, was that what God really wanted? I wiped away the tears with my towel and moved over to the bathmat. I froze. I wasn't sure what to do. Should I talk out loud or talk in my head? Should I stand up, or sit down? I started to sob uncontrollably and before I knew it, I had fallen to my knees.

Hot and sobbing after standing under the steaming water, I found myself on the ground, completely naked. I'd lost the comforting protection of the towel on the way down. My knees hurt on the bumpy surface of the bathmat. My hair was dripping around my neck. The tears were pouring out of my eyes. I could barely speak. I tried, I really tried to make myself feel like it was real. Like God was there. Listening. There was just so much that I wanted to say and so much that I was feeling but it felt like it was all stuck inside of me and I couldn't let it out. Not in the way I could if I was speaking to someone in real life. I wanted to talk to him, I desperately wanted to know if he could help. But I still wasn't entirely sure what I was even doing. I didn't understand the power that I'd brought into our lives. Was this force even God, how did I even begin to summon him if it was?

I was scared. What was I doing? It all just felt so wrong. I murmured aloud no more than a few words before the howls of hurt got the better of me. I simply couldn't find the right thing to say. I wasn't like Brianna; the words didn't flow out of my soul in the way they gently ebbed out of hers.

So I put on my pyjamas, dried my hair and got into bed. I wanted to make a tent. I wanted to hide from the world under my duvet and be back there with George and wrapped around his body, making love. I lay there for a while and tried to sleep but my mind wouldn't switch off. I came up for air, it always felt colder to breathe again after being under the covers. Whilst under there, I'd decided that I should hedge my bets. That if I didn't know how to pray, that I should use the professionals. I knew that I wasn't a master of prayer but I also was pretty certain that I didn't want to take any risks if this could actually work. So at that moment, I did what I knew and asked for help but this time was a little more specific.

If this force knew what I was doing when I was a little girl, then surely it knew about George being so desperately sick. It had to. All of the crazy situations I had found myself in were increasingly indicating that something, whatever it may be, was real. Even though it terrified me and made me feel utterly awestruck, if there was an outside chance that prayer was going to work then I had to do it. I had to communicate with this energy.

I knew that Brianna was my girl because she knew what to do and was just so much better at it than me. And so tucked up in my bed, I decided to play it safe. I decided to text Brianna and ask her to help us.

'Hey lovely. Hope you're home safely? Thank you so much for this afternoon. You've helped SO much, you've brought such peace. I'm still so sad that George is in such discomfort, but he said he loved the time he had with you; it was really calming and relaxing for us both. Please pray for him not to be in turmoil and so much abdominal pain. Please pray that this hideousness ends and he's healed. You were like a little ray of sunshine and hope today, in amongst the darkness and despair. You have helped me find my strength and peace. I'm not sure where it's coming from? I just so want George to find this strength too. I wish I could pray it for him but I'm not sure how? He's not in a good way. He's asked me to take the children to him tomorrow so I'm just trying to organise the logistics of that. Do you know anyone else in Nottingham that we could ask to come and pray? I want to do it again but don't know how? Please keep praying, I think it works. Thank you, Louise x.

Miracles

<u>Saturday 12th November</u>

'Good morning Louise! I'm so excited you want to pray some more, I've found an amazing young vicar (friend of a friend) called Simon, I've texted him. I've been asking God this morning what he wants you to know, I sensed him saying that he is with you. Each day he renews your strength and your hope. Today there is a fresh portion for you. I sensed him saying 'I want you to know that I am with you in the midst of these messy torrents of despair, fear, uncertainty, hope, pain. I love you more than you are capable of comprehending. I've never quit loving you and never will. My heart is a place of rest, a place of peace, of being real and being received. I surround you wherever you go, but if you ask me into your heart, I will live within you, I'm your Father and companion walking through this with you every step of the way. Bri x'

'Brianna, I can't explain what's happening. As I went to bed last night, I thought of everything you said to me, about this feeling being available to me *every-day. I was so desperate and in so much turmoil, that I tried so hard to pray for the first time ever. But it was hard, I thought I wasn't doing it right and that no one was listening. Then this morning, when I got to the hospital, literally as I walked through the front doors, I got the text you sent about fresh hope. The timing was faultless. Literally, as the doors opened, my phone beeped. I'm with George now and he is the calmest, happiest and most peaceful he has been in weeks?! He's so blissful and content and says he feels like he is finally happy too?*

It's CRAZY! Remarkable! He says he has a big ball of light in his chest and that it's pulsing?! I'm mesmerised by the miraculous change in him, he's literally just lying out with his arms open in his bed. It's like he's floating somewhere. It's miraculous! It's amazing! All the pain seems to have gone and he just has this amazing energy oozing from him that I feel when I hold his hand. I think it must be God, is this how he works?! I'm not even sure? George says the boys are with him and he doesn't need to see them; he says they're in his heart, where they will always be. He asked me to check with the nurse and see what medication they had given him. He's requesting more of what he's feeling. I checked; he hasn't had anything apart from a tiny drop of morphine in the early hours! They're not sure why he's no longer in pain? They can't explain it?! Whatever has happened it's beautiful. I think it's his time, which breaks my heart, but something we've done has definitely helped. It's altered him. It's changed him. It's remarkable. No one can believe it!! He's so happy, so calm and willingly wants to accept his fate. I never thought his death could be transformed and become this beautiful, but somehow it has. Somehow it is?! I'm not sure where this change has come from? Was it our prayers?! Is it God?! I'm keen to know more, about the vicar who you think could maybe come and pray? We need more of this, it's working!!! Send help!

Thank you Brianna! Words can't explain how much you've helped us. I know George can't get up from his bed and be cured, but this is just quite simply all I could have ever wished for! After seeing him in such tortuous discomfort, for so long, I can only describe this as a MIRACLE. Louise x'

'I am literally on the floor crying out to God for you. Please keep me updated if you feel up to it, but I totally understand if you need some space. I just got a text from Simon the vicar, he said he would love to connect with you... Can you meet with him tomorrow afternoon? Bri x'

'George is just with his sister, so I am giving them some space. Everyone is just happy that he is finally smiling and at peace!! It's amazing, overwhelming, out of this world! I can't believe it!! Did our prayers really make this happen? I would love to chat with Simon about doing this more. It's madness that this is what has worked!! After everything else we've tried! I've texted Emma in California, we would love to pray with her if she's free? We're just about to take George's drip and feeding line down. He's told us he's ready to stop all treatment too, he's just so happy. It's remarkable, given the fact we know death is coming. When his doctor came in this morning, I could see that she knew something had happened, I told her this was the case too. She looked around the room as if she could see something and then just smiled and said, yes, I feel it too. I was gobsmacked. I still can't explain what's going on, even though I feel the force in the room and know it's there. What's happened??? Is this feeling God? I was dreading this moment this time yesterday when I thought I was going to have to bring the boys in for a painful goodbye, but now it all just feels so right. There's no fear, it's all gone, he's just so happy, so full of hope. He's ready to die. I still can't explain it?

183

I'm in shock?! I don't know what's going on?! Keep walking with us, Lou x'

So glad George is having such quality time with you all. It's SO amazing! I'm praying God orders time and that each conversation that needs to happen will open up. I'm praying time is stretched wide open for you. I've just seen a post on Facebook, from the church in California, who prayed for a lady with terminal cancer in Nottingham three years ago, she also did a skype call and was healed! So, I'm trusting God for his will. I don't want to take anything away from your peace, but am quite simply just walking alongside with you, in the belief that miracles have and can still happen. Brianna x'

'Hi Simon, I hope you don't mind me texting. I'm Louise Blyth, wife of George and I got your number from Brianna who I think has been in touch? I'm not sure how much (if anything?!) you know? We've had a CRAZY 24 hours and God seems to be moving here in a big way, even though I'm not sure I even know him? George was diagnosed with Stage four bowel cancer last Christmas. He has put up a heroic fight, until this point, but it now seems that he's finally ready to let his soul fly high. Brianna came into our lives by what seemed like pure chance! (I'm starting to think it now wasn't? It's all gone a bit mental!) She has given us so much spiritual peace over the last 24 hours and commanded a force called the Holy Spirit? She came and prayed with us yesterday and the difference we've seen in George today is phenomenal. It is miraculous. I can't quite believe it?! He's finally at peace, so happy and no longer in tortuous discomfort. No one can explain it here at the hospital? He's also talking about a light inside his chest and hope inside his heart?! Is this what happens when you believe in God? I'd really like to understand if you could help us some more and if you could come and pray? I'm so out of

my depth! I don't know how to do it! Can you help us find closure and help us keep this force so George's soul can fly high? I'm a Nottingham girl born and bred, it also sounds very strange to say on text, but I overwhelmingly feel that I'm supposed to meet you for a reason. I think that maybe you're meant to help us, then we'll help you, maybe with your church? SO much is going on at the moment, but I'm learning to trust these strange intuitive feelings I'm having! It seems they're no longer a coincidence! I'd love to catch up with you on the phone when you have a moment? I'm sorry that this text is SO random! I've never sent anything like this before! Thanks so much. Louise'

Sunday 13th November

'Hi, Louise. Thanks for getting in touch. I'd love to help you and George in whatever way I can. I'm around all of today if you would like to chat. Love Simon.'

'Morning Brianna! We got through to the healing rooms last night and we prayed for the first time with the church in America. George's mum was there too. She said she saw a beam of light that came across the room and into his heart!? What is going on!! This is AMAZING! I didn't see it as was crying, but the whole moment was just so beautiful! George is at such peace, all of the pain he was feeling has left him! I'm still in shock! I didn't manage to FaceTime Emma; I don't know who it was, that prayed with us from California?! I've also contacted Simon the vicar and we're going to meet. I've asked him to come to the hospital. We turned George's feeding tube and drip off last night. I was told to expect him to be very sleepy today, but he isn't. It's another round of the miraculous. My mother-in-law just texted too, she's with him right now. She says he's awake and so happy and so pleased to have had

a lovely comfy night. WOW. WOW. WOW. I can't explain what's going on, but the energy you brought on Friday hasn't left the room and is just pulsing here. It's all over George. I can feel it when I touch him! I never thought I'd write a message like this either, but I'm quite simply so amazed! Lou x'

'Wow! God is so good! Incredible! It's him that's brought such peace, through the Holy Spirit. That's what you can feel. I visualised George's hospital room before I went to sleep last night, I'm praying that God would allow me to be there in spirit too, I've been praying through the night. Since last night I saw a type of golden aura in the room for you today. Total peace, ease, laughter, happiness, wholeness, shalom. Treasuring each moment for you. The golden light is the presence of Jesus. God wants you to know Louise, how held you are in prayer. The London healing rooms prayed for you yesterday, they didn't know anything about George, but they asked God to show how he had created him. They felt him say that George is a mighty man of valour. He is a fighter. Determined, the direction is always forward. He can extinguish fires in each situation he walks into. They had a picture of a man holding a flag of victory, like a character in a musical. He is a man of favour, that has risen with favour on his life. They prayed to release HOPE and also BLESSING on you and your family. My friend also prayed with me yesterday, she didn't know about the inflammation around George's liver but saw God releasing a healing salve in spirit, something like Aloe Vera on to his abdomen. Know how known and loved he is. Bri x.'

'Wow! They're right!! George is a man of honour, he always wants to do the right thing, the direction is also very much forward for him. Always! He never looks back with regret! The Aloe part is interesting; his mum has always *sworn the blessings of it as a natural remedy!! I'll see if we can bring some real stuff up to the hospital! If the spirit wants it, we should try it here too? Simon the vicar is coming to see us today. George is definitely at peace; I have to admit I'm a bit scared by what's happening? It's amazing. He's like a different person. I can still see how sick he is, but all of the pain, all of the heartache, it's gone! It's just disappeared! It's INSANE! I so desperately want to believe in a miracle cure, but feel like I have to protect my heart and prepare for the reality of the situation we're in. It's all so confusing. Lx'*

'Don't worry. SO many people are praying for you and keeping you both in their hearts. Everyone wants to support you and there are people who will come and sit with you if you would like? We're also sensitive to what you are going through and don't want to intrude. We will keep praying for the miracle and being thankful for those that have already come to pass. This isn't on you, Brianna x'

'Simon is going to come and visit today and that feels right. I'm going to go with that, no more visitors for the time being. Thank you for rallying so many people. It's lovely to feel so loved at this time. I hope their prayers keep working, it's amazing to sit here and see the change in real life! I still can't believe it. It's just SO beautiful! Something out there is doing this for sure! I've never been more certain after seeing so much pain and now all of this glory! It's mental! Lou x'

'You're so welcome. About you feeling scared to hope, I'm so with you and I don't want to build false hope, but I also don't personally want to give up on the miracle of cancer leaving George. I feel that God has given this whole

situation to me and is very clearly asking me to stand in the gap. As imperfect as I am, he wants me to be his representation, so you can hear him, fully, like he is a person standing with you, talking to you. I will believe until the last moment, (even when you maybe can't?) So maybe that takes the pressure off? I pray that you can just enjoy each moment? I hope you can just rest and know that everything possible from a spiritual side, is being done. I think if we both put our hope in God; who is far kinder, more compassionate and loving than we can ever imagine. No matter what the outcome, it will be peace. It seems from your messages this is already being poured out? Putting your trust in God is simple when you know-how. Why don't you try praying again? You could just say, 'God, I trust you are walking this with me every step of the way. I trust in your outcome?' Brianna x'

'Thank you, that makes me feel better! I feel like I'm missing these precious moments of life, as I'm so preoccupied with the amazing spiritual shift that I'm seeing around us. You can see it on George and feel it in the room. It's so tangible, I can't even begin to explain it! I'm so glad you get it! I don't want to overlook the spirituality, it's lifted us to this point, but I also don't want to miss the moments that it's gifted us. Like your note from the big guy said, there is a little part of me that ALWAYS believes in miracles, but I just can't bring myself to completely believe he could be healed?! I want to! But I'm scared it's then going to hurt even more when he goes. It gives me peace to know that you can be the middleman for the moment, thank you. I just don't want to miss these precious moments with my soul mate, whilst he's still alive. Thank you for believing in God for us and bringing this amazing Holy Spirit into the room. Thank you for believing in miracles. Louise x.'

'Aww. I'm so glad I can help you. Praying you find yourself laughing with

George today, really enjoying your time together. Let me know how the prayers go with Simon? Bri x'

'So, George just rang me from the hospital!!!! He hasn't picked up his phone to me for over a couple of weeks! I was shocked when I saw it was him! I double looked in fact! He sounded SO happy. He got to talk to our oldest little boy Charlie over the phone and say goodbye during the call – it was SO sad but so special! It's something I never thought would happen last week, I still can't believe it has! My gorgeous little boy told him that he would get big and strong and look after me when he's bigger and older with his brother. I'm crying so much, it's so nice that we're getting this special time. I can't thank you enough, for everything you've done. For how you've stepped out and in. I so badly want to believe in miracles, the hope has quite literally flooded into George's room. It's all around us in there. THANK YOU!! Lou x'

'I can't tell you what an honour it is to be part of this moment. How precious to hear what Charlie has said. It brings me to tears. How is George's body? Has he tried eating anything, since he's been taken off his tubes to see if the obstructions are gone? Bri x'

'No. George hasn't eaten or drunk, but I haven't seen him yet today. I'm going to take some Aloe vera though – we have our own plants at home, I'll see if it can do anything in the way your friend saw in prayer. I'm prepared to give anything a whirl! Even if they all think I'm a lunatic! Louise x'

'As I was making breakfast, I felt God's pleasure over George and felt

189

that he'd really made God laugh over the years. God loves his childlike sense of humour and feels there have been times when George has got himself in funny predicaments?! God wants you both to know that he's had huge belly laughs watching him in those situations. Brianna x'

'Ha-ha! This makes me smile SO much. He MUST know him. George has got himself into more silly predicaments than most over the years, too many stories for text! But he is a TOTAL joker, this is on the money. Well done God! Lou x'

'I'm thanking God for yesterday's good day and for the gift of today. I'm declaring LIFE GLORIOUS LIFE over George. we need you, God we need you! Keep coming! Brianna x'

'So, I'm here at the hospital. George is happy, smiley and asking to eat!?!?! WTF?

He's been drinking Ribena (you know the one that you blessed in our makeshift communion?!) and the nurse said it's amazing. It's removing all of the toxicity from his body!!!! She was gobsmacked! I've just watched them pull out a load of really nasty stuff through a syringe! I'm baffled, amazed. They are too?! I really think that you're right, that you've tapped into God and then are sending him onwards through me, into us?!

Am I then somehow tapping into George with your help?! I have no idea! It's all so confusing, but it's all real?! We're going to rub some Aloe vera on him soon. I'm believing that something beautiful still may happen, but what has happened already is incredible, beautiful, wondrous!

There aren't even words! I never thought it would be this way. Louise x'

'YAY!!!!! GOD IS AT WORK!!!!!!! Keep thanking him. This is how miracles work.

When Jesus multiplied five loaves of bread and two fish to feed the five thousand he lifted his eyes to Heaven and thanked God for what he was about to do, before he even did it! I know this is all new to you, but I would urge you to lay your hand on his abdomen and say these words.

'God thank you for what you are doing! Thank you, that you are here releasing life. We agree with Heaven and release life in abundance over this body! We break the spirit of death and any darkness. We cover George in love and partner with Heaven to bring life. Thank you, God, that the toxicity is leaving. We speak peace to the inflammation in George's body. We speak alignment of organs and pray that any obstructions leave. We ask that normal digestion and eating return. We declare that George has a destiny to fulfil on earth! God, we thank you, we honour you in all you are doing.' Brianna x'

'I've just done it. It felt a bit weird as I don't usually talk like that!! I asked everyone else to leave the room and I've prayed for the second time ever in my life. It felt so odd, but I did it!

I'm pretty sure I'm speaking to something now so it's a little bit easier, even though I'm not sure what it is I'm talking to? There's too much good stuff happening within George for it not to be real! I rubbed the aloe vera on for good measure too! Thought it wouldn't do any harm!! Lou x'

'I feel God rejoicing and smiling with us. We want to see more of you God! When you see improvement, you have to continue to thank God, celebrate every single tiny improvement with him, keep praying and asking for more. When does Simon get there? Bri x'

'He's just left! He was a legend, he prayed with us which was so beautiful and so healing. I cried loads, but we had SUCH a good day. So many laughs and time for precious conversations I was scared I thought I might never have. George is SO amazing, it's like there's an electric forcefield coming out of him, he's like the Jedi's in Star Wars! He's holding hands with everyone who is coming to see him and helping them feel and see, the beautiful peace and love that is in him. My dad said today after he'd spent some time with him, that he felt like he'd just met the Dalai Lama! The impact he's having on people is not of this world. It's so beautiful, I just don't ever want it to end!! I think it has to though? Simon is so nice, such a cool guy, he's helped us make sense of what's going on. He's clarified that God is moving in a really powerful way, that the light that George is feeling inside him is the Holy Spirit?! He thinks that's what I'm feeling in the room too. Is this what God is, energy?

I had a really long chat with Simon too about how you were and still are, (!!) somehow in sync with us, despite the fact we're strangers! He couldn't believe that you've been texting me at EXACTLY the right moment. I showed him some of our texts, he was amazed by the timeliness and the encouragement you had given. He then came upstairs and sat with George; I've asked him to do the funeral – I feel like I've got to be realistic even though I don't want to be. I am still believing in the miracle of healing; it seems so possible now George seems so happy and almost well in spirit! Generally, he seems SO upbeat today which is utterly heart-breaking when I know how sick he really still is. Yesterday was amazing, I still can't get my head around the way he was speaking and the way he was behaving, it's been ethereal! Today he's like his old self, laughing, cracking jokes, he's just him and ALL of the hideous pain he was feeling has gone! Honestly, it's CRAZY! The obstruction is still there, but it's definitely better. I desperately still want the miracle. I know that

192

something big has happened, we've definitely all felt it and seen it at work. EVERY person who has walked into George's room has commented on the energy. Something supernatural is going on, but I can't quite put my finger on it? It's beautiful, I don't dare to believe that this is real! Louise x'

'AHH! It's SO amazing that Simon is great- I've heard wonderful things about him and his wife. Last Thursday before I came, God told me that when I visited, I needed to change the atmosphere. That I had to fill the hospital room with his presence.

At Emma's church, there is so much of God's presence that people get out of the car to be healed and miracles happen before they even enter the building!

In God's presence pain can leave, emotional peace and healing can happen. It is SO amazing that each person is now encountering this when they come into the hospital room! This is exactly what I prayed for! It's the Holy Spirit! Music helps to welcome this too.

As I mentioned before, I continue to pray that our prayers, can also take the weight off you, so you can be present and enjoy the moment. We are continuing to believe on your behalf, we believe for the miracle of total healing. I hope it's OK for me to send, I have some video messages from friends at Church who have prayed over you and George tonight? I'll send them after this. Bri x'

'Thank you. I LOVE the video messages. You are so in tune. I've just fallen into bed on my own. I felt so sad and these have just broken the fall. He's dying. I know he is. But I know now that he somehow wants to go? The energy is taking him somewhere better; I can see it as much as he can, we're both so OK with it all. It's mad! Louise x'

'God loves you SOOOOO much and he gives me a nudge and lets me know when you need encouragement the most. Sending you hugs. Brianna x'

'I've been thinking about what you said on the music front, about it welcoming the Holy Spirit? I must tell you that George's dad put Classic FM on when he came to visit after you last Friday. He's a musician. George hasn't turned the TV off since that visit. I know I've told you about all of the changes we have seen in George, but weirdly, the part I haven't mentioned, is that the songs have been SO in sync with the moment we've been in. Yesterday, when I walked into the room and saw George SO changed in spirit, the Superman theme tune was playing! I'm not even joking! It's one of his favourite movies and people have always joked that he is a real-life Superman!

Today, I was also telling George about the message you'd sent, about someone praying and seeing him hold a flag – we were joking that it was like he was in a musical. George LOVES musicals! As we sat holding hands, reflecting on how much we loved musicals, the TV started playing a song from West Side Story. We couldn't stop laughing! it was so beautiful!

Pray for more of this. Pray for more of God. I don't know how he's doing this; I don't even know who he is, but something somewhere is helping us, it's beautifully controlling it all! Sweet Dreams. Louise x'

Monday 14th November

'Louise. It was MY privilege to be with you and George yesterday. You're a remarkable couple. I have been praying for you both this morning and read this Psalm, it's meant for you both, so I had to share. "'Those who know your name trust in you, for you Lord, have never forsaken those who seek you." In other words, God is with you both and won't ever leave you. Keep trusting,

keep seeking. No pressure whatsoever but I would love to come and pray with you again if it helps? I'll continue to pray for you each day. Simon x.'

'Louise. I love you. I miss you. I've just had a lovely night drifting in and out of sleep and drinking Ribena, I can't believe it. I'm OK. This is OK. I'm safe, the pain inside me has gone. I will always be there for you. Just talk and I'll listen. I'll be there with God, to embrace you and keep you safe. I'm yours forever. Georgie x'

'Oh Georgie! I love you. I miss you. I'll be with you soon to hold your hand. You're doing great my gorgeous boy. I'm so proud of you, float now my perfect soul mate. Hope is here. Louise x'

'Morning Brianna. Georgie just astounded me and sent me the most incredibly beautiful text about being with God! He's found him. He's confirmed what I thought, that it is him moving in his heart! Simon messaged too, with a beautiful Psalm about trusting. I'm still hoping for the miracle. I can't believe what is happening?! I never knew death could be so beautiful. Louise x'

'Wow, Louise, this is HUGE news. It sounds like George has accepted God into his life. All of Heaven is rejoicing! So lovely about the music too, God has the best sense of humour and impeccable timing. How fun that this was your encouragement. I would continue to thank God for being present and invite him to come even more! Invite the angels too! Keep your eyes out for single white feathers appearing, I have had this happen, both seen and then float out of the air from nowhere! It's beautiful! Praying for you all! Bri x'

195

'I'm at the hospital. Your text came through as I walked through the door! Georgie is very sleepy today but just SO happy. We're praying with Simon again later. Lou x'

'WOW! You're so in-sync! All afternoon I've been feeling how fiercely God loves you, Louise! He hugs you close, you are so treasured! You are doing everything you can and he is so proud of you as a mother, wife, friend, daughter. I feel him giving you the freedom to throw off expectation you have of yourself and simply be – totally present and engaged, loving in the way that only you can. This is so beautiful! YOU ARE DOING SO WELL!!!! Bri x'

'I can't believe this message about God being proud! George is well enough for me to actually talk to him this afternoon, it's such a gift! I've just been sat questioning all of these things with him. It was painful. I was so upset. I was wondering how I'm going to carry on in all of these roles without him. It's literally exactly what we were just talking about. I find it AMAZING that God tells you such things at exactly the right time?! And I mean EXACTLY THE RIGHT TIME!! It's incredible to know he hears exactly what I'm thinking and is helping Georgie so much with this incredible peace he's feeling. Thank you. Thank you for everything!! Louise x'

'WOW! This is why I felt so strongly that I had to text (I'm so afraid that I'm overwhelming you and might sound odd!) But God pushed me because he wants to bring rest to your heart. I hope today has been good even though there is an understandable energy dip from you? God has been showing me what a strong woman you are. He wants to redefine strong for you. It is not

about powering through or having it all sorted, it is how you are at your weakest point, how you still show up. Embrace the vulnerability, still believe, even if it feels like just a shred of courage. Strong looks like God carrying you through each moment. I got a picture of you as you get into bed tonight. God wants you to know that the covers that surround you are like his embrace. Total safety. Be held, be secure. You are in his arms. You both are. Always and forever Brianna x'

'Your words have made me cry. You're SO describing the tension I have going on in my head at the EXACT moment it happens. It's uncanny, even though this synchronicity has now been going on a few days, it never fails to astound me that you know things through him?! It's so odd, it's so brilliant! It's CRAZY! It's saved me! It's saved George! I've literally just got into bed as I read your message. I'm realising more and more that nothing is really a coincidence anymore! It's just too in sync! It's literally the exact moment that I need you the most that you always text. It's beyond powerful, you encourage me when I feel so sad and low and that I can't go on. Just when I feel I might unravel completely you show up? Or are you God?!I'm so confused! I swear that it's only because of the energy I'm feeling through you, that I'm sleeping, eating, doing the basics of living, as well as still smiling at a time when I feel so sad. Thank you. Simon has been in touch again today and is going to come and pray again tomorrow which I'm really looking forward to. I'm trying really hard to do it, pray that is. I want to mean it, I want to say it like you can, but I feel like a fraud! Louise x'

<u>Tuesday 15th November am</u>

'Dear God,

I'm not sure if this is your name. I'm not sure if this is what I want to call you. Are you actually a man? I'm still trying to figure out what this supernatural force is that I seem to have connected with over the last few days and how I personally want to identify with you? I'm not really sure how I'm even supposed to pray? But I think I need to start trying, start learning. You've already given me so much, so this is the least I can do for you. So here I am. Writing you a letter on my phone, I thought it might be good to try writing to you instead of Georgie. That I should give it a whirl, given how you've now shown up.

Whoever and whatever you are I want to say thank you. Thank you for coming into my life at a time when I feel frightened, scared, sad, lost and completely heartbroken. Thank you for giving me hope and happiness in what is undoubtedly my darkest hour.

I tried to get in touch with you when I hit rock bottom. Driving around the countryside in desperation, as I realised that the one person who keeps me going on this earth, was most likely leaving soon. The person who is my rock, my partner in crime, my soul mate, my true love. The person who connects with me on a level I have never felt with anyone else. The person whom I wholeheartedly love. The father of my children, the centre of my world. I love him. I'm not sure how I can go on without him?

I feel so angry that you are taking him from me. I feel so sad about having to live in my current universe without him. I feel so jealous of all the other people who don't have to go through this torturous experience at the age of thirty-three. I feel so sad about all the dreams you're so cruelly snatching from me. It's awful.

But somehow, in all of this darkness, you have helped open my eyes to a power beyond my comprehension. Something that does feel miraculous.

Something that incites fear and hope almost simultaneously. You are making me see and truly believe in a spiritual plain that I always thought was a fantasy to help people feel better! You have shown me a glimpse of a force or a power far greater than me or George. A force that knows me better than I know myself. A force that even in my wildest dreams, I never really believe existed. A force that is pretty magical, supernatural and exciting.

I tried to get in touch with you because there is a small part inside of me, that does want to believe in miracles. I so desperately desired the miracle of healing, that I was prepared to do anything, absolutely anything, to get it. So then somehow and I still don't know how you sent Brianna into our lives. An intense, but amazingly kind and brilliant person. Someone who seems to be connecting with you, in a way I can't at the moment. Someone who is helping me through this. Someone who wants to help you, help me, for no malicious or badly intended reason. I know that Brianna isn't making up the messages she is sending me. I know that they are coming to her from somewhere beyond the world that I inhabit or currently understand. I know that it isn't a coincidence that she sends me encouragement at a time when I need it most, despite the fact that she's really a complete stranger! I know that the messages are coming from you but who are you? Do I know you? Have you been here the whole time?

I know that I'm supposed to do something with this new-found connection that I'm discovering. I know I've got to figure out how to interact with you on my own, I can't be the third wheel the rest of my life. But how do I do it? What you have given me is exciting. It's amazing. It's like a drug. But this drug is distracting me from the present. Somehow eclipsing the most painful and saddest thing I have ever experienced. It's making me feel scared. Scared that I am missing moments in the here and now. Scared that I will forget to say things to Georgie whilst he's still with me. Scared that people will think I'm mad. Scared that I won't grieve properly and I'm going to let this excitement and love for a force that can't even physically be seen, block out the pain.

The fact is, I do now wholeheartedly believe in your existence. I know you're real. Your force, your powers of divine intervention the whole caboodle. I don't know how you're doing it? I don't know how you're helping? I'm not sure what you even are, or how you have moved into George's mind, body and soul? You're definitely not a man on a cloud, although that's how your energy feels; like I'm floating.

How are you helping me? I just don't understand it?

It seems ridiculous to even admit it, but I know I'm currently experiencing your love and comfort. I can feel it. It's an energy flow. It's pure joy. It's unlike anything else I've ever felt, apart from making love, but maybe I'm not supposed to say that? Is that a bad comparison? But letting you in is almost the same as letting in the intense joy of making love to someone else. You have to be relaxed, I think you have to really want it and I also think you have to be open? (Man, now I'm laughing! Totally not how I know it sounds!! But you probably know I'm not hugely PC anyway. Given you're there the WHOLE time?! I mean really??!)

I do also know that you're making me say goodbye to Georgie in the way that I know him now. You have to be because he's still so poorly!! And for that, however wonderful you are now you've shown up; I hate you. However brilliant the powers you possess are, it is still so horrid that he's been so sick. If you're so great, why did you let that happen? Why can't you help even more?

George has endured so much pain and suffering. I know it's going to end with him being taken from us. I think, that maybe you have it in you to heal him, but I also don't think that's the way it's supposed to go? Why not? He is the BEST. Such a good guy, such a wonderful husband, daddy, son, brother, friend and colleague. He really is one of the good ones. I wish this wasn't happening to me. I wish this wasn't happening to him. I wish I could somehow change it. I wish you could change it! Can you?!

I so desperately want to believe in the miracles of healing that Brianna and her friends speak of. The scientist and pragmatist in me, still can't get my head around it though, although I've seen such obvious change in George already?! Complete healing still seems so completely ridiculous and impossible, but yet I want it. I need it. I desire it more than anything I have ever wanted in my life. I crave it so badly, that I would do anything in my power to get it. How do we make this happen? What more do you want from me? From him?

And this is where the tension starts for me. You have opened my eyes to a world of hope, love and compassion, that exists on another plain to the life I have led up until now. I can feel it. I can hear it. I can sense it. Once you catch a glimpse of your world it rushes in. It covers your whole body. It's SO bonkers. It's SO supernatural, that it does spark a flame of hope within me. I feel giddy and excited, but then scared and angry. Are you setting me up for a fall?! What on earth even is this?

I have to protect myself, God! I know George is going. His body is failing him, everyone knows it. You can see it when you look into his weakening face. So, my question to you is this. If you love me beyond measure, then why do I have to lose George? Why can't he stay? Why can't he be part of my adventure on this spiritual plain for a little while longer? Why do I have to be a warrior, when I'm not sure I actually want to be one? Why do my children have to grow up without their daddy? I have been trying to convince myself for the last

201

few days that this was our destiny. Somehow that makes it feel slightly better, but I still don't like it. I've been wondering if George's heart, soul and love, are so wonderfully brilliant that he's on some level too good for the world he currently lives in? That my children, like me and George, are so strong, that they are capable of growing up without one of the most solid foundations and role models they could ever ask for? Their father. That this is just a chapter in my life that's a difficult one and it will get better. It has to, right? Surely there's still hope and happiness to be found? Surely that's one of the reasons why we're here? I'm trying to convince myself that George will live forever in my heart and I will still be able to communicate with him on some level maybe? Through you and through your love.

But I hate it. I don't really understand it. Are you making me choose between you and him? Or do I have to love you to still have him in some way? Or is it that you've been here the whole time and you are our love? So, you are part of this whole thing anyway? You always were? I don't know and I definitely don't understand it! So, I'm scared. I'm so scared. I'm scared of all of the emotions I'm feeling. I'm scared that I have to know all the answers for my children. I'm scared, that I've got to carry on with life without my best friend. I'm scared that I haven't yet reached rock bottom and there's still a pit of emptiness, sadness and grief, that I must fall into before I can get back up.

So, please. Please keep helping me. I beg you! I don't know how you do this, I'm not even sure how I'm supposed to ask for it. Sitting and praying with my hands together and saying big words feels like I'm a bit of a fraud at the moment. I like writing though, so maybe letters will work for now if you're OK with that? Know this then. I wish you could cure George; I really, really do. If you can, then please do it. Make it happen. I'm so scared of what might happen next, please keep the love coming to me, I feel like I'm in the process of falling so hard. I feel like I'm being brave and strong when really, I know my world is crumbling and changing around me. I feel like I am finding happiness and carrying on, even though I'm so desperately sad. I'm the weakest I've ever felt, but somehow still here? Still willing you on? Still feeling hope?

I hate that I've had to give George permission to die. I hate that this is currently my reality, even though what you're showing me is so exciting! Please help me dearest God!! Show me what to do, use the people who can connect with you in a way I can't just yet, to guide me. To guide us both. Make my Georgie be happy. Don't let him feel any more physical and emotional pain. Don't make this be too drawn out.

But if it's at all possible, if it is within your capabilities, then please let my boys have a Daddy a little longer. Please. I'd love that so much, but really can't bring myself to say it out loud, as I know I should really be seen to be accepting of death and not believe in miracles. For him more than anyone else. I wouldn't dare to tell anyone this other than you. I don't want people to know, that I'm crazy enough to be so in love, that it makes me think it might be possible? That hope is coming. I'm not giving up. I can feel it all around us.

But if you can't do any of this - which I recognise is a big ask, even of you, please keep showing me that you love me. Don't ever stop. It's the only thing I've got to live for other than my children.

Show me that you will care for me and protect me. Show me that you will help me not be sad, not be too lonely and not be too jealous.

I love George with everything I have. I want to love you in the same way but don't know how? Please keep helping me and guiding me. With love, Louise x'

'!!!!!!Text barrage incoming!!!!!! Brianna x'

'Ok. This is just too weird. I just finished writing a letter to God on my phone. At the exact moment I pressed done in my notes app you text?! Whaaaat? This is freaking me out! Louise x'

'WHAAT??!!! Even I'm shocked by this?! God is SO good! Am I still OK to send what I have? B x'

'YES!!!! GO GO GO!! I can't believe you have a reply! Whaat this is so weird?! Lou x'

'God knows what you can handle, God allows you to continue to function and smile on the outside, even if you're crumbling in your heart. He gives supernatural peace beyond all possible understanding. I am overwhelmingly feeling God's tenderness for you and how connected his heart is to yours. He is allowing me to feel all of the emotions you are going through and having me send uncanny texts to bridge the gap for you, to know how very present he is. You are not alone. Just as you would talk to your own Dad, talk to God like this, like he's your Father, he's asking me to encourage you that he wants to hear everything. He needs to hear from you. Louise, God has put Psalm 56 on my heart for you, he wants you to read it. Here's the highlight reel… "When I'm afraid I put my trust in you … In God I trust and I am not afraid. Record my misery; list my tears on your scroll, are they not on your record? Then my enemies will turn back when I call for help. By this I will know that God is for me… I will present my thank offerings to you. For you have delivered me from death and my feet from stumbling, that I may walk before God in the light of life." Brianna x'

'I'm crying my eyes out. I've just read the Psalm in full. I'm certain it's the reply to my letter, it has to be, without a shadow of a doubt! I still don't know how this is happening?! How are you doing this?! Thank you God! Who knew the Psalms were so awesome and could answer prayers, through other people, on text!? MIND BLOWN!!!!! Does this always happen with you?! Louise x'

'I know the way that God is moving is a lot for you. It is miraculous. I know that the way I'm interceding is overwhelming – I don't usually do this! I usually hold back a bit more with my faith, but your situation means I'm all out fighting for you and for George. I can't hold anything back, because I would rather put myself out there and have you think I'm odd and know I've done everything in my power to help you, than not try. As me speaking (not God!) I just want you to know, that I want to understand everything you're going through and I'm also here to support you in any way that I can. But I don't want you to pull away from George. Just let me know if there's anything you need. I'm praying. Brianna x'

'Thanks, lovely. You've been so kind. You've done so much; I still can't believe what you have done?!? It's CRAZY! I will never be able to repay you, but I will drink champagne with you and laugh, cry and smile about this whole series of events when it's done. I promise. I love what you're doing for us. Please don't stop. Louise x'

Peace

Dear Georgie,

Even though you're still here I want to let you know I'm OK. I'm managing to sleep without you by my side. I've been wearing your t-shirts and your boxers to feel close to you. I know I'm close to you in my head, in a way I always kind of knew before but had never really realised. I think I know now, that this is what's going to pull me through; your love wrapped up in God's. I know our souls are connected on a level that we used to joke about, it's part of the energy I can feel in your hospital room. We're so different and so in sync all at the same time; maybe we're all more connected than we know? You always said you thought that not many people have the love we have and how right you were. It's a love that transcends our current reality. It's a love that will always bind us. It's an energy that moves in the same pulsating way the force in your room moves. I can feel them both, I can see them both; although not with my eyes. It's so crazy!

206

I'm SO proud of you my love, you have fought so well this last year, I'm really overwhelmed by the legacy you are leaving behind. When I read through the messages from all of your friends, I realise how many hearts you have touched in your lifetime. I know God knew that too, it makes me smile when I think of the note, he got Brianna to write for you. I can't wait to see you today, but I also know you've got to go soon. I can feel it's coming, so for now, I just want you to float. I want you to breathe in the spirit of love surrounding us all and be content with the peace that it brings. I also know that I have to stay here for the time being. I know I have to do it on my own, with the boys to help me. We have to make sense of this INCREDIBLE power that we have evoked and somehow show it to others with our love story. I wonder if others will be able to believe because we have? That's my wish, it would make all of this, every last drop of pain and heartache worth it. If I'm honest, I sort of want to come with you but know I can't. I know I have to stay for our boys, for our gorgeous beautiful babies, who are still too innocent to understand what's happening. I need to help them understand when they're old enough to process it. I want them to feel this force too and to help them see, that your love will be with them forever.

This morning Charlie and I looked out of his bedroom window. He saw your car and said,

'Oh Daddy's car! Where's Daddy?'

Last week these six words would have destroyed me, they would have thrown me into the pits of despair! Today they didn't, I was able to be Mummy and really tell him from the heart what was happening. I told him that you were getting weaker and your body wasn't working in the way it should anymore. This would mean that you would die soon. That dying and death are what we call it. But I also told him that your soul; that's all of the best parts of Daddy - your love, the boys' love, our love, your humour, kindness, generosity and freedom- would fly out of your body and go to Heaven. Charlie asked me where Heaven was, I said I didn't know. I'm still not sure where exactly you're headed, but I just know if it's anything like this spiritual force then it has to be great! It's so magnetically beautiful it has to be! I told him we couldn't see it in our earthly bodies, but we could feel it if we really wanted to. It was most likely all around us, the whole time, but we could pretend it was in the sky for the time being if he liked, that way we would have something to look at? Charlie then asked me what it was like. I said more beautiful and more amazing than we can ever know and full of the most incredible things. I also promised him that you would show us and tell us what it's like in your new home. So, there's your challenge. I know how much you like those. Charlie asked if he could go there too, go to Heaven and see you, that made my heart ache with sadness. I said one day, but not just yet, I've told him we've got lots to do here first. I said that we need to make yours and Jamie's souls full of happiness, just in the way Daddy's is now. We need to have SO much fun and laugh so hard that our tummies hurt that way, we'll know that you can hear us, see us, be with us. He liked that, it made him smile and he did the little happy dance you taught him.

Georgie you are so loved, you know that already and I know you now know this isn't the end. It's just the beginning. The best is yet to come. I will ALWAYS love you; I know you now feel that too. I will use your spirit and your love, to guide the three of us, with God. You have my word. It's funny that our wedding vows said until death us do part. That is so suggestive that it's the end. I now know there's never an end for the love I have for you. It's eternal, powerful. Enough to help me transcend into a universe and feel a power I never knew existed. Your love taught me to feel it, your energy taught me to know it. Life isn't as black or white, right or wrong, fair or unfair as I perceived it before. You will forever be in my heart and I will forever be guided by you. I love you, always, forever and then some more. Stay safe with the Big Man, he's got you. I trust all that he brings, it's such peace and beauty. L x'

Dear God,

Turns out the stuff you can do is pretty damn cool!! I never thought that I would find something this brilliant, when I went looking for it on that rainy, dark depressive night. I'm still struggling to comprehend that you actually heard me?! Is this how you work then, this energy? This amazing feeling of pulsating love that I can feel that Brianna and Simon have told me is the Holy Spirit? Mental!

Do you work through other people too? I mean Brianna is definitely following something that she's hearing from somewhere else? She has to be! Her messages of encouragement and the timing of when I get them are too perfect! It's like you're here with me, cheering me on the whole time! It's amazing! Have you always been here? I think maybe you have, but I just didn't know you? I thought you were a man on a cloud, when in fact the force I can feel is more of bright energy. It's formidable. Do you actually see everything? Do you try and control things through us and it's up to us if we respond? Do you hear everything? Do you know all of my jokes, bad parts and even the things I do that I think no one else sees?!

It turns out you do answer prayers! My word you're good! You've shown me you're here, that's for sure. But now what!? Where do we go from here? I didn't know how to talk to you before, but I'm getting it more now. You just let go. Do you just say everything, even your deepest darkest secrets? This whole thing is just totally insane, it's sort of like you're an imaginary friend? I *definitely don't understand how you work. I feel like I know you, but don't know you too, so if it's OK with you, I think I'm going to carry on writing letters for the time being, hope that's alright? I feel I can only pray out loud, when I'm with people who know what they're doing, the professionals. Otherwise, I feel like I'm trying to say lots of big words, but am not really sure what they mean? I also feel so sensitive to what I might look like, how I might sound and what other people might think. I know I shouldn't, I know it should just be the two of us, that's why I like talking to you here. I feel much more connected, when I talk to you like my friends, like my dad. That doesn't mean I'm not interested in your holy book or its various translations. You know me, I like books and words, I love searching for meaning and debating what my interpretation of that meaning might be. But I want to use my own words, I want to talk to you just as me for the time being, not using somebody else's script from a long time ago. I think it's a bit more down with the kids this way? A bit less pompous, a lot more real and authentic? Which is what I'm all about really. So, I'm going to keep writing. I feel like I am talking to my dad that way, he likes writing too.*

Today I've got a few questions for you. Well, in fact, I've got about twenty-five million, but these are the ones I'm prioritising today, you probably know what the others are anyway and have already told Brianna the answers!! Is it a coincidence that the man I love and you, both have names that start with a G? I mean it's actually been making me chuckle when I really shouldn't be laughing at such a time, but I really don't think it is?! Is George's love for me, really your love? Is that how you actually work? Is that why I could feel you because I could feel him? You showed up in Brianna, she's definitely channelling you, so can you show up in other people too? Do they have to ask for it? Do they even know when it's you?! Or is it just their intuition? Is their kindness, their feeling like they have to do something really you willing them on? This is all such a head-fuck, (sorry, but I really like swearing, so I hope that's OK?! I know I probably shouldn't, I don't think your book approves, but it's how I talk, so I hope that's OK for now, I'll change I promise!) I also need you to know that just because your heavenly squad, think that Georgie has led a full life and needs to leave my current reality, that I will never stop loving him. I will always need him to guide me and to help me. There will always be a part of him that's mine only, not yours. I'm pretty certain this has to be how it works anyway if part of his spirit is you and part of you is in him? So I've just got to figure out how I have a relationship with two people, who actually aren't physically with me. Is this the weirdest three-way ever? (Now I'm laughing, seriously are you actually there the WHOLE time?! Do you see EVERYTHING?! Man! This is SO weird for me to know!!)

Deep breath. So today I want to pray for this. I want to pray for the continued peace and happiness that George is feeling. I want to say thank you for the prayer that Simon did about downloading knowledge and talking to my boys. It's working. I'm listening to my heart in a way I haven't before and I can tell Charlie things without being sad. Who knew I could do this? Turns out you did?! Is this you in me?! Are you in me? Can I channel you? I pray for rest and continued calm. I have no other words other than I'm completely fucked (sorry for my language!) I'm asleep standing up and not one hundred per cent sure how I'm even still going? I know it isn't a coincidence that my little Jamie has been so unsettled whilst all of this storm has brewed around us. I love the calm and serene. Please let it continue. Please let it help me through these weeks to come. Please help Jamie feel your love and sleep too. He's just a baby. I want him to feel protected and safe. I ask you to give him that now. I pray for you to help me grieve properly too. Don't let this enlightenment overshadow the fact that I have to honour a goodbye. Let me feel sad but happy. Let me feel lonely but with love. Let me feel despair but with hope. If you can help me make sense of my emotions, that would be great. I pray for you to keep showing George that he has permission to go too. That he can float, that he can be with you and your crack team of Angels, that what he feels from you is so good, that he knows he must go. That it's meant to be. I want to see no pain, no discomfort, no fear- he's already had so much of this and he deserves no more - if you give him anymore now, I will be totally pissed off with you! So please, let him be at peace. Please let him feel loved, please just let him be.

I also want you to continue to show me your power, if you do that, then we can have a kind of, I'll help you if you help me thing going on? I'm not sure how your relationships usually work, but the best duos work on give and take right? I think you need my help a little bit because lots of people have lost their way with you. I think we need to show them how you feel about them in fresh new ways. I think and hope I can help you with that. So, I think that's it for now. With love, Louise xx

PS thanks for the despair weight loss plan you've put me on. I've been trying to lose weight all year and it's finally happened. Death has the bonus of helping me get rid of my baby weight. YAS! (sorry for being so vain! But I think you can somehow read my thoughts anyway ;-)'

Thursday 17th November am

'Louise my darling, this is for you. I want you to know how much I love you. How much I will always love you. I don't believe in perfection, there's always room to climb a hill faster, make a tastier steak, or crack a better joke. But I feel blessed to have found one life-changing exception. You and our *love. I remember the favourite part of my day, when we started at the chocolate factory, being when I could ring you for a chat on the walkie-talkies. We would have spent all day together, but then would spend another hour putting the world to rights! Then finally I got my kiss at Hogmanay and our perfect love began. You are the most amazing person in the world and to me you are perfect. Perfect in how you tackle life with such love and passion. Perfect in how you helped me follow my dreams, even when some of them seemed quite mad! Perfect in how you sacrificed everything to be the most amazing mother and wife. Perfect in how you are finding immense strength, at times where others would crumble. Perfect in how you have given me so much of God's love, that my soul is bulging and bringing me such strength, to allow me to go at peace, with no regrets but instead with love, Joy and completeness. I know you will take all of this perfect love and spread it through our friends, family and of course our beautiful boys. All my everlasting love, Georgie x'*

'Dear God,

The enormity of this situation is starting to kick in, George just sent me a message and it's floored me. There's been so much excitement this week I've forgotten myself a little. I've forgotten how much I miss and love George even though he's still here. How I'm still in utter disbelief that this is really happening?! How I'm actually watching my one true love die. The person who was so full of life, up until so recently, is now so weak and he's only thirty-four? I'm so sad. I want to howl out loud, but I also know there's not space for two babies in my house, Jamie already wakes and cries most of the night, but of course, you see that. I think you see it all now, but you don't always intervene? Why? Is that because this is meant to be too? Is that because death is healing? That Heaven is better than here?

I can't believe I'm going to be a widow. I'm going to have two small people who are completely dependent on me and I'm going to be without my partner in crime. It's completely brilliant, that I've figured out he will still be here in spirit and that you will be by my side too, but he's not actually going to be here? To help me? He's not going to be my husband?! I'm exhausted. I have a house to run, meals to cook, children to care and pay for and at some point, I will have to go back to work. How will I do this? On my own? Who will be there for me? Who will put their arm around me and protect me? I'm so so scared. I'm so sad. I miss my best friend already. I miss lying next to him in bed and hearing him breathe. I miss him smiling at me in the morning. I miss him finding me in the middle of the night for a cuddle. I miss his physical presence. His gorgeous blue eyes, his athletic body, his super-soft neck. Yes, I can maybe connect with him in a way I hadn't realised before through you, but once he's gone, I can't have him. I can't touch him; I can't make love to him. He's really all yours. That hurts. WHY?

I'm thirty-three and I'm going to be a widow. I'm thirty-three, I have two young children and I'm going to be a widow. I'm starting to love you too and I don't want you to go, but I also need to understand why have you done this to me? Why are you taking him now? Why have you given me this incredible relationship only to abruptly end it? The events of the last week have been amazing. Beautiful. Wonderful. I love you so much for opening my eyes. I also love that you have taken away George's suffering. That's so kind, THANK YOU. But now I'm suffering and that makes me sad. Can't you do anything about this? Surely you can?

My heart hurts when I see other people in love and I see them with their person. I'm so completely outraged that this is happening to me?! Are you really OK with this!? It's so sad. I love George. George loves me. I now understand this love transcends into you and me, from wherever you are. You've helped me see that and I really want to thank you, that in amongst all of this hurt, you can still bring hope. Bring peace. You're the only force that's managed to do this. To somehow make it all OK, even though it isn't? I can't help but feel that I'm on to something pretty special?

But, just because I know you doesn't mean that I'm going to be alright! That I'm not breaking inside. Do you think that I don't need someone to share the weight of bringing up two young children with? How do you OK these problems in your heavenly realms?! I mean can you even rubber-stamp it? I want to understand your decision-making criteria because it seems pretty hideous! Stick that in your pipe and smoke it God!! How do you solve the practical and physical things that I want and need!? That my children need! Why do you want to see me live like this?! It all just seems so unfair, even though you're so beautiful!

It's currently completely awful and it's going to get worse before it gets better, I'm sure. I don't see that this is going to go any other way. I'm embracing talking to you like a dad, but just because you are starting to feel like family doesn't mean I'm not mad. I'd ask my dad these questions in this exact same way (probably with a few more swear words if I'm honest!) I want to know what you think! Why are you doing this? Or are you not actually in control of death? Is that something else? Another department? I know I'm maybe a little bit ungrateful, I'm sorry, but lots of other people are seeing the tragedy of my situation. Just help me through it OK?! Help me find a way to not feel this hurt. I'm annoyed but I still want to talk to you, I just need a bit of space. Give me some time to feel less angry. Louise xxx

PS if you could also organise a bit more sleep for me, I'd like that.

PPS I'm starting to question where your influence starts and stops. We need to look into that. Road traffic accidents have been playing on my mind today Are they even accidents?!! And what about Natural disasters? Is that you? Or is that us? This is all just so confusing? Is the whole point that I'm not even supposed to understand? You're a total enigma? Why?'

'Good morning Louise! I was thinking about you all of yesterday evening and this morning. You say you don't know how to pray but I think you do. Jesus taught us to pray like kids, it can be messy, angry and emotional. Prayer is simply bringing your heart to God. I know that you're seeing now that he answers back – it's never how you expect it, but you will start to get to know him and see how he shows up! Prayer is a relationship and he wants to reveal himself to you as you get to know him. I'm praying that God gives you peace, as you walk through this supernatural experience. I pray that you don't feel guilty for feeling joy at knowing God at such a sad time. He wants to bear the burden. There is a way to stay connected to George and experience what is happening around you. Supernatural creates depth and beauty to situations, but it's not separate; it's very connected in fact. Almost like you live in-situ where you are, with greater colour and meaning. As an aside, I've realised you and G answered a prayer I prayed a few months ago. For many reasons, I asked God to show me an example of a good marriage. I am captivated by your relationship, how you love him with every fibre of your being. Seeing this depth, this commitment, it's incredible. It makes me realise that this is the kind of depth and connection I should wait for. Thank you for the gift of witnessing the beautiful, powerful, awe-inspiring way in which you love. Brianna x'

'Aww, thank you. You're SO in sync! I just wrote a long badass prayer to God. I'm so mad with him. Really mad in fact. It's the best love that George and I have, you've made me blush and brought a tear to my eye. Our love is true; I can't think how else I explain it. I think George might be sleepier today, I'm not sure what to expect. I'll let you know when I get to the hospital. Louise x'

'Hey Simon. Thanks so much for coming to pray. My mind is buzzing with so many questions about God. Yesterday my heart sang at such a time of sadness. More things happened after you left, mind blowing-wonderful things. It's like my soul cried so loud when I went out that night, that I've had enlightenment? Is that how this usually happens? How people meet God? Somehow, the power of the love I have for George has allowed me to transcend this world and have, as well as feel, intense communication with a force I never even knew existed? Is this usually how it goes? Please keep praying for us whilst I figure this out! I would never EVER usually send texts like this. I also realise I've become everything that George and I said we hate in terms of over-sharing, but I'm not really in 'normal' life at the moment, so I hope you don't mind me sharing! Keep praying for us. Keep the encouragement coming. It means so much to us both. Thanks, Lou x"

'I'm praying that you are engulfed in the Holy Spirit's incredible compassion. That it would make sense to you. Brianna x'

'As ever your timing is impeccable. I've just been texting Simon and then crying in the shower. I read your message the moment I was dry enough to see the screen! G's sister just texted to say he's weakening but still peaceful. I'm still hoping for that miracle. Louise x'

'I'm sending you some video messages we've made for George, only if he's well enough to see them? I hope it comes through to you? Tell him I'm praying. Brianna x'

'IN SYNC!!! I have just walked in his room!!!!!!!!! I'll tell him. Lou x'

'Ha-ha ha-ha! Brilliant timing again! Thanks God! Just to encourage you, that the pain, loneliness and heartbreak that you feel, is a sign of the big and beautiful way in which you love. It shows the depth of your connection to each other, how much George means to you and how much love you both have in your heart. Brianna x'

'Thank you for the video! It's the most beautiful prayer EVER. I love it! George LOVED it, it's made him so relaxed and peaceful. All of the nurses are crying today because they love everything about him and the aura he's giving off, as well as the feeling that's in his room. It's such beautiful energy, it's there but so unseen, even though it's recognised by everyone who sits with us. He just keeps smiling when he's awake, it's like he's glowing; he told someone today that he's going to Heaven tomorrow! God also just sent the sweetest member of staff to come and talk to me! I'm pretty certain it was him! She was the lady who found George loads of pillows the night he first arrived. She walked up out of nowhere on the corridor and just hugged me without even asking! I'd literally been talking to God just before, about who would give me physical comfort! Then there she was! She told me that she never usually hugs anyone at the hospital because it wasn't what she was supposed to do! She said though that she just had this overwhelming sense that she should do it?! She also told me that she knew I had children and it would be hard for me on my

own, but she knows I can do it. I was so amazed, I asked her if she believed in God, I thought that she must do given she was saying all of these things! That maybe she'd listened and he'd told her to come! She said no, but, was so intrigued about why I'd asked her?! I told her I'd prayed for the hug just a few minutes earlier? We were both as amazed as each other! Is this how God rolls?! Is he sometimes people's intuition? I think it is? I told her she was the answer to my prayer and that God was moving quickly around us at the moment. I think I'm figuring out that God works through other people? Based on this conversation, it seems like they don't even have to believe? Is it just when they listen to their instinct?! That overwhelming sense they get inside them? Is that what the Holy Spirit is? Or is that the force I can feel in George's room? This is all so confusing!! I'm now back in George's room, holding his hand. Classic FM is currently playing the Romeo and Juliet theme tune, as I sit here on my own with him asleep. I'm bawling my eyes out. God's ultimate playlist strikes again. Louise x'

'How are you doing now? Brianna x'

'I'm OK. I'm wobbly but I'm OK. I'm with a friend. Georgie is definitely in transition. He keeps talking to someone? But he is happy. SO HAPPY. At the hospital, they're utterly gobsmacked. They've said they wish everyone could die like him. They're calling it, 'doing a George.' He's going, his soul is on its way. I can see that, even though I've never sat with anyone who's died. We've said our goodbyes in this reality. He isn't saying much now, just mumbling and then every now and again, it's like he's having a really animated conversation with someone, saying things like "yeah obviously," and "I know!" Really clearly. It's like he's here but not here! He loved your prayer

SO much I can't tell you. There was a definitely a physical change in him when you said to fill his body with pure love!! It was remarkable, I saw something move over him. I'll tell you about that over some wine some time, I feel like I'm going mad! His body is starting to not look like him now, I can't explain it. Parts of him are in transition and the part that makes me sad is the fact that his body looks SO unlike him. I know it's because the best parts of him, the George I know, are going somewhere SO much better. I think some of him might already be there? That peace is comforting. It's beautiful. I couldn't have asked for anything more. Keep praying. Louise x'

Thursday 17ᵗʰ November pm

Dear God,

Thank you for giving me today. Thank you for the beautiful souls that enrich my life - my friends are helping me through this so much, more than they realise. Thank you for letting them bring fun and laughter in my darkest hours. (Oh and wine, trifle and chocolate too.) Thank you for helping me, help my beloved Georgie, find peace and fill his heart with pure happiness. He's such a good man, (even if he still bosses me in his final hours, about how to make Ribena!) Thank you for this special time of memories and goodbyes. It's a moment in time I know I'm going to savour and relive forever. I love it. All of it. Thank you for helping me find light in the darkest of places. You've helped me so much.

Death always used to fascinate, but terrify me, I'm now seeing it in a whole new light and understanding, in a way I never thought possible. Thank you. You've got me here. This did not feel possible last week. When it was so black. So helpless. You're a legend. Please keep helping me, keep holding me, keep doing what you're doing. Whatever and however you do it, something is working, just don't let go, don't stop. I'm in a holding area now and I'm not sure for how long? I know I'm waiting for news of his death, but until then there's nothing I can do. I've seen a glimpse into a new world, which I still can't comprehend or quite come to terms with – but maybe that's part of the point? Can we ever fully understand the supernatural realms, when we live such a natural life?

I also know that this white space of George's hospital room, the current epicentre of my universe isn't really "real life." But then in what sense should I now be experiencing real? Everything is so far from reality right now. I haven't seen my children properly in two weeks. I have no idea what food I have to eat in the fridge. The hospital staff, a vicar I've just met and a lovely American girl who sends me messages from your beautiful world, have replaced my old life. It's definitely a big deal kind of moment. I have completely missed the entire new season of 'Keeping up with the Kardashians,' and I have no desire or inclination to sit and watch it. (As an aside, don't let that be forever, I really LOVE watching reality TV.) I'm lost but I'm found. I'm sad but I'm happy. I'm excited but scared. Don't leave, Louise x'

Dearest Georgie.

I love you. Always. I don't want to let you go but know your body is broken. I wish so badly I could fix it, but I know I can't. It's time my love, the moment we've been talking about. You are the master of your ship and the captain of your soul. Fly high. Send me messages and signs- in a good way! Keep loving me in a way that transcends everything. Keep me in your heart, tucked up, cuddling. My life on earth will not be the same without you. I ache for your touch even though it's still possible to grasp it. Fly now my perfect soul mate. God's got you gorgeous one. Louise x

Dear Louise,

I'm holding your heart in my sleep. I love you. George x'

'My Gorgeous Boy!! I love you. I shall say goodbye now, I'm yours forever. I don't know when I'll see you again but I love you always, forever and a little bit more. Louise x'

After

The morning George died was odd. Even though I knew he'd gone, I didn't get the official confirmation from the hospital until the early hours. That was because the night before when we'd said goodbye for the last time, I'd organised with the nurses what would happen when he departed for Rose Cottage. That's how Rachel had referred to Heaven and we had both smiled when she'd said this. The hospital staff and I had been loosely making plans all week and I was prepared in as much as I could have been for what was coming. But really nothing and no one could ever have readied me for what happened after he went and how remarkably different our lives would be.

It had been so strange walking out of the hospital knowing it would be the last time I'd see him. We were both so certain it was our last goodbye when I'd leaned in to hug him on that Thursday night. He'd even got out of his bed to put a clean T-shirt and socks on,

'I've got to look my best for the Big Guy,' he'd said, with a cheeky grin written all over his ghostly looking face.

It was odd, hugging the remains of my husband for one last time. His broken body had felt so different and bony next to mine, but his soul remained so unaltered and powerful: so full of everything that was uniquely him.

The week leading up to our last night together had taught us to trust the voice inside our hearts in a way we never had before and George was so sure and certain of what would happen next, it brought calm and peace to us all.

George knew just as much as I did that God was real because of everything we had felt. Despite the fact he was ending his adventure in his human clothes he was also so expectant about starting a new one in another dimension with God. As I made my way down the stairs to the exit that night, I was unsure of what I felt. There was so much on my heart after our last goodbye; sadness, horror, uncertainty all beautifully and yet bizarrely intertwined with elation, peace, hope and trust. It was unlike anything I'd ever felt before and I hadn't even had a moment to process my unravelling thoughts before I looked up and saw her at the reception desk.

If I could have planned the time when our paths would cross again it wouldn't have been the moment I'd have chosen. And yet the beauty of what unfolded next was too perfect. There she was, the receptionist I'd spoken to all those months ago on that night when I'd forgotten the three-point-plan and had searched for time and time again on all of our hospital visits and never seen. She was busy and had a queue of people standing in front of her, my heart was in my mouth as I went over to say hello, I knew I *had* to speak with her. It was one of those, 'I just know I have to do this,' moments, the types of feelings I was beginning to listen to more and more.

As I walked towards the busy desk I wasn't sure if she would remember who I was and yet before I even opened my mouth she spoke up.

'I remember you,' she said, as she quietly placed her telephone receiver down and shuffled the immense amount of paperwork on her desk. She was looking down and frowning ever so slightly.

'There are some days at work that get to you more than others,' she continued as she looked off to a point in the distance whilst mindlessly moving the paper in front of her.

'That night, when I met you and you cried with me is something I'll never forget and will be with me forever.' She looked away again and then back at me.

'I had to phone my daughter when I was on my way home that night and ask her to come and sit with me after we spoke, I was so distraught. We drank almost a whole bottle of wine.' She veered off into the distance again and gazed. 'It's so precious life, isn't it?' She stopped and took in a deep breath. 'How are you?' She asked looking me straight in the eyes with a directive sort of tone, 'how is he?' I think she knew it wasn't going to be good news. I think she already knew that death would inevitably take hold.

'He's upstairs.' I paused. 'He's dying.'

Her face looked ashen, shocked and knowing all at the same

time. It was only when I softly said,

'But I know that this is going to be OK,' that her expression changed from pity to curiosity. 'I've got hope that this isn't the end,' I said, staring into her eyes with passion and conviction. She held my gaze as my phone rang. 'I'm sorry, I've got to go,' I said.

That was the last time we saw each other and she was the last person I spoke to outside of our close unit of friends and family before he died.

The same ring tone woke me from my restlessness as I lay with Jamie snuggling in my bed the next morning at 6 am. He was as sleepless as me and I'd brought him into my room just a couple of hours earlier so we could snuggle together and wait for the phone call I knew was coming. When I heard the phone buzz I squeezed him tight and breathed the smell of his hair,

'Daddy's gone to be with God in Heaven,' I said behind tears as I gripped his body close to mine, 'Let's see what the hospital have to say.'

My eighteen-month-old son didn't have a response to this overwhelming piece of information I had just whispered into his ear. But I knew in my heart that the words had soaked into his soul, sometimes you just have a sense with these things.

The phone call was brief and full of love. I didn't recognise the voice of the nurse at the end of the line,

'He died just after midnight,' she said, 'we tried really desperately to be with him, but he slipped away when we were out of the room,' the unfamiliar voice sounded broken.

'I already know,' I responded trying to muster a matter of fact tone, 'I knew the moment he went.' I paused, I recognised that I sounded slightly unhinged. These words were not something I ever thought I would utter as I had never previously understood it was possible to feel someone else die when you weren't with them. But that's exactly what had happened; I'd felt him leave and cried out on my own in the dark to God. There was a pregnant pause on the end of the line,

'It's what he wanted,' I continued, reassuring the nurse who was audibly upset and muting her sobs.

'He wanted to be by himself, he wanted to be alone when it happened, just him and God.'

She went on to give me some information about what time his body had been taken to the undertakers and asked if I had any other questions.

'No,' was the only reply I managed to get from my lips.

There really wasn't anything else left to say. After the call from the hospital, I phoned George's mother who was staying in a hotel next door. I also phoned my parents who'd returned to their house as I'd requested.

'He's gone,' was all I could say to both sets of parents. There were no tears from me. Just cool calm collection and focus.

That morning I still had to get up and get dressed; Jamie and I decided to do this despite the fact it was still dark outside and Charlie was sleeping. I wasn't sure what other routes to direct myself towards and the certainty of knowing that the breakfast cereal had to be poured, the milk had to be drunk and the nappies changed felt purposeful. The house felt oddly quiet. My best friend and nanny who were both staying with us were still sleeping upstairs. As Jamie and I tiptoed around our home it felt oddly empty and unfamiliar, the quiet though was soothing and was exactly what I'd requested; I'd wanted to be on my own with God just like George had when it happened.

As I sat in the playroom watching the trees move in the breeze and Jamie playing on the floor with his older brother's cars, it was then that the realisation dawned on me tat I wanted the world to stop. I wanted to curl up in my bed and pretend that all of what was happening was a bad dream. But in my heart, I knew that this would be the first sunrise of many that I'd have to see in without my soul mate.

Somehow, I had to prove to myself that I could live and I had a peaceful sense of confidence that I could now my eyes had been opened to so much more truth and hope about our existence. At that moment I don't think I truly comprehended what his death really meant and what our lives would really be. It was simply as if he was away with work somewhere and might still be coming back, striding through the door with confidence and his dazzling smile. It was utterly impossible to believe he was never going to come home again and light up our hearts; that prospect just didn't feel real. Somehow, in amongst all of these thoughts, God felt more real than ever though.

As I sat and watched the trees dance in the breeze, I decided to send Simon and Brianna a text. I'd told all of our close family now, the rest of the world could wait a few more hours, but the two of them had walked the last week with us. I felt it was only right that I let them know. I also needed to tell them how God had comforted me, they were the only ones who I assumed wouldn't think I was mad.

<u>*Friday 18th November am*</u>

'*Good morning my friends. After everything you've done for us, it felt right that you were amongst the first to know that Georgie flew to the angels at half-past midnight last night. I wasn't with him, but I knew. The moment it happened was odd. I sat up in bed and turned my light on and asked not to be scared. I felt a rush of energy into my bedroom, it was utterly overwhelming. I was SO frightened; it was like something slammed into my personal space. God came and got me though. I can't explain it. It was like there was someone in bed with me. I know that sounds SO ODD, but I could feel the energy. I slept restlessly until the phone rang at 6 am. I knew it was the hospital before I even looked at my phone. Jamie was with me, so I wasn't by myself when the news was confirmed. When they told me the time he'd passed, I knew it was the exact moment some kind of force had rushed into my room. Keep us in your prayers today. It's going to be rough. Louise x*'

I re-read the message after I sent it and looked at my clock. It wasn't quite 7 am. Before I had a moment to think what next, my phone pinged. I knew it would be Brianna.

'*I'm covering you in love and prayer. I know this might seem a lot right now, but I have to tell you something too. I think I've mentioned before, that God speaks to me through pictures and visions? Last Saturday when I was praying for George, the spirit took me to a place by the water, there was a woman with a small wooden boat. I sensed that the water's edge was symbolic and it was a meeting place. Last week the boat was empty and I didn't see George there. Throughout the week, I've kept going back to this place, praying for more time. Last night from 11.30 pm onwards, I saw that George was in the boat. He was exhilarated, like a young kid, his hands were on each side of the craft and he was rocking it back and forth and up and down. He was beyond excited about the adventure he was going on. It was strange. I was on a train, on the way home from Cambridge and cried all the way back home, I couldn't understand it, but now reading this it makes sense. Praying God holds you today and always. You are loved beyond measure Louise. I'm here for you too as a friend. This last week has been a lot to process, but when you want to talk it through, I'm here. Brianna x'*

I was stunned by the message and as Jamie continued to play and the others continued to sleep, I typed ferociously back. I couldn't quite believe what I was reading. The image of the water had spoken to my soul.

Thank you, Brianna. I can't believe what you've just said about the water and the boat! It's crazy and totally not a coincidence, that I chose this exact picture to put as my screensaver at 12.30 pm. It was the one photo that felt soothing. It was just before the crazy energy rushed into my bedroom. Now I think I know why. Keep praying. Louise x'

I sent Brianna a screenshot of my phone's home screen. The photo in the background was a picture taken on our family holiday just a few weeks earlier. It was George on his own, but it was different from most of the other shots I had of him. He was floating on the water whilst looking happy, relaxed and serene. He wasn't someone who spent a lot of time in the water, or even on the water but when I'd been looking longingly at all of the photos of him, this was the one that felt like it fitted. I hadn't taken a moment to think about why I'd chosen this particular image until then. As my hairs stood on end and I looked incredulously at my screen I realised it wasn't a coincidence that this was the one photograph that felt right. It spoke to me and gave depth to my situation in a way that I hadn't even understood just a few hours earlier. As I stared at the picture I realised that because of Brianna's text the photograph really showed me how George was feeling: that even though he wasn't here with us on earth, he was at peace. I sat dumbfounded in the armchair and unable to move as I heard Charlie wake up on his monitor.

I made myself get out of the chair, clicked the child gate to leave Jamie playing and went to see my biggest boy. Breaking the news to him as he woke with his sleepy eyes and kissable cheeks, was the hardest thing I've ever had to do. I knew that he would understand the concept of what I was saying more than Jamie and that the words I had to say to him would mean more. As I brought him down to the breakfast table rubbing my eyes and looking at my best friend who'd heard us getting up and come into the kitchen for encouragement, I knew I had to say it. I closed my eyes and thought of the peaceful picture as I uttered the words,

'Charlie, Daddy died last night.' As I said this, I put my arm around him and hugged him close.

'His body was very broken, remember that I told you that it was starting not to work properly and was really making his arms, legs and tummy hurt? Well the cancer that was growing inside him finally made it stop working whilst we were asleep last night. His heart has stopped beating. His body has stopped working. He's died.' I swallowed the lump down in the back of my throat as I went on.

'But he's safe now, you know. He's gone to be with God in Heaven.' I pulled back to look him in the face and check if there was any response. There wasn't really anything, I wasn't even sure if he'd truly understood.

'Daddy won't be coming home to our house anymore,' I went on, trusting my heart to find the words.

'His soul, that's the best part of him that we spoke about before remember? His soul has gone to live in a place called Heaven now and his body will turn back to dust like the ground.' Charlie held my gaze with not an ounce of emotion on his face.

'Poor Daddy,' was all he said as I hugged him and cried.

'I'll learn all about God and Heaven,' I desperately promised through the heartbreak and tears that were dropping on the breakfast table, 'so I can teach you all about it.'

My friend put her hand on my shoulder and passed me a cup of tea. It was all we could do at that moment, there was nothing else left to say.

As we ate our breakfast I don't think either of the boys noticed the blackness I felt, they were more bothered about having chocolate cereal and toast, disbelieving that we were eating the most amazing breakfast food I could find in our cupboards. I had wanted to give them a treat and it felt like we deserved the sticky

232

sweetness. As I looked up surveying the chocolate mouths in front of me it brought a small smile between the tears, all I could think was that George would approve. I tried to think of him, floating on his boat, at peace but without us. This was the start of the painful realisation that every part of our life was going to be altered from this day forward; he wouldn't be with us anymore. He was floating in another dimension

The reality of our lives since project Invictus had started meant that George had quite often been absent from family life; silently feeling and suffering from the side effects of his disease in another room. But as I sat there in a daze, both present and not present I looked at my children's delighted faces as they devoured and licked the chocolate toast on offer and couldn't help but find peace and strength.

I looked back at my phone with the relaxed and serene picture of my husband on water staring back at me. The whole situation just seemed so weird. George had died with no pain and in a state of sheer joy. This crazy force called the Holy Spirit had shown up in his room and into my bedroom last night. I was completely broken. George was dead but God it seemed, was real. He was speaking to us in so many different ways - through texts from Brianna, through photos, through words and visions. What did it all mean and how could he help me now George was gone? Was it even remotely possible for him to help with this amount of pain? I didn't know, and then I saw Jamie waving and licking something that made me sit up and brought me instantly back into the moment.

Since receiving one of Brianna's many texts a few days previously I had been on the prowl for white feathers; I wanted to be shown that they were a sign of Heaven. I had been willing them to appear and asking in my mind for them to be the confirmation of the supernatural existence I'd felt all of the week previously.

In my head, I had been silently daring this Holy Spirit force to do more and more outlandish things to show me God was real. As my mind wandered over the crazy events that had unfolded and the sterile nature of the conversation I'd just been forced to have with Charlie, I'd felt so alone.

Meanwhile, as I felt absent and numb, pondering over what on earth had happened Jamie was in his chocolate paradise living his best life, scrunching his toast in his hands and spilling the milk from his bowl all over the cloth.

When he looked up, his hair smothered in butter, crumbs hanging around his lovely toothy grin and chocolate smeared all over his face, I noticed something in his fist. It was poking out of the top. At first, I couldn't quite make it out.

'Open your hand JJ,' I said, 'show Mummy what you are holding.'

As his chocolate-covered fist unfolded, I realised he was clenching a fairly sizeable, white feather. He held on to it super tight, almost sucking the edges, trying to get every last drop of the chocolate spread onto his lips. I was stunned. I burst up out of my chair as this was simply amazing. Just when I'd stopped willing it to happen Brianna's prayer had turned up in my son's hand,

'Well done my little J,' I said lovingly to my chocolate-coated boy, 'You found the feather Mummy's been asking for. What a clever boy you are!'

It was the final bittersweet confirmation I needed that George was safe. I texted Brianna to let her know.

'You're not going to believe it! I just got the sign you asked for! Out of no-where! Jamie handed me a beautiful white feather at the breakfast table, he was almost eating it! I still can't believe it; we have no feathers in anything in that part of the house! He doesn't have them in his bedding either! I still can't get my head around what is happening! I've lost the love of my life but gained the greatest love you can ever know. This is all so odd! How did I not know any of this was real before? #IBELIEVE. Louise x'

That feather would be the start of many white feathers that would crop up into our lives out of nowhere; they still do in fact. It's funny how signs can sometimes go so unnoticed until you need them the most. I would never have thought twice about a white feather before. I would have assumed it had come from something in the house. But I knew that this feather wasn't from a cushion. As we sat in our breakfast room with its tiled floor and wooden benches there was nowhere obvious that this large white feather could have come from. It had to be from somewhere else. Surely it had to be the answer to Brianna's prayer? This would be how life would unfold; sadness boldly sitting alongside hope. The emotions beautifully leaning into one another, intertwining energies into our very altered lives.

The rest of that day was a blur. My best friend stayed with me in our house. My nanny kept the wheels of routine rolling for our children. I had already asked all of the family to give us some space and go back to their homes until the funeral. It all just felt so empty and yet there was so much to do. I had to visit the funeral director, talk to our bank to secure cash flow and still find time for my boys and my emotions. My parents stayed close and moved back in the next day as soon as my best friend returned home to London. Everything just felt so surreal, time passed so slowly around me and the days felt like decades

As the sympathy cards started to pile into our letterbox over the next few days there were two that stood out. George's mum and another one of my best friends both sent me the exact same card. They knew nothing about the text conversation I'd had with Brianna. They knew nothing about the symbolism of water and boats that we'd discussed. They didn't know about my picture of George on the water that was still the screensaver on my phone. Both of the cards had a picture of a small rowing boat tied to the side of a quay. I was dumbfounded as I placed them on the mantelpiece. Is this how it worked I wondered as I gently placed the cards side by side. Did other people hear this force, this Holy Spirit and not even know that's what it was? Is this how God really spoke to us? As I stood staring at the cards Mum wandered into the dining room and smiled.

'It's so strange how people send the same greeting cards,' she said tenderly, examining the boat cards that I'd just displayed. In that moment it felt like I froze to the spot I was standing on.

'You're not going to believe this,' I said as I looked at her in disbelief.

'What is it now?' Mum asked looking a little worried.

I confided in her and told her what had happened. I told her all about Brianna's vision of the boat and how it matched the cards. I also showed her the picture that I'd chosen as my screen saver on my phone, the photo that had spoken to my soul, in the exact moment George had died just a few days earlier.

'That's so strange,' she said reaching for her phone and looking bemused. 'I chose the exact same photograph!'

We stood in silence looking at each other's phones, gobsmacked at what we were seeing. Mum pulled me in for a hug as we both cried feeling thankful; all of these synchronised signs were just too perfect not to be real.

Life it seemed was destined to spin in this new way. Just a few hours later I was sitting holding my parents' hands as I registered George's death. The pity, despair, sadness and shock were just so tangible in the eyes of the registrar as she wrote the official details of George's passing with her large traditional fountain pen.

'He was so young,' she said in obvious horror and an unassuming quiver of disbelief.

I gripped Dad's hand forcing myself not to scream. It would be the first of many moments I would feel like this. I was so mad that she didn't understand that George had been saved and was still here with us, but not in a human way. That he had gone and while I would never see him again in his body, God had him now.

I wanted to tell her that Heaven really was where we could all be headed if we were prepared to accept the truth and allow for the supernatural and God in our hearts. I wanted to tell her that maybe, if we opened our eyes to allow the thought, Heaven was better than where we were currently.

I wanted to tell her that God was real and that I had proof and had felt him, seen him and knew of his power. That a random person we didn't know had brought him to us because I had asked. I wanted to tell her so desperately that George had gone from being in indescribable pain to pure and perfect peace and was filled from the inside out with a beautiful, glowing, electric type of love and hope. That it was God who had made it all happen and saved him.

I wanted her to know that I'd seen a door open into another world from his hospital room. A door that I never even knew existed. A door that wasn't a real door like I open in life, but a door of energy. A door of connection that I banged upon with all my heart and begged and screamed to be opened.

I wanted to tell her that I'd been asleep my entire life and only just woken up because he had died. I desperately wanted her to wake up and see it too. I wanted her to know, just like I did, that George was wrapped in perfect love now. That his spirit was finally safe and that unequivocally I knew no harm could reach him because I'd caught a glimpse of his force. I'd felt it in my heart, on his hands, all over his hospital bed, his dying body and in my bedroom the night he died.

I also wanted her to know that it had taken this door to open for cancer to finally stop screwing with our lives. I desperately wanted her to know that nothing could screw with my life now. Not even death. Love had won.

But at that moment, I didn't find the courage to say any of this. I simply clenched my dad's hand and said, 'I know.'

I feared that if I'd really told her how I felt then I would have sounded weird. Like I'd been brainwashed and that the courage of conviction in my heart was a result of serious trauma.

That conversation was like so many others I would be forced to have and so life without George continued. Slowly, in between the surrealness of it all I began to learn how God was there in amongst the chaos of loss.

My parents stayed with us as I cried and shook with sadness. They kissed my boys and tickled them when I was so tired that I couldn't move. They wrapped their pure love around us; it was just what we needed and they put us first. They were amazing. I slowly came to see that their love was much like God's. Completely unconditional. Was their love his love too? It was all so confusing! Were these feelings of love something I'd learnt from him before I'd even become me and known my parents? I had no idea.

In between all of this figuring out in these early stages of loss I felt bad that I needed my parents to look after us. I felt like a child and hated it. Needing them was another manifestation of the distinct loss of who I was. I could understandably see the stress in their faces; their hearts had also been broken by the loss of their beloved son-in-law. It hurt them that they couldn't fix this for us and it broke my heart to see them hurting for me. It was brutal but I kept telling them I was OK because I believed and had hope. Because I knew God was real. He gave me purpose, unlike anything else I'd ever felt before. That's because deep down, in spite of the pain and deep anguish I felt, I knew that he was there.

I desperately wanted them to believe in the way that I did. I wanted everyone who was sad to have the same salvation I had found in my heart. The same love and hope that could sit and be with them in the darkness and help them feel protected in the way it was binding up my hurt.

The texts of encouragement kept coming from Brianna at the exact right time and moment. There was the afternoon we spent watching 'The Jungle Book,' with the boys, snuggling under a fur blanket and she texted. '*I see you wrapped in Fur. B x*'

I couldn't believe the message when it came through and simply replied with a photo of the three of us wrapped together on our sofa under the fur. It was all just too amazing and always gave me goose bumps.

It also seemed that whenever I questioned if everything we had experienced was real or begin to wonder if it had all been a dream, I would be sent a reminder that would incite fear as well as awe and wonder. The synchronised encouragement from Brianna still came in the form of visions or explanations of my emotions and continued to be SO in touch with my heart. It was all so real.

Then, there was the prayer she sent for me to read to my mum. It talked about her wanting to protect other people and contained the image of a glove. Brianna told us that God wanted her to know that he could see her trying to take away the brutality of the heat out of the situation but that sadly my heart had to feel. At the exact moment when I went down to the kitchen to read this prayer out loud Mum was at the sink. She had her back turned towards the window and was washing-up. When I started reading the words she turned around in floods of tears and held up her hands. She was wearing yellow washing up gloves. It was another sign. We were so seen yet unseen by this force we were coming to know as the Holy Spirit. It was utterly bonkers.

And yet despite the messages of encouragement from Brianna that continued to allow the flames of hope to burn in my heart and my eyes to be opened to the wonderful signs of love around me, I still felt so black. It felt great to know that God was there but I was still angry at him. I was hurting so much and still couldn't believe that he had stood by and allowed George's death to happen. It was all well and good that this Holy Spirit force still seemed to know the specifics of what I was doing, but that didn't stop me from feeling utterly abandoned.

The grief and sadness also meant that I felt more closed. I struggled at times to feel close to God in the same way I had in the hospital room. His presence had been so tangible and obvious there. The magnitude of the energy had been electric when George was with me.

'Was that because George was in transition and this is what happens when someone dies?' I thought out loud most days.

I'd walk on the country lanes around my home and wonder if part of Heaven came to earth in the week that George had died.

Or was it that the door to this realm was simply left ajar and the breeze of peace from this glorious setting was able to stir around my heart because I was willing to be part of it now. I didn't know.

All I knew was that I wanted that peace again. I wanted the feeling of the force that I now knew was the Holy Spirit. I wanted it in the way I'd witnessed it that week because it was the only thing that made my life worth living. I needed to get closer to God and I knew that I couldn't rely on the luxury of having Brianna forever. So I kept writing. Even though at times I hated him I still wanted to strike up a friendship with this love. A love that I could sometimes feel, never really see and still didn't really know.

<u>*Wednesday 23rd November*</u>

Dear God,

Where are you? I want you to stay as close to me as you've been this last week. I need you now more than ever! I can't do this without you! I won't cope if you're not here by my side! Walk with me, I beg you! I'm overwhelmed with messages of shock and anger from all of our friends and family. I've even got messages from people I don't know! It hurts. No one else really knows how beautiful George's death was. No one else really understands that it wasn't you who took him. I know you saved him. You saved us all. I want to run away. I want to hide out with people who don't know me, to allow me to feel my grief and my hope in you without it impacting anyone else. Please help! I feel empty and I can feel your presence less. I don't like it. Show me you're still here, help me still hope. I beg you. Louise x

Dear George,

*I keep waiting for you to walk through the door and tell me it's all OK.
I keep waiting to give you a cuddle. I know you can't do that either. I miss
you terribly. I miss you more than ever before. I love you. I'm carrying on
because I have to. I'm annoyed at the world's anger and I'm angry at God
too. Come and lie with me, even though I can't see you. Find me, hold me,
keep our hearts close. I love you. Tell God to help me through this. Tell him
I want to get to know him better. Tell him, I need him as my friend. L x'*

The next day rolled around and I had to focus my brain on
organising George's funeral. He'd been very clear that he didn't
want it to be a completely sombre affair but a celebration of
everything that was wonderful about his life. He wanted us to
show that death wasn't the end. That's why we decided on one of
the beautiful days in the previous week as the beautiful golden
energy had flowed out of him, that his funeral wouldn't just be
about him. It would also be Jamie's baptism - his official welcome
to the world and our line in the sand that life continues. An
indication that we wanted our children to be raised knowing God,
so they could feel him and make a decision for themselves when
they were old enough to choose. It would be a funeral and a
baptism in one. It would be the 'Cycle of Life.'

We were animated as his sister and I plotted what this event
might look like whilst sitting next to his hospital bed, we even
looked up ideas on Google together. It turns out though
organising the party that we had so excitedly discussed just a few
days ago was pretty depressing without him being there. And
while I knew that his spirit would be seen and imprinted all over
his event, he wasn't actually going to be there in the way he always

had before. That hurt my heart so much and yet I also felt and knew that he had passed the baton of encouraging and inspiring hope over to me.

Just a few days after his death, George's sister returned to our family home to help me organise his send-off. It also meant I could send my parents back to their home for a few days. On the afternoon of her arrival, we went over to Nottingham to see the church where we hoped his celebration would be held. As we walked through the town centre, arm in arm, the people around us hunting for Christmas presents and admiring the sparkly lights it all just felt so wrong. We were having a nice time together. Arguably, I was having a nicer time than the previous Christmas when George had been diagnosed and everything felt so bleak. I thought back to that shop assistant and how her words had floored me as we strolled through the city. Somehow, I was stronger now, more experienced, more resilient. Was it because I felt like I had to be this way for George or was it God-given armoury? Maybe even both? Either way, a knowing will was wrapped around my heart and cheering me on. I just couldn't figure it out.

As we continued along the cobbled streets, my sister in law talking about options for food after the service, I found myself blurting,

'It's sort of like a reverse episode of 'Don't Tell the Bride,' don't you think? We've got just a few weeks, to organise the send-off of a lifetime! The only difference is I don't have my groom!'

We looked at each other and belly laughed. It was bizarre.

Feeling happiness when we were so devastated. This mix of emotions is a strange part of life that people never talk about, but really this is what grief is. Such complex emotion that is so often shelved and over-looked by others and at times outwardly and obviously un-invited into their lives. So uncomfortably isolating when you already feel so alone and so alien about feeling happiness. Fortunately for me love kept on shining through.

It was the vicar Simon who had set up the meeting with the church that we were headed towards that day. This was because his church was yet to be renovated and was still an empty building on the other side of the city. In the days following George's death, I had come to know Simon and his family a little better. They had prayed with me and continued to help me piece together the crazy series of events that had unfolded around us. I also began to realise that when I'd first sent the text asking him to come and pray I hadn't at all appreciated any of his circumstances. I was far too into my own story to think of anyone else's life in that week.

What I hadn't known when George was alive but was learning now he had gone, was Simon's story. He and his wife had only very recently relocated to Nottingham. His church was still only a few people who gathered in his front room and he'd never actually ministered a funeral or a baptism before. He was an exceptional leader who was still very much finding his feet. I came to realise that what we were going through was as new to him as it was to us. God it seemed was working his magic in all kinds of wonderful ways.

As we got to know one another in the fleeting moments we

spent organising George's celebration over the phone and face to face, I became increasingly aware that Simon had been sent to help us. It was obvious that he had been positioned to stand with us and be our friend. There were just so many beautiful parts of our lives that linked together; I was the same age as him and his wife, our kids' birthdays were not that far apart, he didn't know Nottingham and I did. He was trying to establish himself in the local church community and then we had shown up with nothing short of a miracle.

That day we sat together in a church I'd never visited before. The meeting was the two of us plus George's sister and another vicar who I'd never met. This was because the church we were hoping to use for George's service belonged to this experienced minister. It was interesting that he spoke to the synchronicity of the situation we had found ourselves in before the meeting had even begun. It was him who pointed out that,

'It's not a coincidence we're all here today.' I sat on the edge of my seat as he continued, wondering what on earth he would say next.

'I was actually supposed to be in another meeting today, that meeting was cancelled at the last minute. It's the only reason I'm sitting with you all now, it's the only reason I fully believe that this is all clearly meant to be. Only God knows why we're all here. Why we've been put together. But here we all are and I'll take this as a sign that I'm supposed to host this service here in my building. You can use my church.'

We all breathed a sigh of relief and Simon looked over at me and smiled. It was what we'd been praying for.

In that meeting, we could all feel that something was binding us. As we walked towards the exit, feeling thankful that we had finally set a date for our event of a lifetime, George's sister excused herself to go to the toilet. Simon looked at me, took a deep meditative breath inwards and began to speak.

'It can sometimes take quite some time, you know, to get close.' I looked at him confused and blankly as I wasn't really sure what he was referring to.

'Forgive me, but in your relationship with George did you feel more intimate towards the beginning, or as your lives grew together?'

As he asked the question, still unsure of the path he was trying to lead me down I felt like I was watching the movie of our old life flash before my eyes. I could see George and I walking hand in hand on the streets of Edinburgh; I saw him drunk and eating pizza and me shouting at him; I was back on the bridge the night when he had asked me to marry him; I was on the aisle walking towards my future husband; I was in New Zealand looking up at the stars by Lake Tekapo on honeymoon; I was inside one of our duvet tents; I was giving birth to our children; I was talking to him on the phone, hearing him tell me he had cancer and I was in the hospital, sobbing, as I watched him die.

'Well we were obviously much closer towards the end,' was all I could say. I didn't really know where else to begin with all of the images I had seen in my mind's eye, these beautiful moments just felt stuck in my throat.

'Well this is how it is with God,' he mused, looking at me squarely in the face.

'Your relationship never stays the same. As you change, so too does your love. It's much like a marriage. You have to get to know him in the way he knows you. You have to be with him in all of the moments life throws your way, to really *know* him.' He looked towards the stain glass windows as he tailed off.

'It's an interesting line of work, my job.' He had a faint smile on his face now and I looked at him, confused. He was just so opposite to everything I had ever expected a vicar to be. He was cool, he wore trendy clothes, he was like so many of our friends. He'd also been so kind, just like Brianna, and asked for absolutely nothing in return.

'You see the thing is,' he went on, shifting on his feet and scratching his beard.

'I haven't told you, that you guys have also answered some of our prayers.' He looked down again.

'What do you mean?'' I asked.

'Well,' he said, 'you know Claire and I and the kids. We've only been here a couple of months. It was, I mean it is a big move for us all. We've been asking God to show us, we've been praying for signs that he's here, that he's moving in this city. And then, that night when I got your text…Well, I was overwhelmed. It was Claire who said I had to go, that I had to go and meet you both. As soon as I had spent some time with you, I knew that you were the sign. That this was God confirming to us he was here. That he was alive in this city.'

I swallowed the lump in my throat down. I had never really thought about the fact that even clergy needed encouragement. It sounded so obvious once he said it, after all, even clergy are still only human. And faith is such a delicate balance to walk.

'Woah, I had no idea,' I said not believing what he was saying.

'You wouldn't,' he went on, 'but this is often how God moves. So knowing but unknown. George also answered another deeply personal prayer of mine. A prayer about death. It's something, like most, I've always been afraid of. Yet now having sat with him, having seen him. Well, it was all just so beautiful. It was so full of glory.'

At this moment my sister-in-law returned from the toilets.

'Ready to go,' she asked, cheerfully.

'Yes, I'm ready.' I replied.

I looked over at Simon who could see I was figuring stuff out at a rate of knots. He smiled, as he waved us on our way.

As we walked back to the car in silence I couldn't stop thinking about the conversation I'd just had. I was learning more and more, about the tightrope of this thing called faith. It hadn't even entered my mind that George and I might have been signs to other people. I still find it crazy, that even when we didn't know that God was real, we were still the bearers of such hope to others and could even answer their prayers. I was slowly beginning to realise that this was how he worked.

As the funeral date came closer, despite trying to seek the positive and knowing that I'd made some new friends everything still felt hard. I'd be lying if I said I felt really close to God at this time, despite the fact that I believed more than ever that he was real I still didn't *know* him. Because of this he sometimes felt so absent even though he was supposed to be there. It was almost like he'd dropped us back off into real life but not the life I wanted. I felt abandoned and wondered on a daily basis if this is what it would be like forever? A giant George-shaped hole and a nice benign force just watching over us? I already knew I wasn't interested in that. I wanted it full throttle. Full power. I'd seen God move in the hospital room and knew what he could do, I wanted that all the time as it was the only part of life that breathed hope and excitement into my soul.

And so I realised that if I wanted to live in a relationship with God then I had to find my own way with his divine power. It was just like any other relationship. I couldn't expect it to be all on him even though I'd somehow been brought up to believe that maybe it should. The texts from Brianna had started to lessen too and I had felt the drop in God's presence because of this. And then I thought about what I would do if this had been George and his communication had dropped off. I would have always looked for new ways to find him.

So that's what I set my mind to but I didn't really have the know-how. My heart was drawn to the Psalms as I found the words so comforting. When Brianna and Simon had shared them with me in the last moments of George's life it was as if these beautiful words spoke to my soul. Brianna had also ordered a book of Psalms for me to read. So I took it as a sign that maybe I should try when the Amazon Prime delivery driver showed up with my Bible that day!

At first, it was hard. The only time I had the chance to read was when I went to bed and I was already tired from putting one foot in front of the other and organising George's celebration. I was mentally broken. But every time I asked anyone who believed in the way I now did they told me to read these poems. And so I found the time and forced myself to stay awake and soon I was hooked. Somehow they said everything I wanted to say but couldn't find the words to express. Just as the Invictus poem had made George and I feel like someone had been through what we were feeling, that's how I felt now when I read the Psalms. They connected to my hurt and brokenness but also wonderfully spoke to the hope, love and expectancy I was feeling. It was the first time I'd seen anything in words that felt the same as what was on my heart. It felt good that someone else was expressing it for me and that they understood it. That I didn't have to delve into the depths of my soul to find the words that sometimes just wouldn't come. The Psalms carried me at a time when my own words couldn't.

So I kept on keeping on. The days felt like months. The routine at home was incredibly brutal, as well as uplifting. The boys were happily kept to their routines with the help of our nanny, my parents and George's mum and didn't seem too concerned that Daddy hadn't come home. I think it was largely because I kept on reminding them that he had died. We played acting out the 'Cycle of Life,' with our 'Happy-Land' set and we pretended to bury our 'Toy Story' characters when I had time to play in between the seemingly endless death-min tasks at hand.

In amongst this grief and precious time with my boys, I began to find my own way with God. I wondered about where he'd been in my life this whole time. I wondered how he worked. Why I could go from feeling him and knowing he was there, to not feeling him and not knowing where he was, all within the space of an hour. It was unlike any relationship I'd ever had before, and completely out of this world. But one thing I knew for certain was that when I felt him, in the same way I'd felt in that hospital room, it gave me peace and hope unlike anything else. The love I felt was unmistakable but was it only because I wanted to receive it that it was so strong? I couldn't figure it out, so I kept writing.

Dear God,

I'm sorry it's been a while. Life after death is busy, but then I think you know that better than anyone. I really miss our time together; sorry it's taken a while to get back in touch. I've been starting to tell some of my friends about you. Some people get it, others don't. They think my strength is inspiring- they don't understand it's not me but really you. I don't know why, but I still feel quite shy talking about you, it's almost exactly how I felt when I met Georgie! I suppose there's some fear, that if you fall in love too much, then you'll leave yourself open to more hurt? Or that maybe others will think you're stupid? I think I feel a bit like that at the moment. I'm scared to give everything to you, in case I don't get back what I need. In case I get hurt in some way. In case other people think I'm mad?

I just can't hurt any more than I already do at the moment. I miss George SO much. I know he's here, I can feel him, sense him, he alters my mood. Just in the way you did on the night that George died. You made me feel safe and happy. Is it bad that I want that the whole time? I don't know if I'm even allowed to say that or ask for it? But I want it. I want you like this every day. I know that's maybe pretty selfish. I know that you have billions of people to tend to (which blows my mind by the way, so much! I mean how are you always there for everyone?!) It truly is supernatural!! But then your existence is so spiritual… Somehow George is helping me see this more. I think you work a little bit like him, you're always there but sometimes you're more there? I'm not sure why though, is it because I invite you in? I just don't know. I can't comprehend it even though I'm trying.

I have so many questions about how you work, it's so real but not real, so tangible but not tangible? I do love you though, I hope you know that. I believe in you with everything I have. I wish everyone else could believe in you too. The world would be an incredible place if everyone knew your love! But sadly, I think it's maybe not supposed to be that way? I'm not really sure why though? So I simply trust that you've put me on this path, even though it's incredibly hard. I trust you know why this is happening and that all parts of our life stories, the good and the bad, happen for a reason? I trust you, I want you to know that.

The worst part at the moment is that I'm really struggling. I miss my cuddles and kisses. I miss laying my head on his chest, his lovely smell and seeing the way he looked at me; knowing just how much he loved me. I still can't believe it, I just want to see him, but I feel like I can't even remember our life before cancer. It's all a blur. All I feel like I can remember is stress. Horror.

I know you didn't make George get cancer; I understand that now. But did you maybe always know he was going to die young? Was this part of the purpose over his life, to teach everyone he left behind something? I know that

253

you helped him die the most beautiful death, it really was so extraordinary, the way you moved into his body and into his room. It still feels like a dream! I also know that if it wasn't for George's death, I would never have found you; but that's the part I keep coming back to! I feel angry about the fact I can't have you both. I hate you for it. I also feel like George is trying to show me he's here with us? But maybe somewhere else? Because of that, I feel like I get the whole Jesus part of the Bible, more than I ever really used to. I mean he quite literally put his finger up at death!! I know that was you in him! It has to be, it's the only way his stories are even possible? You are him and he is you? He showed us in very real and concrete terms that death isn't the end. I mean he CAME BACK!!!! It's off the hook crazy, but it's the same crazy force I've felt! I know it!

I'm sure I have a lot more to learn. I always thought what Jesus did wasn't really possible; all those miracles, walking on water! I mean it's mental to think about. But now I realise I was just missing the supernatural point. You and him, were trying to show us, in a human way, in a way we'd maybe understand the true strength of your powers because he is you and you are him? But even though Jesus came, maybe it is still a little out there for people to get their heads around? I mean it is when you think about it? But I think I get it now. I still feel like I'm waiting for a miracle though? Why? I really am just like the girl in the card you made Brianna write! I can't explain it, but I feel like what you've done with George isn't actually all you've got up your sleeves? I don't know why I think this is? It makes no logical sense, but I feel it. I know it in my heart. I still feel like I haven't seen your true capability and maybe you haven't seen mine? I'm expectant. I want more!

Then I think why me, why now, why my children? I just can't make sense of all of this!? I'm open, I'm ready, I'm willing to learn but I'm scared. Scared of loneliness. Scared of hurting. Scared of being on my own for the rest of my earthly existence, but then scared that by being close to someone else, I'll stop being close to George. I hate this confusion. Please help me. There is so much going on right now, I'm struggling to cope. Such excitement tenderly next to such fear. Such hope coupled with such intense grief. Stay with me, always. Your love gives me wings. It's mad I've fallen in love with something that I never even knew was real, a force you can't even see. But my word can I feel you. I love you. Give all of my love to George. Louise x'

My prayers always got a response. It wasn't always as obvious as a text, in the way it had been in the hospital, but it also often was. It wasn't with the same regularity, but the super-charged, intricate connections that I had made during the week when George died continued to spark around me. Simon and Brianna continued to give words of encouragement. It was always when I felt that I was scrambling to see the light, that they would message.

'I don't know if this is right to send, but I sensed an awful lot of sadness from you yesterday at the church. God will be and is your comfort. He will always be close to you, even when you're most sad and feel most alone. He loves you and is for you. Don't ever forget that. We're with you. Simon x'

There is so much sadness every night. I never get the chance to cry in the day as I have to keep on keeping on for the boys. Going to bed is the worse, it's part of the reason I'm so tired as I get upset before I sleep. This text is spot on, thanks so much for sharing. Thanks for the encouragement. I know I'm loved. I wouldn't have got this far without God; I just couldn't have done it without him. What's hard is I'm now trying to figure out my relationship with him as I move into widowhood (I hate that word!) I suppose because I've lost George and gained God, I expect him to support us in the same way? I know this sounds so bonkers, but I don't know what else to expect?! Lou x'

'Perhaps it was God supporting you all along? He will now find new ways to support you all, differently, in a new season of life. That doesn't mean it has to be just you and him. It will be other people too. We're here. All of our church as it stands is here with you too. We're around you. We're praying for you. Oh, and I want to encourage you to continue to expect great things. "The Lord is close to the broken-hearted and saves those who are crushed in spirit. The righteous person may have many troubles, but the Lord delivers him from them all. He protects all his bones, not one of them will be broken." Psalm 34. Simon x'

Life moved fast and slow. I wanted to find the way through and there was a stubborn part of me that knew I had to be on my own. I needed to see how it would feel and how I would cope. I wanted to invite the pain of total isolation into my home so I could move past it. I loved having my parents around, but I also knew they couldn't move in; neither of us wanted that for one another. I knew I just had to get on with life as it would be now and that it would be a million times worse if I dragged it out and I had my parents stay with us indefinitely. It was totally like the feeling of wanting to take a plaster off; I just wanted all my hurt out in the open, even if it was the most agonising thing I'd ever have to do. I felt like our little family had been trampled and broken and that there was never a moment or a day off from that. I was on my own and I couldn't even go out of the house for milk if I wanted to. I was solely responsible for two very small, very beautiful and very dependent humans. It was inescapable grief everywhere I looked but I knew I had to feel it in the same way I could now also feel the inexplicable hope of God. This was the only way I knew how to survive.

A Celebration

Twenty-eight days after his death, the 'Cycle of Life' arrived, it took so long to co-ordinate a church that had the capacity and space on their calendar so close to Christmas that it was a longer wait than we had all anticipated. Simon and I had been so very thankful to the experienced vicar whose meeting had been cancelled that day. It was thanks to him and God that this event had even got off the ground. As I focused my mind on what was coming the day before this big celebration, I decided to go and sit with George's body. It felt right to sit with him one last time on our own and I needed to see what his coffin looked like before everyone else would see it. I needed to prepare myself before he would be carried into the church, inside a box, by his friends.

Our funeral directors were amazing, so full of kindness, so in step with what I might want or need and I recognised that it took a special person to do the job they do each day. Undertakers are required to navigate deeply personal and alien moments simultaneously and the day I arrived in the funeral home and was ushered quietly into an oddly cosy waiting room, I felt so safe. When I was ready and had taken the biggest deepest breath imaginable, I went through the connecting door to be with him in his coffin. I was taken aback at how beautiful it was seeing the design in real life for the first time. As an artist, George's sister had taken on the responsibility of creating the artwork for her big brother. I'd seen mock-up designs of what his box might look like but the beauty of what she had created still took my breath away in real life. His coffin was blue, his favourite colour, and covered in photographs of his life, beautiful memories that he'd made with others and a striking picture of the moon. I had asked for the lid to be closed as I didn't need to see his face in death. I had already seen it so many times in life that I didn't want this to be how I looked at him in his human clothes for the very last time. I'd already had that moment in the hospital and didn't need to see his body without his soul inside.

Mum was with me and made sure I was comfortably seated on the wooden chair next to his coffin and then, as I had requested, she left. George and I were on our own then. I admit that it was a bit eerie. Here I was with the man who I loved more than anyone else, with whom I had shared the most intimate moments of my life and he was gone. It was clear that even though his body was there, I knew he wasn't. I smiled as I thought about how much he would have loved his box. As I touched it I couldn't help but think it was absolutely perfect, so full of life, happiness and him. I sat with my head lowered for a while, I wasn't sure if I should pray out loud or pray in my head. I wasn't sure if I should speak to

George or speak to God, I mean, they were in the same place after all and this might be the last time we'd ever get to talk, just me and him. And then my phone pinged. The timing was too perfect. I knew exactly who it would be. I took my phone from my pocket and read the text'

'*God wants to encourage you. I see a glow of heaven around George and the spirit rejoicing that he has finished the race. I feel God's very tender heart towards you, like a Lion protecting her young. He is feeling all that you feel and is very watchful over you to keep you safe. Sending so much love. Bri x*'

'*OK, this is weird. You are too on the money. I'm just sat wondering how I pray next to George's coffin. Man, you're good! L x*'

'*Oh wow! I see in spirit butterflies lifting off George's coffin. When a caterpillar transforms it is a complete breakdown and death of the former self before it then flies. I see so much life and beauty being released in the spirit right now. When there is death, there is a dramatic multiplication in life. Thank you God, for George! Thank you that even in death his life is infectious, bringing so much to so many. Brianna x*'

As I put my phone away I suddenly felt the rush I'd so desperately been longing for again. The peace, hope and love I'd felt in the hospital room slammed into my body, it was an overwhelming comfort. It's what I'd been looking for, praying for and wanting more than anything else. It was like a warm energy wrapping around my body and lifting my soul. The ebb and flow of a force field that was like magnetic power spinning out of control. It was pure perfection. It was God.

I'm not sure how long I sat with George and the Holy Spirit in that state. Time is irrelevant in these types of moments. Once I felt ready though, I went back through the connecting door to my mum.

'Are you OK love?' she said reaching her arms out to hug me.

'You're not going to believe what just happened when I was in there,' I said.

'Brianna knows, doesn't she?' Mum simply responded.

I nodded and we then made our way back to the car in silence, our arms linked. It wasn't a bad silence; it was a reflective pensive kind of one. I texted Brianna.

'I love your messages. I don't know why but they still keep surprising me, lifting my heart up in ways I can't explain. I could totally feel the Holy Spirit after you texted. You opened up its way back into my heart. To be honest, I sometimes get confused, if it's George or if it's God, but either way, it's a beautiful and happy presence. It lifts my soul. Thank you. L x'

And then the big day arrived. Thursday 15th December 2016 is a date like so many others that will stay imprinted on my soul for all eternity. No one likes going to funerals. You never hear about a funeral and think 'Oh great!' in the same way you do when a wedding invitation drops through the post. I was astounded by how many people felt the need to tell me they weren't going to come to George's funeral because they didn't like the idea that he'd died, they couldn't cope with the service because it was too sad.

At the time I was livid, but with hindsight I know that it was their own fear of death speaking into their hearts. I was also fully aware that there would be so much grief and sadness about what we'd all lost that it might be overwhelming for some. After all, it was the first moment that George's death was going to become real for all of those who hadn't watched him die.

Amidst this, I also knew that I had a responsibility to carry God and bring the Holy Spirit into the celebration. It was all I could hope for. I knew I had to show the entire congregation what death and grief, with God, could look like. It was the Big Guy's first moment to really shine through me and for me to wear his colours. I was determined not to mess it up. For George or God. If it worked, I knew it could be the first part of creating hope for so many.

I got to the church early that day and had made a plan with our nanny that she would bring the boys later for the 11 am start. It wasn't a hard decision knowing that they should be there with me. It was important for them to understand the act of how we formally said goodbye. I'd even done a dummy run a few days earlier so the boys could run around the church and familiarise themselves with the surroundings. On the day itself though I wanted to get there early as I couldn't face being with everyone else's sadness as we waited for the service to begin, so I'd asked the more experienced minister if I could sit alone in his vestry. I wanted to sit with Brianna and Simon whilst the church filled up behind the closed wooden doors. I wanted them to pray over me because I knew that prayer was the only thing that would lift me and help me feel the hope I so desperately wanted. Here I was, a woman who until a few weeks ago had never even prayed sat with my eyes closed and palms open upwards. Simon and Brianna spoke beauty and love over my soul that morning, it was so unlike my corporate routine before big public speaking events and yet perfectly beautiful. I could still feel the pulsating force around me as I stepped back out into the packed church before George was due to make his entrance.

As I walked to my seat with every chair in the church occupied, I could feel people's eyes watching me. Everyone felt so heartbroken for us, but I also knew they needed to see me. They needed to know how I was doing and see how death had altered me, changed me. They needed to know what grief looked like. Because of this, I had been very deliberate about what I had chosen to wear and how I had shown up. My make-up was faultless, my hair freshly blow-dried and my dress a carefully chosen grey number. I wanted people to see that mourning could look different from what they thought. I sat in my seat next to my parents and Dad gripped my hand as the beautiful music we had chosen for his entrance began to play.

Classical pieces have this calming effect on your soul and the music we had picked, 'Benedictus' from Karl Jenkin's 'The Armed Man, A Mass For Peace,' was majestic and ethereal. As George's friends entered carrying his coffin, there heads bowed down, I looked over to his parents, brother and sister. It was every part as painful as you can imagine. I could see people I know and loved breaking down in front of me. I could see their hurt, horror, disbelief and shock and my heart hurt for theirs. At that moment, hardly anyone knew the beautiful way in which George had left us. They didn't understand that his final days were spent in God's glory. So I kept my head held high, I knew that hope was coming. I knew that God would show up in our readings and messages. I knew that we could all still feel light, in this terrible darkness if we opened our eyes. I clenched Dad's hand tighter and focussed on the stain glass window in front, muttering under my breath, 'Come, Holy Spirit, come.'

As George's coffin was placed in between the beautiful road bikes we had asked to be covered in flowers, I took a deep breath and surveyed the scene around me. To my right were all of George's friends from university; tall, masculine guys crying into their hands. I could audibly hear the sobs around me as the music quietened and the experienced vicar began to speak.

'Of course, you shouldn't be here today,' he said sensitively. 'There's something about being at the funeral of a thirty-four-year-old man that's very, very wrong. It's just not how life should be. And so, there's a great deal of sadness here today, but despite all of this know yourself blessed.'

The minister continued, 'I was talking to George's mother just before the service about how we all often talk about living in the right way, but we very rarely talk about dying in the right way. You're going to hear more about this later and I know that you will be blessed. This is not only a funeral service and a time of thanksgiving for George and for his life, but it will also be a baptismal service for his youngest son Jamie. You will see that the whole thing is called the Cycle of Life. Which as you know, are words that hold a huge amount of meaning for George as a keen cyclist. So, I wonder, can we bring our emotions and our memories together today. Can we gather together for a short moment of quiet and of prayer before we begin.'

The quietness filled the church. The crying was still tangible as the organist stepped over to his instrument and began to play, 'Lord of all Hopefulness.' I fingered the beautiful order of service that I hadn't seen in print until now and was so was happy to stare at the gorgeous illustrations of pizza, Peroni and bicycles. They were gorgeous memories of happy times lived that pulled me through that first hymn.

After the first song it was the readings. Invictus was read by George's best friends and I'd also asked a colleague from George's work to read a Psalm. These words had comforted me so much in the days after his death that I wanted others to feel this comfort too.

After their speeches, it was time for mine. I had known even before George had died that it would be my responsibility to help deliver a message of life in his eulogy. I had to tell them God was real. I had to tell them there was still something left to live for and that we could all still feel light in this terrible darkness if we opened our eyes to see it. As I looked down at my printed notes on the lectern, took a deep breath and began, I pieced together some of the story that had unfolded around us.

I told them in brief what had happened: That we'd asked for God to show up and that he'd arrived in miraculous and remarkable glory. I told them about how George had the most beautiful opportunity to say goodbye and died in peace and hope. It felt good to say everything I'd been feeling out loud for the first time. All of the thoughts that had been swirling around and burning deep inside my heart liberated my soul as the words found their way out of my mouth into the crowd sat in front of me. As I finished my speech to a round of remarkable applause, I sat back down in my chair and breathed as the photo montage we had made played on the big screen in front of me. I had done it, it felt good.

As the music that accompanied the montage ended Simon spoke up for the first time.

'Father God we thank you for George, we thank you for all the ways in which he touched our lives.'

I slowly came back down to earth as I let these words wash over my soul.

'We thank you for the vitality and energy that was seen in George's life. We thank you most of all for love, for his love, for your love which we experience through him.'

My mind was still buzzing as I listened intently to the prayer.

'We thank you that love is stronger than death. We thank you that your perfect love casts out all fear. Give us grace to live our lives in the same spirit as George. Give us grace so that we may too be prepared to face death when it comes with peace. We bring these prayers to you through Jesus. Amen.'

I was still amazed at how beautiful prayer was when it was done right. Simon had a way with words that was just so incredible at condensing everything you were feeling in a really amazing way and as I sat there wondering if I would ever be able to pray like him, he began his sermon.

'I don't know how I'm supposed to follow Louise or speak in full sentences after that moving video montage,' he delicately began.

I looked at him and smiled, willing him on with my eyes.

'I didn't know George very well at all, but I met him at one of the most important times of his life,' he continued. The emotion was palpable.

'Knowing him for that short period was one of the greatest privileges of my life. And in fact one of the first things that I should tell you that George said to me after I met him, when he asked me to speak at his funeral, was that it was going to be and I quote,

"A tough gig."

The audience started to wipe away their tears and erupted into laughter. Simon continued.

'Thanks George, this is actually my very first funeral so what a way to start!'

He looked at me again as more laughter rippled across the room. Bringing joy to other people's hearts was exactly what we had prayed for. I smiled back at him again encouraging him.

'It is however, an extraordinarily tough gig for all of us all today,' he went on, his voice quivering with sadness, 'a momentously sad and tragic occasion. Yet as we are about to see, George didn't see it exactly like that and in fact, he wrote a message to be read out here which sums up his unique perspective on life and on the events of his own death. Before we get to that though, I want to spend a few moments reflecting on George's key qualities. George was incredibly talented, he had so many incredible qualities it was hard to pick out just one or two. He was driven, a dreamer, a risk-taker, he was fun, positive, courageous, kind, devoted, generous. I want to focus on three of these qualities that were evident throughout his life and the first was kindness.'

The crowd sat glued to their seats as Simon went on.

'George was a very kind man, something which was obvious to all of those that knew him. He was someone that looked out for the needs of others, he wasn't self-absorbed or self-obsessed. He was a kind husband to Louise, an amazing father to Charlie and Jamie, an amazing son, brother, friend and colleague. His kindness will be greatly missed by all who knew him. He didn't have a lot of patience for those who weren't authentic and I discovered this in the short time that I knew him. He wanted to know who somebody really was, even if it wasn't a polished presentation or version of reality. George could handle that, in fact he welcomed it.'

'Secondly his courage. Anyone who knew George would have seen that he had a taste for risk taking,' the laughter erupted again all over the room.

'He was immensely courageous and determined and was known by his friends as Superman because he seemed to be able to take on all kinds of risks and get away with it. He was diagnosed with bowel cancer last December, but he didn't let that stop him. Nothing could get in the way of George pursuing his dreams and his goals. He wanted to take part in the Ride 100 across London. His doctor said no. George said yes and that was that.'

Simon was easing into this sermon now, he looked comfortable out front and the crowd felt that too.

'There's a similar story later in the summer when George was due to ride from London to Paris with his work colleagues. The only problem with this of course, was that he'd just had a liver resection, only five weeks before he was due to set off. On the pre-op notes the nurse wrote the following words in capital letters, 'this man thinks he will be riding to Paris, I have told him this will not be happening.' She was wrong.'

It felt so right that Simon was telling these stories about George. He'd spent a lot of time in prayer with us and really made an effort to get to know the man behind the illness in those days when we'd sat around his bed covered in the Holy Spirit and said goodbye. As he continued telling George's exploits, I remarked how bizarre it was that I was the one who had spoken first about God to our friends and family. It felt a little ironic that the ordained minister was the one who was speaking about George. It hadn't necessarily been planned that way but it was how it was meant to be. I'm pretty certain it was what God wanted.

Simon's commanding voice brought me back into the moment, he had found his flow now.

'Thirdly George had hope. He was someone who enjoyed

thinking about the possibilities of life. He was a dreamer, someone who was able to see beyond what was immediately obvious to others and embrace what might be. George's attitude meant that he got a heck of a lot done, Louise spoke with me about this. In the last five years, he'd got married, had a hip replacement, a collar bone plating, two children, renovated a house and lived through a year-long cancer battle. He was planning to buy another house up until a couple of weeks before his death. He simply believed more was possible than most people imagined.'

'But George didn't just exhibit these qualities in his life, they were also evident in his death too.'

This was the part of Simon's speech I'd been waiting for. I watched him take a deep breath before he boomed,

'Kindness. As I spent time by George's bedside I was struck by the immense amount of patience and warmth to those that were with him. Whether they were members of his family or members of the staff at the hospital. One thing I'll never forget was the second time I went to see George. We finished by praying together and he asked to hold hands. I held his right hand whilst his mum held his left and Louise was holding his feet weeping. In much the same way that I'm trying to do now, I was trying to articulate some simple prayers. Nothing had prepared me for this and it was all I could do without breaking down into sobs without words. As I did my best to contain myself George, who was holding my hand tightly just gently stroked it. I thought to myself, I'm here to look after you and here you are expressing this incredible kindness to me and here we all are, being comforted by him. It's something I'll never forget.'

The tears began to roll down my cheeks at this point, Simon hadn't shared this part of the story with me before. He continued.

'George was courageous. He lived a remarkably courageous life and died an even more remarkably courageous death. There was no measure of fear whatsoever around him. How did he find this courage? Was it a natural gift? Yes. Was it learnt from his parents, his family? Yes. But beyond these reasons George had found a great source of strength and courage. This was because in the last week of his life he'd encountered a love he'd never known before. The love of God,'

Simon looked at me as he said these words.

'It was George's experience of God's love that made him able to face his death with such peace, confidence and courage. He trusted in that love which had become apparent to him so recently and he was able to die with great courage because of it.'

The silence was tangible in the church I turned to look and take in the faces of those around me, they were all listening intently.

'And finally hope. It is a great tragedy that George died so young, but he packed a tremendous amount into his thirty-four years. Even in his death, he wasn't at all negative but full of hope. When I met him for the first time, he said he had no regrets, he said 'I've done everything I wanted, it's been frickin amazing.' Only he didn't say frickin.' The congregation burst into laughter once more.

'Where was this hope from? It wasn't hope based on wishful

thinking. The words of Psalm 23, the Psalm I read to him at our first meeting contain the answer, "even though I walk through the darkest valley, I fear no evil, for you are with me. Your rod and your staff comfort me. You prepare a table before me in the presence of my enemies. My cup overflows for you are with me."

'George had experienced the truth that God would be with him through everything. Even as he passed through the shadow of the valley of death. He'd seen God prepare a table before him and that table was a place where he found deep joy in the midst of the most unexpected environment. The table was God's own presence, the kind of thing that only God could have done. Kind, courageous hope-filled lives. We can all live like this, we should all honour this. Perhaps it's therefore appropriate that this final word be given to George.'

Simon looked at me once more as he took out the neatly folded piece of paper from his pocket. It was a message that George had insisted on writing in the days leading up to his death.

During this time he was so weak but so full of joy that he'd asked me to bring a pen and paper to his bedside. As his sister and I sat by his side he told us that he wanted to write some words that would be read out to the world. He was very specific that his thoughts could onl be read aloud after he had died. In his last few days on earth George had personally asked Simon to read the words at the cycle of life. It was exactly how he'd wanted the first part of our service to end, no one outside of close family knew about the message, Simon delivered it word perfectly.

THE WONDERFULNESS OF LIFE

Death at a young age brings terrible grief and terrible loss. This can't be ignored or not felt.

However, the greatest gift we have in life is choice. I am clear that I want everyone to choose love, laughter, peace and happiness for the future. Park the grief and inject your sparkle to rain upon my family.

I want you to share your magic, share your gifts and share your perspective with them as they move into a new chapter. I feel so incredibly lucky to have such a diverse group of family, friends and colleagues with such brilliantly different strengths. Now is the time to use them.

So today do let out the grief and cry happy tears for the incredible memories we have made together - no one can ever take those away. But then, make the choice. Make the choice that from this day forward you will bring your brilliance and love to all around you. When there's a choice always laugh rather than cry, always dream rather than accept, always look for the positive in every single situation and always, always look forward.

When I'm on my bike and it's feeling tough my mantra is always don't stop spinning. This is what I ask of all of you today. Don't stop spinning forward. I know that the future is full of beautiful things.

GEORGE BLYTH

273

Grief & Gratitude

'The Cycle of Life,' was such a beautiful day. After the words George had written had soaked into everyone's souls we began Jamie's baptism. Walking towards the front of the church with Jamie on my hip and Charlie holding my hand as our friends and family watched our every move was a surreal experience. The boys were wearing matching gingham shirts which I had picked out especially for the occasion. They were George's favourite colour, blue.

Their innocence and love for life felt beautifully at odds with the tears we had shed whilst saying goodbye a few moments earlier. As I walked up to the front I couldn't think of a more visible and fitting tribute that would show how we would spin forwards as a family. By declaring that I wanted to raise Jamie to know and understand Jesus was the best and most fitting way I could find to show my gratitude for life, love and God.

The baptism was short and uplifting. Charlie stood on the stage comfortably holding on to his Daddy's coffin; he bought an easy wonder and understanding to death which somehow made it feel more acceptable and OK. As the service closed I was asked to parade Jamie around the church so he could be blessed by the crowd. George's coffin was then carried back out to the beautiful tones of a flash mob choir singing, 'All you need is love.' It felt like the party George had wanted as the undertaker came over and whispered in my ear,

'I've never quite been to a send-off like this before.'

As we moved back the chairs and tucked into the delicious food, I was overwhelmed by the outpouring of love that came from so many. People hugging me and thanking us for the hope and light we had given. Some told me it was the best funeral they had been to. Others told me our words had made them really sit up and think about God. It felt like we had done George proud and for that, I was exceptionally grateful. We had shown others how to grieve with gratitude and with God. That was all I had ever wanted.

In the days, weeks and months which followed I tried my upmost to stand firm with this belief. I called it being sad but choosing happy. I soon came to realise that grief wasn't at all linear and it also wasn't always wearing black. So much of what I had always perceived grief to be was not at all the reality. Sometimes grief was freedom and brought new perspectives. On other days it was all-consuming, taking my soul to places of despair and dark hurt and even though I had God on my side it was and still is so very hard.

Grief is a curious concoction of emotion. It is sitting by the light of the stars and crying alone with hurt. It is finding myself completely overcome in the strangest, most inappropriate of moments. It is feeling out of control when the vast oceans of anger, pain and jealousy swirl around like torrents inside of me.

I realise now that when I allow the pain it actually makes life sweeter. Grief is feeling sad but then feeling immensely thankful for all of the minutiae of everyday life. It is loving everyone else who is left, in a fuller, more three-dimensional kind of way. It is remembering to look up, even when it feels like my entire body is being pushed down. I figured out that grief was and still is just another expression of love. It is the beauty of everything I'd ever felt about George in reverse and was and is as unique and individual as our relationship.

As we were slowly forced back into reality, it was hard to understand where the boys and I belonged. Every single part of our life was not what I had ever anticipated. Our loss was everywhere - in everything we touched, in everything we looked at. No part of our world was left unaltered by the devastating bomb that had detonated. And there was no longer an us, just me.

It was solitude. It was an overwhelming sense of responsibility. It was lack of sleep and loss of appetite. It was crying and wishing it was a dream. It was waking in the morning and feeling free for a few seconds before remembering the pain. The searing hurt which would slam into my heart like a high-speed train and leave my chest feeling suffocated. It was unbearable unspoken sorrow that not many people knew how to invite into their hearts.

In the aftermath, because of my new-found hope and faith in God, I was fast-tracked into living with a curious mix of emotion. For a long time though, the sadness outweighed everything. I'd get in my car and drive. I would never know where I was headed and often pull over in lay-bys, churches or sit by open water and simply cry. Remembering the night that I had gone out and called for help and hoping that no one but God would see me as I sobbed out the unspeakable pain and hurt that was within my soul.

I was by myself for much of this intense grief but never on my own, despite the loneliness I always felt. I knew God was with me, I could feel him and there would always be some declaration of his presence. Sometimes it would be a message from Brianna. Other times it would be a text from someone else I loved. On certain days he showed up as words of encouragement from total strangers, or sometimes the way the birds swooped around me whilst I was walking in the fresh air. Into this deep despair, God kept showing up to be counted in the most gentle and beautiful ways. Over time I had to learn to see it was him. Learn to read him and know his ways and while it wasn't easy as he wasn't always as immediately apparent as I'd been shown when George died, I had a head start. I knew what he felt like and I knew that he was often unseen. I knew that he could speak to me through words, coincidences and dreams I observed, as well as through conversations and signs from different places.

After spending so long in the confines of the hospital and watching how death had crept into George's body, I found the gift of the sun shining on my face each day so much sweeter and the beauty of the natural world would always raise a smile. Even on the darkest, blackest of days, God's hope had taken up residence in my heart. I couldn't help but feel gratitude despite the fact I was burdened with deep grief. This hope didn't always burn fiercely and on some days it would be the tiniest of flickers. But it was always there. It never went out and it never left me. It was always tucked up inside me, even if it was hidden behind despair.

At times I'd wonder if God had been there the whole time and as I got to know him more I came to realise that he had. I'd just named him as hope before, never realising that this feeling was actually coming from him. It just seemed so very intangible to get my head around such a concept, that some of what I was thinking and emotionally responding to had always been fuelled by a force far bigger and stronger than me. A force that lived in my heart that was a feeling and a connection just like the love I will always have for George.

I also accepted that God couldn't take away the physical loss I felt. Only George re-appearing was ever going to do that and I knew that wasn't going to happen until I went to Heaven. But yet I still believed in God's hope, love and in his power. Everything we had experienced in that hospital and afterwards was so real that however much heartache I felt, it was never enough to extinguish the hope the whole experience had given me. The understanding of how life and death really worked. The knowing that there was more to life than what meets the eye and so much more wonderfulness left to discover in ourselves.

So I kept on putting one foot in front of another. One

moment, one minute, one hour and one day at a time. I kept being encouraged by new friends from Simon's church that God could be like another Father to me. At first, it was an incredibly hard notion to understand to reconcile how you could be in a relationship with something that was almost like an imaginary friend. But then, I watched how Dad responded to my grief. I could see and understand what he could and couldn't do and as I observed this, God's love began to make more and more sense. I could never have expected my dad to take away the hurt I felt over George's death. That was an impossible task and I couldn't expect a magic wand to be waved and for it to be stopped. Feeling the fall out of my emotions was quite simply part of the gift of being alive.

But I began to learn that God, just like my Dad, could walk with me. He could be there, arguably in an entirely different way to a human being, but equally, he could sit with me in the dark. Neither of them could ever take away the hideous pain of what had happened. All they could do was be there and show me how to live, with kindness and grace, in spite of George's death. They could keep reminding me how love felt and show me how to live with the black mark that I was rapidly accepting would forever be engraved on my heart.

Living with God and living with grief were relationships I had to work at to understand. I had lost so much love yet was still surrounded by so much compassion. In the early days, I'd often find myself musing, how God was so very much like grief, in polar opposite ways. It wasn't in the way he felt or behaved, but in the way the rest of the secular world approached him. I'd see this in my friends and family who approached the divine just like grief. They carried so much fear, anger, reserve and wonder in their hearts. I never perceived this as a bad thing, because I understood the outlook, it was oh so familiar to me and was exactly how I had perceived life before cancer, death and ultimately God took hold. I had never recognised or appreciated the full wonder of the life we all live before then. I had thought it was all mine for the making and thought I could create my own luck and happiness in people, achievements and things. Not in him. Not in myself.

I know now that both God and grief are relationships that you have to fully live with. Fully be present with. There's something quite beautiful about the ambiguity found within both, that is of course when you get to the point of being able to accept them for what they are. On the days when I found it hard, I always made sure I mustered the strength of spirit and resolve to lift my hands high in praise. I wanted to always acknowledge that there was more to life than maybe any of us in our earthly clothes would ever realise. I also always felt such peace in those moments, such joy and gratitude. I was always left wanting more even if I still felt knotted with sadness.

It was odd, grieving the loss of the love of my life, but feeling the greatest love anyone can *ever* know. But just because I couldn't see a physical person with my eyes, didn't mean he wasn't real. The force the Holy Spirit continued to bring, bound me, replenished me and energised my thirsting soul; even on the most disgusting of days. Other people noticed it. They would remark on how strong I was. Maybe how inspiring. I would always laugh. I knew it was never me. I knew it was God. But I also knew that most people weren't ready to hear that. They didn't understand. Yet I knew, it couldn't have been anything else, how else could I feel so bad, yet so good at the same time? I could see a tangible impact on my life. It was evident in my relationships, in my parenting, in the way I continued to live. It was all around me.

Living was still tough though. God was amazing, but I was still on my own. At every avenue, there was always something to remind me of the loss. That wasn't just because I now had to fill the box marked as 'widow' on every official form I completed. It was in how I slept, how I dressed, how I ate food, how I managed my life, how I looked after my children. In the early days, I desperately used to seek spaces where I could forget what had happened. I quickly realised though, that when you lose someone who is as much a part of you as the air that you breathe, they will be everywhere you go forevermore. Be it the knowing glances and touches you observe in other people's relationships, the happy families shopping in supermarkets, or the shows you choose to watch on TV.

Increasingly I recognised that the only way of coping with the loss was to turn to God. This was because I recognized what it felt like when you caught a glance of his kingdom. Whenever I had a taste of his power and could see the remarkable way his glory filled my mind, body and soul, it was life-giving. I became increasingly conscious that I felt like I had a foot on either side of a bridge that spanned humanity. I understood all too well what it was like to not believe, but I equally understood the fierce fire of hope, peace and contentment that now burned in my heart. All of this, in spite of the trauma I had lived through. At times, my sadness about this was just so very acute. I realised that I wasn't just grieving for George but that on some level I was also grieving for everyone who wasn't in a relationship with God. I felt sad that they didn't know him in the way I did. Why was that? Why had I found him and they hadn't? I prayed to try and make sense and continued to write.

Dear God,

I'm figuring out how deeply personal your presence is. It's such a very intimate thing. Your force. Your power. Your greatness. I know you can inspire people. You can drive people, you can even propel people, but the irony is, so many people don't see it as you! They don't feel your force in their hearts. They miss the point. They miss how you really talk to them. People only talk about you when it's convenient, when they can blame you for bad stuff that's happened; when acts of unkindness potentially disprove your existence. But they're forgetting that we're all creatures of free will?! That was the gift you originally gave us! Surely this utter disregard for who you are and how you work, makes you sad? It has to? This total neglect of understanding for what you've given us is odd. It makes me so sad. I can't believe so many people don't get it. That they don't grasp you?! Why!?

I know when you're around. The feeling is indescribable and unmistakable. You were there the whole time, but the feeling wasn't burning quite as strongly as it is now! I wish I could help other people, feel your force in the way I can. I wish they would allow you to carry them too when they're hurting and broken. I'm starting to accept that George isn't coming home. His spiritual presence, that I felt so much of in the beginning seems to be lessening now. You're showing him too much of a good time, I think! What does everyone do all day in Heaven anyway? Are there even days there, or is time just irrelevant? Do spirits have jobs? Is it quite full? I'm trying to figure out how everyone fits in and it still feels beautiful without being overcrowded? But then I think that's maybe the point. I can never figure it out. I can never truly understand until I go. It's supernatural. That's why I can't get my head around it. I'm maybe not supposed to understand it fully just yet. Maybe that's it.

Don't you wish more of us realised though? Don't you wish more people had the faith that George had? That I now have too? Don't you wish more people knew you? This faith is carrying me, in a way that is so different from others who live out their grief without you in their hearts? Why did I get to meet you and know you? Did you pick me, or did I pick you? Why do people that have known you their whole lives, sometimes lose you when they need you the most? I know, I can never know how anyone else deals with loss, I also know that grief is unique. But I do know the anger, the hurt and the pain that I feel and so many others feel too. I see it and feel it from them. I know, that you see this sense of loss. That's because you're with me when I'm crying. You're helping me. You're walking with me. You always send signs and encouragement, to help me know I'm surrounded by your grace. It's beautiful. But why me? Is it just because I asked? Is it just because I looked and then opened my heart to see?

Your presence is pure perfection. A thing of beauty, love and healing hope. I think I'm becoming a little addicted. I crave it, as it always makes me feel better. To be honest, it's the ONLY thing, other than cuddles with my boys *that does. It's protective. It's caring. It's awesome! I feel weird to say it, but at times the pleasure is as good as making love, I know how bonkers this sounds! I also don't know how else to describe it so hope you're OK with this.*

So today, I'm praying for hope. Hope that more people will find you. Hope that you lift those in their darkest of hours. Hope that we continue to get to know each other a little better. Hope that George is living his best life in your Kingdom. Hope, that my children and I, continue to make sense and find peace in what's happened. Hope that the best is yet to come.

Thanks for the last few months my friend. They've been a roller-coaster. You have kept me standing. You have kept me sane. I'll drink a large glass of champagne in yours, your son's and the Holy spirit's honour tonight — what's your tipple? Or are you so good you never drink!? Surely you have some fun sometimes? I'm now wondering what a party in Heaven would be like and how much George would love it! I'm sure he's dancing on the tables and getting told off! You Rock, so just keep rocking my world OK?! Louise x'

Inside, my heart was being crushed but somehow God helped me juxtapose the joy of life and still allowed me to feel the beauty of living. I had to be Mummy, but also reinvent myself as a solo parent. I was lucky because I had help. I had the support of my parents. I had our nanny. I had my friends, my family of colleagues from the chocolate factory and I also had Patricia my psychologist who I carried on talking to. All this richness of support carried me when I needed it most.

I also had Simon's church and its growing community. A new group of friends that were all getting to know each other. It was odd having to walk into a social group as just me, a new widow who was a person they'd never known with George. In some ways it was nice not to be known as a couple, but it was also so very difficult having to explain. Having to tell the story of how I knew Simon, how I'd found the church. It all just seemed like I was slightly unhinged when I declared that God did it and this was to a group of Christians. I desperately wondered how they all knew him and if he had moved into their lives with the same power and velocity that he'd slammed into mine. I wondered if he felt the same way to them as he did to me. I wondered if they spoke to him at bedtime every night and wrote letters like I did.

I struggled to come to terms with the dramatic shifts that had gone on. I wore Nike air max trainers yet was a widow. I had disco dances with my father-less children before bed and then went to bed alone and read the Psalms. I felt the love around me rather than made love to my husband. I went to church every Sunday but still loved drinking wine on a Saturday. I had to find a way to mix my old life with my new life, to re-build. As time went on my written prayers became more and more erratic, but that wasn't because I stopped praying or believing. It's because I learnt to talk to God on my own terms, in my own way.

The insane amount of texts from Brianna stopped too; neither of us could continue to live our life on a day to day basis in the way it was in the hospital. Even to this day, every now and again, I get messages which make me sit up. She still knows stuff about what I'm doing even when she's not with me, it's mad, as well as utterly supernatural! Her messages always make me laugh as well as feel encouraged.

Brianna has become a great friend. She was by my side at George's funeral. She visits us from London regularly and always showers the children and me in her love and wisdom. I've learnt more about God and Jesus by talking to this woman than anyone else and will be forever thankful for all that she's done for us as a family. Quite simply she helped us receive the best gift ever, hope that there's more to life and for that, I will be eternally thankful. We still text most weeks as well as speak on the phone regularly; our conversations aren't always about God these days although he does always come up! They're also about clothes, hair, makeup and the latest TV shows. But we've also become such close friends that we share some of the deepest parts of our soul. God didn't just gift me someone who could hear him in those last weeks of George's life, he also gifted me a great friend to walk alongside me in this new season.

Simon, his wife and his family are great friends too. We see them every Sunday when we go to our church, the church that I've watched grow from a few people in Simon's house to a packed-out hall each Sunday. I sometimes forget that Simon spent so much time with George as he was dying. This is because my life with the church was never part of George's identity. The church and my faith have moved on so much since he passed, I often muse that they're at times in-sync.

Kate, her sister and her mum are still hugely important to my family. Every time I see them it makes me smile to think that they were part of how I ended up with so much hope. My mum feels the hope and comes to church every weekend too, what happened to us was as real for her as it was for me.

There are still days though, even surrounded by this loving community, that I fall into bed after a long day looking after my kids, working, grieving and wondering about my future and I am exhausted. I don't always have the appetite to pick up my phone and ferociously articulate in prayer everything to God in the way I did at the beginning. I don't want to read the Psalms every day either, there's too much other good stuff in the Bible to look at. I'm OK with that though and am learning that it's almost the same as when you first fall in love with a guy.

In the beginning, you're all over one another. Texting as soon as you've said your goodbyes, wishing each other goodnight every day. But for anyone who has been blessed to have a relationship longer than a few months, you'll know that this type of passionate connection doesn't remain forever. That it moves into more of a quiet knowing, an unassuming force field of support and understanding.

I've never felt annoyed by the fact that my hotline to God has become a little less intense. That's because I know we are still talking every day. Sometimes it's in my car, sometimes in the shower. Sometimes it's out loud, sometimes it's in my head. Other times, I just lay back and look at the sky and ask to be with him. I have started to learn when he's more obvious and also when I need to ask him to show himself. I continue to summon his help, although it's never on quite the same scale as it was that rainy night when I stormed out of the house.

Faith, hope and love are a lifetime's work and a lifetime's

adventure of discovery. I'm still on my own little voyage and most certainly don't have it all mapped out. There are days when I know the Kingdom of Heaven is real and yet there are other days when I search for signs and more proof. On the days when I question, I always get something. Sometimes it's big, sometimes it's small and it's almost always never what I would expect or choose. It's much like my life now, but I shouldn't wish to alter it. That's not the plan, that's not how God wants me to roll.

As the time between George's death and my future life without him expands, the wonderfulness of life is very much touching my soul again. I've learnt how to slowly let light beam into my heart, whilst honouring the heartbreak and loss I've lived through. I've also discovered that when it comes to the passing of time, that is not a healer. But God is. He heals, he helps, he stands in the gap of hurt.

Life I've come to realise is as great as it is gruesome; this is all part of the gift that is being human. I think I've weathered the centre of the grief storm now, but the sadness is still there and at times the storms still brew I know they always will. Even now, the rain clouds can gather and hang over me. My grief still has the power to sweep me off my feet and suck me up into oblivion, spinning me around, battering and beating my body with anxiety and leaving me sobbing on the ground desperately asking God for his help. But I've also experienced first-hand that it's always in these moments, of falling on the floor, that you learn the most about yourself and that you really begin to understand what you're made of and the magic God put inside your heart. Like all of the best survivors and warriors, I've learnt to predict now. I've learnt to know myself better and have figured out signs and potential causes of what might trigger a fresh storm of grief to brew. Best of all though I now understand what I must do to take cover and I also understand that storms can't be stopped, but they can be survived. I also know grief hits my heart ten times harder if I try and pretend it's not there. So I allow myself to feel and I ask God to sit with me whilst I cry.

Loss is powerful. It is to be respected, it is to be allowed and it is to be handled with great care and great love. Sadness has important lessons to teach us and when the sunshine reappears after great pain life is SO much brighter, so much more loving. It's also how I've come to know God better. I let him soak through me in these dark-blue moments and I feel him more afterwards. Love and light are so much sweeter once you've truly felt the dark and let it breathe into all the parts of your soul.

Living life in faith, brings a fresh perspective. I've never been one for rules or one that likes to be told what to do. What I'm realising though is that my friends who are also believers are some of the least judgmental people I have ever met. They're not at all what I thought.

Slowly, I'm also figuring out my own thoughts and responses to the commandments and ways of life that the Bible lays out. Overwhelmingly though, despite the loss, I feel more gratitude, just like I did on the day of George's celebration of life. God has taught me to look each day in the face and know that I can and I will, whilst honouring my past and recognising the depth of what it gives my soul, but fiercely keeping my eyes locked on spinning forwards towards the future with my boys.

The Wonderfulness
of Life

At times when the sun glistens on the river, or the leaves dance on the trees, I wonder what it's like in Heaven? If I'm honest there are days when I wish I could visit so I could be with George and be with God. That would be bliss. The more I read about the divine the more beautifully abstract and brilliant the heavenly kingdom sounds. But I know that's not the plan for me just yet. I know there's more purpose over my life – my boys need to be raised, cocktails need to be drunk, life needs to be lived and there is so much more learning to do.

George lived a beautiful life and died a remarkably courageous death. There was no measure of fear whatsoever about him in the end. Just peace, just glory, just love. We both found such courage, hope and strength from the fact that we encountered a love neither of us had ever recognised before. It was our experience of

God's love that made us able to face death and grief with such peace and confidence. We both trusted and I continue to trust this love implicitly every day.

The power of faith, hope and love, is what makes our tragic story so bearable. These emotions, these connections and flows of energy are so powerful they transcend us all and this is what allows me to live. I have experienced profound peace and deep joy in the most unexpected of environments and the most difficult of moments. Everything that happened was miraculous. All of it and yet, did it only happen because I asked?

I would never wish my circumstances upon anyone, but I do, longingly wish for you to experience this hope and love for yourself. The truth that God can and will be with you through everything if you open your heart to allow him in. Even now, at times it still doesn't feel real. I still can't believe that everything I've just shared happened. That George died. God found us. That he texted me on a phone, through a stranger and healed my husband from all of the pain he felt.

When I reflect on our story I always find myself smiling because George was a truly magnificent man. He fitted. He helped me make sense of my thoughts. He supported me when I doubted myself. He was my cheerleader, my rock, my constant. He was undoubtedly my God. I worshipped him. But then maybe that was the point, maybe his love was wrapped up in God all along.

I'm still getting my head around all of the stories in the Bible. It's a beautiful, but at times difficult book to read and identify with today. There's so much teaching that needs to go alongside it to allow your heart to truly understand the truth and instruction at it's centre. But there's been one story ever since the beginning of all of this, that keeps coming up. I'm taking this as a sign that you need to hear it. Your soul may be open to what I have to say, it also may not. Only you can decide what you want to believe and I respect that more than most. But what I will say, is that all of us have a spiritual connection, far deeper and wider than maybe you have ever even realized. Ultimately we are all connected by love and by light in a way that beautifully defies life and death. I have seen this and I have felt this and if you're ready and willing to see it there is a force out there that you can feel in your heart too.

In the second part of the Bible Jesus speaks about his impending death. People have come to see him and he starts talking about dying; it's not at all what any of the people who are gathered expected him to say. Jesus makes his point using an agricultural analogy. He talks about crops and seeds. In the winter, he tells us that as plants die, their seeds fall to the floor and become buried under the earth. He tells us that it's this death and this burial of seeds, that allows for new life to begin; new life to emerge from the underground, in the next season. Although the plants remain invisible for a while, as something else is growing and forming and only death itself is visible, he talks about how new life will emerge in a few months' time .

Jesus is talking about his own death here. He died, so that other people might experience a new life of connection with God. He wanted to show us that death wasn't the end. He says that he is going to die and that he will be invisible for a while. But his death will allow many others to experience new life both this side of death and beyond. This analogy helps me understand so much about George's death. His end was, of course, tragic, but it also birthed so much that was new, for him and me. So much love, purpose and hope.

George himself had real hope that his death was not the end of his journey. He knew it was not the case. I could see that he felt this through an inexplicable peace that oozed out from every part of his being. On the day before his death, when we were alone, he raised his head off the pillow as if looking toward something.

'The angels are here,' he said, leaning back and smiling.

'I'm going tomorrow.'

And I believed him. I wasn't scared and I wasn't concerned by his observation. It gave us both such peace and sure enough, he knew almost to the exact time when he would float into his next season.

George taught me that life is to be lived.

'Live hard, laugh hard, dream big,' I can still hear him say.

None of us can ever know, what truly lies around the corner, that's in God's hands, as much as it's in our own. All we all have is the moment, our daily bread. Therefore, I urge you to live like George! To seize the day and not spend your time doing things you passionately dislike. Dream and find the fun but above all be gracious and thankful. Always recognize what you have and always give thanks, before you ask for anymore. The flip side of this mantra is also exactly what it says on the tin. Life is to be lived, therefore know when it's your time to call it quits. Know when it's your time to fly high, know when your fixed-term contract with your body is up and accept the next part of your exciting adventure with God beyond death. I've seen first-hand that death can be beautiful. It's not to be feared. I want to die like George: peaceful, content, happy and so full of love, glory and the Holy Spirit.

I recognize that all of what I am sharing is so very hard to get your head around. But in some of his last days, before he died, George spoke about how while he had always been so logical, always so ready to see the science and black and whiteness in situations, now knowing that he was dying meant that his logic could no longer serve him in ways it had done previously. He was therefore forced to switch on his spiritual brain and talked with me openly about how he had opened his eyes to see what was wrapped around him in a way he had never done before.

So next time you talk about fate, you observe a coincidence, or you feel an overwhelming sense of purpose or calling towards something, all I ask is that you think about where it might be coming from. Whatever the name is that you want to call it be open to that fact that God does drive us forward and that he is beyond our earthly comprehension.

Everlasting love and the infinite possibilities this offers is liberating and life-giving. Love is a powerful connection that can transcend death if you allow yourself to see past the heartbreak and gaze into the beauty.

George led a relatively short life here on earth but it was

beautiful and amazing. I will always love George. He will always love me, our children, his family and his friends. Our love for each other is exactly like that of God's love for you. That is something death can't take away from any of us.

I now know that the only forever we all have, the only certainty over each and every one of our situations, is love. Whoever lives in love lives in God. So that's what I do. I wrap myself up in it. I douse my boys and myself in the love we have from old and new places. Natural and supernatural realms. Familiar and unfamiliar friendships. I hold my head high and graciously accept that our circumstances have been commissioned for a reason far bigger than any of us can ever know.

Most of all though I continue to live. I continue to love. I continue to embrace the beautiful wonderfulness of this life and live in relationship with God. I see the beautiful everyday miracles of laughter, friendship, nature, literature and good food. That's what George and God want for us more than anything else and so together my boys and I choose life. We choose happiness. But above all we choose hope.

Epilogue

I'm found. I hurt, but I'm liberated.

I'm strong but I'm weak.

I never knew I could live in this place.

Where these emotions would meet one another so tenderly.

For everything to feel so wrong, but so kind of right.

Hope can be found in despair.

Love can be found in heartache.

You are found when you look.

You just have to open your eyes.

Look up before you look down.

And search.

Then trust the light to beam into your soul.

Even when it's hard and feels like there's nothing left.

Don't waste time on the what ifs or the what could have been.

Know that the rich tapestry of what is within you,

is very much there for a reason.

All of your story.

All of you.

We all have a role to play in the wonderfulness of life.

Are you even aware of how you've been positioned?

Know that every part of your story has been planted.

Even the bad bits, the parts that you inhabit in solitude.

Know also that the callings you feel,

the fire in the belly.

They're not just a hunch.

It's how he lives in you.

It's part of his wonderfulness.

And it's because he loves you.

Be known because of this love.

Enjoy every precious day.

Create selfless acts towards those you love.

And always, always be thankful.

But know also, that spiritual breakthrough isn't easy.

It's hard, just like life.

You have to be patient,
and respect there is no ceiling.

You have to want it.
REALLY want it.
So the only question left is,
do you want in?
He wants you.

Just be.
Just ask.
Just love.
Just hope.
Just look inside.
Your heart knows the way.

I then promise, that whatever you have to endure,
The best is most certainly yet to come.

$What\ next?$

If you have enjoyed reading this book
as much as I've enjoyed creating it,
I would love for you to write a review.

Please do this via your online retailer.
Alternatively connect with me through my website
(www.wonderfulnessoflife.com) and let me know your thoughts.

You can also find me on social media;

 @wonderfulness_of_life

Further information

If you are concerned that you may be presenting with the symptoms of bowel cancer please make an urgent appointment with your GP. More information can be found at www.bowelcanceruk.org.uk.

The symptoms to be aware of are;

I. Bleeding from your bottom and / or blood in your poo.

II. A persistent and unexplained change in bowel habit.

III. Unexplained weight loss.

IV. Extreme tiredness for no obvious reason.

V. A pain or lump in your tummy.

If you are interested in exploring some of life's big questions and you would like to find a welcoming space where you can talk about God, if he's real and other thoughts this book might have raised please visit www.alpha.org to find a welcoming local meeting that I am personally nviting you to..

Acknowledgements

To Mum and Dad, you taught me about love and for that I owe you everything. Your unfailing support is life giving, I love you both always.

To Charlie and Jamie, your love gives me wings and purpose. I pray that it's your hands that will continue to hold this book and share this story with future generations when I'm kingdom living too.

To Kerry, thank you for having the faith to step out and save us.
You allowed us to receive the greatest gift imaginable and for that I'm eternally grateful. You rock my friend.

To Jonny & Amy, thank you for having the faith to step in and help us and for creating and building a church that loves, values, supports and teaches us. I'm so grateful for our church home and family.

To all of those who walked shoulder to shoulder through the valley of the shadow of death with me. Especially Bep, Tanya, Alexis, Simon, Bex, Sam, Jane, Laura, Karen & Katherine - you all did more than you'll ever know and offered support when my world was unrecognisable. You've imprinted love and understanding on my heart that will remain always.

To my very own superhero Katy. You've kept us spinning when we didn't know how. You're our family forever and we love you.

To all of those who have helped and encouraged with the writing of this memoir: Dave, Andy, Jess, Dom, Abi, Matt, Laura, Gillian, Rachel, Jane, Emma and Martyn especially. Your support, championing, questioning, critique and feedback have been faultless. This book has been shaped by you and the hours you have poured into it.

To Georgie, thank you for sweeping me off my feet and blessing me with your love and beautiful soul. I'll say your name forever.

To Coco, thank you for breathing life into my heart and getting this book to the finish line. I know the best is yet to come.

To Jesus, thank you for always having the last word. Thank you for letting your love triumph. I'm a witness that miracles can and do happen and for that I'm eternally grateful. You're the bomb. I'll love you always.

Printed in Great Britain
by Amazon

Ghosts

of

Lincoln

BY

JENNY BRIGHT, PSYCHIC MEDIUM
WITH
DR. DAVID CROSS

Printed & Published by Casdec Ltd
22 Harraton Terrace
Birtley
Chester-le-Street
Co Durham
DH3 2QG

Tel: (0191) 410 5556
Fax: (0191) 410 0229

Written by Jenny Bright & Dr David Cross

First Published October 1995

© Casdec October 1995

ISBN 0 907595 95 2

CONTENTS.

INTRODUCTION.

Ghosts exist.

That is the inevitable conclusion reached by anyone who undertakes a serious study of the field. They have been reported in every civilisation since the dawn of time. Professor H.H.Price, a former President of the prestigious Society for Psychical Research, once said: *"The tea-party question, 'Do you believe in ghosts?', is one of the most ambiguous which can be asked. But if we take it to mean 'Do you believe that people sometimes experience apparitions?', the answer is that they certainly do. No one who examines the evidence can come to any other conclusion. Instead of disputing the facts, we must try to explain them"*.

In 1994, the authors appeared on a TV programme with Peter Underwood, Chairman of The Ghost Club Society and author of some forty books on the subject. In reply to the question, "But aren't ghosts just all in the imagination?", he replied: *"... there is no shadow of doubt, if you look into the evidence, that many people, with healthy minds in healthy bodies, do see ghosts. It's absolutely overwhelming"*.

"What are ghosts" is the question, rather than "do they exist". You may find some answers in these pages. We have collected here some fascinating stories concerning the supernatural inhabitants of Lincoln, to provide both resident and tourist with evidence of the paranormal phenomena they might possibly encounter in this ancient City. "What are ghosts" is a deep and sensitive question and will be the subject of a later and more detailed book by the same authors.

We have not made anything up for this book and have ignored any tales which we considered to be purely fanciful. Many of the stories are most certainly true, the authors having spoken to first-hand witnesses. You must make of them what you will. But you may never walk through Lincoln in quite the same way again.

Jenny Bright and Dr. David Cross.
June, 1995.

ABOUT THE AUTHORS.

Jenny Bright is a professional Psychic Medium and has been highly psychic since childhood. She conducts private readings on a full-time basis, as she has done for many years. Her reputation alone ensures that she is always booked many weeks in advance. She has two grown-up sons.

Dr. David Cross has a Ph.D in Chemical Oceanography (applied analytical chemistry) and a life-long interest in the paranormal. Following a highly successful Industrial career, he now devotes his time to Hypnotherapy, psychical research and writing.

Jenny and David are married and together run their organisation 'Ghost Tours of Nottingham'. This includes both the Lincoln and Nottingham Ghost Walks, 'Ghost Evenings' in locations such as Nottingham Castle, Ghost Weekends and Workshops for developing people's own natural psychic abilities. (Details can be obtained by phoning the 24 hour Information Line on 01773 - 769300.)

If you have any ghost stories or paranormal photographs of your own, the authors would like to hear from you. Please write to them via the Publisher.

ACKNOWLEDGEMENTS.

We would like to thank all those who were kind enough to tell us their experiences and give us their encouragement to write this book.

In particular we would like to thank the following for their assistance: The Green family (Norman, Margaret, Jonathon, Lottie and Sara); Sarah Christopher; Derek Chantrey of Smith Clayton Forge; Becky and all the staff at Watsons Face Place; the previous staff of the Black Horse Chambers; the Manager and Staff of The White Hart Hotel; Sandy and Mark of Browns Pie Shop; Brian, Pauline and staff of The Lion and Snake; Anna at the Cornhill Vaults; Art Walker at the Theatre Royal; Andy, Jayne and staff at the Green Dragon; Rosemary Robb, author of "Ghosts and Legends of Newark" and "Ghost Hunting"; Terry Lambley, author of "Nottingham: A Place of Execution"; Butterly Aggregates at Greetwell Quarry; David Lanes and staff at Lincoln Castle; David and Kate Thompson at the Sun Inn; Roy Bradley, The City Of Lincoln and all staff at The Tourist Information Centre, Castle Hill; Herbert Sharman; Fred Turner; Joe Cooke; Eddie Burks; and the many people who have attended our Lincoln Ghost Walk and told us their stories.

We have also been helped by many others, whose stories are not included in this book, but will hopefully be compiled into a second Volume.

In particular, we would like to thank our 'friends on the other side' for their constant love and support.

AUTHORS NOTE.

For privacy, the names of living people given in our stories have been changed. The exception is that of Andy McLaren, Manager of The Green Dragon Inn. Some locations are not specified for the same reason.

THE PHANTOM RIDER OF CASTLE HILL.

Dawn was breaking as the young man puffed and sweated his way up Steep Hill in early 1992. Never was a road more aptly named; to the locals it was known as "heart-attack alley". He was in his early twenties and enjoyed the fitness of youth, so there was little chance, he thought, of this nickname applying to him. That morning he was very nearly wrong, but not for the reason he might have guessed.

He reached the top of the road and began to make his way across the wide, cobbled area that is Castle Hill, heading for Bailgate opposite. The pale sky silhouetted the Cathedral to his right, with only the very top of the Observatory Tower of Lincoln Castle to his left catching the first rays of sun. He had come off-shift at his work in the 'downhill' area of the town and had enjoyed the peaceful silence of the streets on his walk 'uphill' to home.

The horse barely missed him.

The deafening sound of hooves on cobbles suddenly rent the still air and he had to leap to one side to avoid being run down. The rider had appeared as if from nowhere, seemingly having galloped through the central arch of Exchequergate, in front of the Cathedral to his right. Looking up, he saw the rider's cloak billowing out behind him, the black stallion fierce in its haste.

As the rider sped towards the Castle, his terrified observer heard a shout of "Open the gates! Open the gates". But as the figure thundered over the Castle forecourt approaching the gates, both horse and rider vanished into thin air.

This ghostly rider is said to be that of a messenger of some centuries ago, who had been dispatched to the Castle carrying a pardon for a condemned man. He never completed his journey and the innocent man perished on the gallows just after daybreak.

Various tales tell of the reason for the rider's disappearance. Some have it that in his haste to deliver the pardon, the rider spurred his horse on too much and his mount stumbled, throwing him to his death by a broken neck. Others however paint a less heroic picture. Stopping at a coaching Inn for a fresh horse still some way from his destination, the rider judged he had time for brief refreshment. But the ale with his supper turned to two, and then to many more. The next thing the messenger knew, it was already day-break and he had no chance of delivering the pardon in time. He galloped away from the Inn and was never seen again.

Whatever the reason for his failure in life, it seems that the rider's ghost still tries to deliver the pardon, just as dawn is breaking ..... .

"Castle Hill"

BROWNS PIE SHOP.

The fire blanket flew through the air and hit Simon firmly on the back of the head.

He had just been about to go through the door out of the kitchen. Instead he spun round, flushing automatically with annoyance as he searched the room for his assailant. Then he remembered that he had been quite alone in the kitchen and nobody was there to throw anything. Except, of course, for Humphrey.

Simon had been Head Chef at Browns Pie Shop and Restaurant for some years. The old timberframed building dated back to the 1400's, as did many of the buildings adjacent to it at the top of Steep Hill. He had eventually got used to the fact that the third floor room at the very top of the building was always cold. The room with the name "W.Bailey" mysteriously carved into the glass pane of the window which overlooked the Castle. None of the staff liked going up to this room on their own. He had also had to get used to Humphrey.

On many occasions Simon had been working alone in the first-floor kitchen when he would suddenly feel that he was being watched. Looking up, he would see no one. But he would not find himself looking up to the height of a normal adult. Instinctively, he would find himself staring into empty space about four feet off the floor, where the face of an eight or nine year old child might be. This feeling of a presence was so often around that Simon had felt obliged to give it a name; Humphrey.

The fire blanket was a typical Humphrey prank, but Simon had made a discovery. He was the first one to enter the building every morning, to prepare the vegetables for the day's menu. He had taken to shouting a cheery "Hello, Humphrey!" on walking through the door, not minding feeling a little foolish as no one but Humphrey was there to hear him.

When the ghost was greeted in this way, fire blankets would remain in their holders and all would be normal.

One morning however, Simon was not the first one in. He was ill, so the Manager had to open up and set about the vegetables. The Manager did not know of Simon's ritual, so Humphrey did not get his greeting. About midmorning, he was hard at work on the vegetables when he heard the phone ringing downstairs in Reception. Putting down the large chopping knife, he hurried down to answer the call. When he came back up again, he was in for a surprise.

"Browns Pie Shop"

The knife which he had left on the worktop was sticking in the floor, point-in, waving menacingly as if it had been flung there in warning. It was several feet away from where he had left it and no stretch of his imagination could persuade him that it had fallen there on its own. It seemed Humphrey was annoyed at being ignored.

On another occasion, Simon was working into the early hours of the morning, during the very busy period of the famous Lincoln Christmas Market. He had again not been first in that morning. While working in the kitchen, Simon heard the front door of the restaurant, down on the ground floor, slam loudly. He was alone in the building and knew he had locked the door, leaving his keys in the lock on the inside. He rushed downstairs, meat-cleaver in hand, prepared to meet the burglars he thought must have smashed the door open. He found however that the door was still locked and that his keys were now some yards away across the floor. He decided to leave further work until daylight and hurriedly went home.

Even though Simon had become quite used to Humphrey's antics, his experiences had not prepared him for what was to prove one of the phantom's more accomplished feats. Needing to ask the Manager something, Simon heard the clinking of coins coming from the small room used as an office, above the kitchen on the second floor. Thinking the Manager must be up there, Simon ascended the spiral staircase. There were no doors on the rooms off the narrow staircase in this part of the building, so as Simon's head rose above floor level he could see straight into the office. It was obvious that the room was empty.

Gradually Simon's eyes focussed on where the noise was coming from. He suddenly saw several dozen coins dancing about in mid-air, all on their own, as if suspended by a myriad of unseen wires. As they swirled about they were clinking together. As he looked on, they all suddenly fell to the floor with a crash. This proved too much even for the hardy Simon and he rushed down the stairs three at a time and out into the street. It was some time before he ventured back in to explain to his curious colleagues the reason for his strange behaviour.

A lady who had a considerable degree of psychic ability once dined, alone, at the Restaurant. When paying her bill, she was asked as usual whether she had enjoyed her meal. "The food was excellent" she told the waitress. "But I was a little put off by the ghostly figure of a child who stood next to me, watching everything I ate!".

Perhaps if you dine at Browns, you might care to set an extra place ... .

THE LION, THE SNAKE AND THE GRANNY.

Knowing that the others were all down stairs, Robert came out of the bathroom dressed only in a towel tucked around his waist. He had just started up the corridor towards his bedroom when, to his great embarrassment, he saw the old lady. She appeared a typical 'granny', perhaps in her mid-70's, slightly stooped and with grey hair tied at the back. He had to press his back against the wall of the narrow corridor in order to let her pass, pulling-in his bare and rather generous stomach as best he could.

Robert had been Relief Manager at The Lion and Snake pub on Bailgate for just over a week. The normal management couple, Terry and Liz, were taking a well earned few weeks off. Instead of going away somewhere on holiday for the entire period however, they were travelling round visiting relatives and taking it easy. They had been away for some time but had now returned for a couple of days before going off on their next trip, so for a brief time they were all in residence at the pub together. Robert had not realised that they had their grandmother with them, or he would have been more circumspect about his half-naked journey from the bathroom.

It was late afternoon and he had showered in preparation for the evening's business. As soon as he was dressed, he went down to the private lounge where Terry and Liz were relaxing. "You might have told me you had your Granny with you, I just all but exposed myself to her coming out of the bathroom!" he complained. Terry looked meaningfully at Liz before saying "Oh, you've seen her then, have you?". But it was not a relative of theirs that he was referring to.

It was the ghost of an old lady which they had themselves seen on many occasions in the pub, especially in the corridor near the bathroom. They had said nothing to Robert about her, not wishing to worry him on the one hand, or appear foolish on the other. They now told him the story and

Robert had to sit down for some time to recover his calm. "But she looked completely solid" he protested "just like a real person". That was how they had seen her too, they said. But 'real' she was not.

This occurred in the mid-1980's and it would seem that the phantom granny is still in residence today. In the middle of 1994 a new couple took over the pub and they too have encountered the old lady, often hearing her footsteps as well as seeing her on occasion near the bathroom. Their pet dog's hackles often rise as he trots through this part of the building and guests have mentioned experiencing the feeling of something brushing past them as they walk to the bathroom.

"The Lion & Snake"

The Lion and Snake has a good claim to be the oldest Inn in Lincoln, having been built specifically as an Inn in the 1400's and having been used for no other purpose ever since. It is built directly on top of the old Roman road through the City; the line of the thoroughfare has moved to the west over the centuries so that the modern road today runs by the side of the Inn. This could account for the sound of horses and chariots which has been heard inside the building in the still of the night. And also for the Roman soldier who is said to haunt the cellars.

Customers may get their own chance to see one of the Inn's ghosts, as some of the public areas are also said to be haunted. The main bar, which runs towards the rear of the building, is the haunt of a rather bedraggled-looking man, who has been seen on several occasions disappearing through the rear wall towards the right hand corner. This is where the doorway to the kitchens used to be until recent times, when it was moved to the middle of the wall and the original blocked off. A young barmaid saw this gentleman in the early 1990's, but during our researches in late 1994 she was still so perturbed by the event that she refused to talk to us. One of her colleagues had to tell us of the incident.

The oldest Inn in Lincoln? Perhaps one of the ghosts would know.

GHOSTS ON THE STEPS.

Today, the Greestone Steps are a relatively little used route for climbing the hill to the Cathedral. Tucked away next to the College of Art halfway up Lindum Road they go through an archway and into a tiny road known as Greestone Place, which eventually leads to the south-east corner of the Cathedral. Most visitors to the City never find the Steps, following instead the main thoroughfare of Steep Hill and The Strait between 'uphill' and 'downhill'. Long ago the situation was very different.

"Greenstone Steps"

The steps you may walk today date from the early 1300's, but the route they follow is more ancient still. It traces the outside edge of the eastern wall of the old Roman city of Lindum Colonia. There was of course a major road going right through the Roman city from south to north, but this main route had certain disadvantages. The gates of the city would of course not always be open. Anyone using the city road would not only have to contend with the general traffic and bustle of the settlement, but also with possible security checks by the Roman authorities. A firm, mud-free route from downhill to uphill, avoiding these impediments, was therefore an important thoroughfare. When you walk the Greestone Steps today, you therefore tread in the footsteps of at least two thousand years.

Not surprisingly perhaps, this ancient route is credited with a good number of ghostly happenings. Greestone Place is now lined with buildings and one of them, near to the Cathedral, was the scene of midnight hauntings during World War Two. The inhabitants of the house were woken in the early hours by very loud banging noises, which they described as being "like the sound of large trunks being thrown around". They were so alarmed that they rushed out into the street in their nightclothes. A thorough search of the house however revealed nothing; no damage, nothing moved and no sign of intruders. (This is a common theme in many haunting stories. People report hearing noises of furniture being thrown about, all the plates in the kitchen being smashed to pieces or similar, but on investigation there is not a trace of damage anywhere.)

More recently, in the early 1990's, a young woman was scared out of her wits on Greestone Place, just above the archway of the Steps, where Greestone Terrace leads off to the east. It was late one summer's evening and she had just ascended the Steps on her way home. Suddenly the air became icy cold and she found herself rooted to the spot in terror. The normal sounds of the world around her seemed to fade into silence as she saw the apparition of a woman float in front of her. The ghostly lady was wearing long, flowing robes, like that of an old fashioned nurse or nun. The figure was holding a small baby cradled in her arms as she drifted a few inches off the ground. The phantom turned into the Terrace and vanished. The young woman fled up the street as soon as she could move and has not gone up The Steps alone since.

Rosemary Robb, in her book "Ghost Hunting" (Hall and Sons, 1992), described the sighting of a ghostly old gentleman on the Steps. He was seen by three young nurses just below the archway before disappearing through a solid stone wall. The man was dressed in the costume of a cleric from the 1600's; could he be the man who is reputed to have hung himself from the archway above the steps some centuries ago?

That the steps are indeed haunted is something we can attest to personally. On Saturday 8th April 1995, we were in Lincoln in the early evening, walking the final route of our forthcoming Lincoln Ghost Walk which was starting at the same time the following week. The area was quiet with hardly anyone about, the now light traffic on Lindum Road below barely disturbing the stillness of the early evening. We had come from the Cathedral, down Greestone Place and through the archway, and had just begun to descend the Steps. Suddenly we stopped and listened. We then continued down, stopping again another dozen or so steps on. We finally paused a few moments later near the bottom of the Steps. Our reason was the ghostly footsteps. Although no one could be seen, footsteps had followed us down the Steps. They had stopped when we stopped, with a sort of brief sliding sound. They had been quiet until we started again, when they had also started. This had happened on all the three occasions we had stopped. The atmosphere was watchful and eerie. Perhaps, we thought, there would be more than one "Lincoln Ghost Walk"; ours, and the ghost's.

FOOTPRINTS AT WATSONS.

"Watson's Building"

Immediately opposite The White Hart Hotel on Bailgate is Watson the Chemist. To the left of the shop entrance is another door leading to the second and third floors of the same building, which are occupied by "Watsons Face Place", a prestigious beauty salon. As well as exhibiting typical haunting phenomena, Watsons Face Place is, so far, unique in our experience in that it has what may well be ghostly footprints on some of its carpets.

The salon consists of several different rooms, all laid out with a variety of beauty therapy equipment. There is one particular room in which clients often mention that they do not like being left alone. This is where most of the strange marks are found. They consist of a series of parallel lines of differing lengths and the impression they immediately give is that of footprints. Imagine a shoe or sandell, perhaps of an ancient era, which has on the soles ridges, or perhaps lines of hobnails, going from side to side. The main sole of the shoe would have three or four ridges, the heel perhaps two. Imagine such a shoe had walked in mud or oil and then trodden on a pale coloured carpet. These are exactly the kind of marks which have appeared in the room.

Are these ghostly footprints at "Watsons Face Place"

The "footprints" appear so close to the walls that it would be impossible for anyone to leave them accidentally, as no one normally walks so close to a wall. They occur at several different angles, so that they would not appear to correspond to any regular feature which may be on the floor beneath the carpet - grippers, for example. The marks were first noticed some years ago, a year or so after the carpet was first put down. The marks became gradually more prominent until some while ago the carpet was cleaned in order to remove them. Months later however, they began to reappear and when we saw them were quite pronounced. We were told that they had in recent months begun to appear in the room opposite as well, for the first time.

We psychically probed the room and Jenny picked up an interesting event. She 'saw' the room as it was centuries ago, when it was a bedroom. A man was asleep in bed, his clothes draped over a chair. Another man crept stealthily into the room and began to go through the pockets of the clothing. The sleeper was disturbed and a heated fight broke out between the room's occupant and the thief. It resulted in one of the combatants crashing through the window and falling to his death on the street below, two floors down.

Could this be the owner of the footprints? The incident may at least explain the feeling of being watched, which some clients have reported in this room in modern times. Or could the marks on the carpet come from an even older inhabitant? In 1884 excavations below the building revealed remains of a Roman crematory furnace together with several jars containing funeral ashes.

What ever period the ghost dates from, it still seems to be very active today. The staff frequently hear footsteps along the top floor corridor, which leads from the room with the footprints, when nobody is up there. During recent redecoration work, a painter began by working Sundays, so as not to disturb the normal business of the place. When he heard the footsteps however, knowing he was alone in the building, he packed up and left; the work then had to be done during normal hours - when there were plenty of other people about for company!

In addition to walking about, leaving footprints and watching people, the ghost here also seems to steal things.

It was shortly before Christmas 1994 and the staff had arranged to go straight from work to a local restaurant for a few drinks and their Christmas dinner out. Linda, the manageress, told the others that she needed to stay behind for a short while to finish something off, so everyone else left for the party. As Sarah, the assistant manageress, was just about to go out of the door, she shouted back up to Linda: "I'm leaving the keys in the box here by the door for you, see you in a bit". Linda shouted back "OK" and heard the doorlock click shut as Sarah left.

About twenty minutes later Linda put out the office lights and went downstairs to the door, to leave and join her colleagues. But there was no sign of the keys. She looked on the floor and all around, but they were not there. Sarah had set the latch-type lock on the main door as she had left, but the keys were needed for the main deadlock and to set the alarms. Without the keys Linda could not make the building secure and therefore could not herself leave. "Sarah, you fool!" she thought "you forgot to leave them!". She went back up to the office and phoned the restaurant, quickly getting hold of Sarah. "You forgot to leave me the keys, dumbo!" she said jovially, but Sarah's response was more serious. "No I didn't, I left them in the box by the door as I went out, when I shouted to you". "You couldn't have done Sarah, because there's no sign of them" Linda replied, and the two women began to get a little short with one another.

"I'll tell you what" said Sarah, "I'll come back and show you where they are and then I'll buy you a new pair of glasses for Christmas". Linda let her in when she arrived a few minutes later. Sarah was then as confused as Linda to find that the keys had vanished. "But I left them there, in the box, they must be here!" Sarah protested. The two women searched the stairs, the office, their handbags; they even searched through the rubbish bags they had put outside in the yard, but there was no sign of the keys. Linda eventually had to phone the owner of the building, who had a spare set, to come out from home so that she could secure the premises.

The keys were never found. To this day, Sarah will swear on a mountain of Bibles that she left them by the door as she went out - and we believe her.

"WADDINGTON TOP".

Waddington Cliff, known as 'Waddington Top' to the locals, is an open area of high ground just south of the City. The old Viking Way runs across its top. Peter's house in Laurel Close lay at the foot of the cliff, its rising mass making a scenic backdrop to the property. With no roads, houses or street lights on this part of the Top, it was pitch black after sundown. Yet very often, Peter would see lights moving across the area after dark.

They would flicker as if they were a lantern or flame of some sort and would move slowly, as if being carried. One evening, before daylight had failed completely, Peter saw a group of white-robed figures actually carrying flaming torches, walking in procession along the hill top.

Rumours abound concerning secret sects holding ceremonies in the area, but Peter thinks the figures may be far more ancient. The place where he had seen the figures was very close to the site of St. Catherine's Priory, an ancient church destroyed about 450 years ago during Henry 8th's dissolution of the monasteries. Peter discovered that the monks at St.Catherine's had been Benedictine - who used to wear white habits.

THE WHITE HART HOTEL.

The children laughed and giggled as they chased each other up and down the corridor outside of Margaret's room. She and her colleague, Catherine, were in Lincoln for several days to set up a new branch of the Travel Agency firm for which they worked. Being away from home only two weeks before Christmas was not what they would have planned, but at least they had the consolation of being able to stay at The White Hart Hotel, a famous Lincoln landmark in the shadow of the Cathedral.

They were sharing a twin room overlooking Bailgate and had just put in a twelve hour day; the new computer system had been proving rather petulant and had for hours refused all efforts to make it talk to its big brother at head office. Jokes about their new offices being haunted did nothing to improve the computer's mood. Communication had finally, and mysteriously, been established and the two ladies had gratefully retreated to the comfort of their Hotel for a meal and an early night.

They had just settled when they heard the children. They seemed to come from the stairway end of the corridor, jumping and thumping their way along, before going into a bedroom further up the corridor. The children sounded to be around 8 to 10 years of age, perhaps an older girl and a younger boy, and seemed thoroughly at home. It was long past most children's bedtime, and why their parents let them disturb other residents in this way was a question very much on Margaret's mind.

The children continued to play up and down for some time. Margaret decided to try and ignore them, but to no avail. Reluctant to get out of bed and dress in order to admonish them, she waited, thinking surely someone would stop them soon. Catherine was too tired to care and advised her colleague to go to sleep, in a voice which indicated that she herself very nearly was. Margaret was just on the point of getting out of bed in a fit of indignation when there was a longer than usual pause in the children's escapades. The minutes passed and Margaret heard nothing. Finally deciding they must themselves have gone to bed, Margaret snuggled down to her well deserved slumber.

First thing next morning, Margaret found herself still annoyed about the disturbances of the previous night. The women still had a couple of nights to go at the White Hart and did not want further noise. On their way down to breakfast they called at Reception, where Margaret explained what had happened. "Could you tell me what room the family is staying in please, because if they are still here tonight I would like a word with the parents" she asked.

The receptionist told her however that no family were booked in. There had been no children staying in the Hotel the previous night. When Margaret insisted that they had been going in and out of a room just up their own corridor, she was advised that the Hotel was rather quiet at the moment and no other rooms on their corridor were occupied. And most certainly, no children could have got into the Hotel and played for some time without being seen (or heard) and evicted. From then on, Margaret made sure she never had to walk along that corridor without Catherine beside her.

There has been a "White Hart" on the same site since 1387. The first one was founded in commemoration of the visit in that year of Richard II to the Cathedral; his emblem was a White Hart. The current collection of buildings dates back only to the early 1700's however, the original old coaching Inn having gradually taken over adjacent properties to become the Hotel of today. The Orangery is the centrepiece of the current building, being the old coaching yard roofed over and made into a dining area. It is here that a ghostly highwayman has put in more than one appearance.

Highwaymen have tended to be romanticised over the centuries into 'gentlemen of the road', often depicted as characters of wit and charm into whose hands rich ladies would press their jewels with expectant eyes. The truth is that most highwaymen were simply ruthless killers. Any coachman who could shoot first would have no pity for these villains of the open road. One highwayman was indeed worsted by his intended prey on a dark night some distance from Lincoln. Having been ordered to "stand and deliver", the coachman seized on a split-second of inattention and thrust a flaming torch into his assailant's face, horribly burning him. Leaving him to his fate, the horses were whipped and the coach and passengers delivered to their destination of the White Hart with all speed.

This highwayman is still said to haunt the old coaching yard to seek his revenge on the coachman who burned him. The ghostly figure has been seen on several occasions, but not his face; he holds his cloak up so that only his eyes are visible, not wishing his terrible scars to be seen. He is even said to have appeared on a photograph taken in the Orangery - but only from the chest down.

Spectres are said to abound at the Hotel. In addition to those above, the "mop-cap girl" supposedly inhabits a landing on the stairs in the north-east corner of the Hotel. Legend has it that she was a child murdered by the Inn's very own rat-catcher, centuries ago. She appears cowering in a corner, looking terrified, as if awaiting the final blow. She wears an apron and mop-type cap by which she has become known.

A previous owner of the Hotel is said to haunt his old apartments, high up overlooking Bailgate, wringing his hands and beseeching his observer to "please help me find my ginger-jar". Another room is said to have a sad atmosphere following a suicide there some decades ago. Some friendly and rather helpful ghosts have also been reported in property just opposite the Hotel which is used for staff accommodation.

A young man in military dress of the early 19th century has been clearly sighted on the top floor. He might be connected with another ghost there, that of a lady in full crinoline-style dress, who seemed to become fond of the small son of one of the managers who lived there. The boy would talk about "that lady" and often draw a figure in a long, flowing dress. One evening she even apparently tucked him up in bed. In the middle of the night, one of the managers sleeping in the building was woken up by things quite literally going bump in the night. On getting up to investigate, he found that a log had fallen off the open fire and was smouldering the carpet. Had he remained asleep, the consequences might have been serious. It seemed that the ghosts had made a disturbance specifically to wake him and prevent an accident.

During the author's own psychic investigations at the White Hart, some previously unknown ghosts were discovered. In the passages beneath the building, a clerical-looking gentleman of about the 17th century was seen striding purposefully along an underground passage, believed to have led to the Cathedral. It has long since been sealed off. One of the second floor bedrooms was also found to have a ghostly resident - a fluffy tabby cat. It trotted up the corridor and straight through the door to the room. This is of course one of the great advantages of being a ghost cat; you can no longer be shut out from snuggling down on your favourite bed!

"The White Hart Hotel"

THE PHANTOM FIELD.

It was a frosty November evening as Barbara walked her dog across the fields behind her house on Bunkers Hill, the main road east out of Lincoln. Half a mile away to the south through the dark, beyond the copse known locally as "The Hedgehog", lay the quarry. Around its edges you could still pick up pieces of quartz crystal. A vein of quartz ran through the whole area amidst the iron ore, which lay beneath the limestone of which much of Lincoln was built. A century ago at 6am, you would have heard the tramp of hundreds of hob-nailed boots along the Wragby Road, as men came from the nearby villages to start their morning shift at the quarry. The area from which they had won the precious ore was now fields again, the active quarry having eaten its way much further south.

Nearly two millennia earlier, this field had been the site of the home of a rich Roman family. In 1884, the quarry workers had unearthed the remains of an extensive Roman settlement. In daylight, the brown ploughed soil could be seen to be widely scattered with brighter red, fragments of Roman brick and pottery shards. Tonight though, the only thing to be seen on the ground was the whitening of the frost as the temperature dropped still further.

The fields surrounding 'the Hedgehog', together with the copse itself, enjoyed a mixed reputation with the locals. Strange tales concerning the area were as numerous as the Roman fragments in the soil. Everyone seemed to know at least one person who had had an experience there which they would rather forget.

In the mid-1980's a young woman had been riding her horse across the fields at a gentle trot when it suddenly stopped dead, almost throwing her into a bed of tall nettles. The horse was obviously frightened, yet they were alone in the middle of the field. Then she saw them.

On the opposite side of the bed of nettles, about ten feet away, she suddenly noticed nine dark figures. They seemed to be human in form, but with shapeless black clothing. They had human-like heads - she could see their outline, the shape of the ears. But they had no faces, and no hair.

They did not appear to be aware of her and there had been no sign of them before this moment, but the horse had obviously sensed them. Horses, together with dogs and particularly cats, are generally considered to have strong psychic perception, in the same way that dogs can detect sounds inaudible to the human ear. Strangely, the young lady did not feel in any way threatened by the figures and eventually managed to persuade her horse to move off.

In the midst of the copse known as The Hedgehog was a circular depression in the ground, roughly big enough to fit a motor car into. It was a favourite 'den' for local children and after dark hosted the occasional camp fire for the braver teenagers. On one such occasion several boys sat watching the crackling flames when they became aware of a dark figure, sitting in the shadows on the opposite side of the firelight. They felt the figure was of evil intent and their dash back across the fields would have broken several sporting records. Rumours abounded concerning The Hedgehog, but the common theme was one of a feeling of being watched, with malicious intent.

Numerous incidents of people being followed by invisible figures have been reported in this area. On one occasion a group of three people went for a walk across the fields, all the time seeming to hear footsteps behind them, but being unable to see anyone. On making their way back the way they had come, they could clearly see their own out-going footprints in the heavy frost. They could also see an additional set of footprints, which followed and crisscrossed their own, which had not been there before.

During the time a new building was being put up on Bunkers Hill, which backed on to the fields, a ghostly black labrador-type dog was seen and heard on several evenings by a local resident, while walking his own dog.

Why "ghostly"? Because the dog was seen to trot happily straight through a solid fence surrounding the building site. On one occasion the man heard the dog clearly but could not see it, but then felt it brush past his legs. This occurred in a part of the fields where crop markings appeared one summer, as strange depressions and formations in the growing vegetation.

Barbara had never particularly taken any of these stories very seriously, and had walked her dog countless times over the fields without incident. Tonight was to be different.

Some distance from the back of her house, a thorn hedge divided two of the fields. This hedge ran directly away from the line of houses, so that as you walked along the hedge, you got further and further away from the buildings. About a hundred yards away from the house was a large opening in the hedge, which farm vehicles used to traverse the fields. There were no street lights here and Barbara's dog was black, so she always took a torch with her to keep track of him. The dog's eyes would flash eerily as the torch beam found it's head in the darkness.

She had been walking for some minutes and was in the middle of the field, near the opening in the hedge. She could hear the dog trotting and snuffling about close by her as she walked. Then she suddenly heard it scamper off and everything went quiet. "Damn" she thought, "the dog has decided to go on one of his solo expeditions!". The dog had a tendency to trot off on his own occasionally and experience showed that he would be out for hours, until found and brought home by a family 'search party'. Barbara wondered if he had just started through the gap into the next field, so she went through herself, shining her torch about in the hope of catching the flash of eyes. She began to walk back in the direction she had come, but following now the far side of the hedge. It was then she heard the footsteps.

The hard ground betrayed the foot-falls with a crunching sound. They seemed to be following her, a few yards behind. She stopped to call the dog, then listened intently. The footsteps had stopped. As she started walking again, so did the footsteps, keeping the same distance. Barbara was a mature woman and while naturally cautious, certainly not of a nervous disposition. She knew of no one being followed or assaulted in this area. If it was an attacker, why were they keeping their distance and not striking? She was after all quite alone and out of earshot of the houses. No, it was not fear of assault that worried her. It was the overwhelming feeling of a presence, which had been with her since she had first heard the footsteps.

Had she suspected a real assailant, she would probably have shone the torch around and challenged them. This was different. She continued up the side of the hedge, the presence following her at the same distance. She was however boxing herself in. She had walked through the only opening in the hedge and although getting steadily nearer to the houses she was on the wrong side of the hedge. She was now in a different field, from which there was no exit to houses or street. Every step took her further away from the gap through the hedge and her route home.

Suddenly in the torchlight she saw a thinner spot in the otherwise dense and impenetrable mass of thorns. The gap would have been a tight squeeze in her youth, which was further away than she cared to admit and when she had weighed a few stone less than she did now. None of this was on her mind however as she instinctively launched herself into this gap, scrabbling on hands and knees over the cold soil until she found herself on the other side. Bursting from the hedge bottom like a sprinter from the blocks, she dashed across the field and home.

As she rushed, panting, through the back door her teenage family observed her with incredulity. Here was there normally sensible, orderly mother, covered in mud, hair all over the place, stockings hanging in shreds and looking like she had been 'dragged through a hedge backwards'. How nearly right they were. When she told them the story of how she came to look like that, they could not stop laughing. To this day, they still joke about it at her expense. But Barbara did not care about their ridicule. The sheer feeling of relief at escaping from 'the presence' will, she says, last her a lifetime.

Interestingly, Barbara found the dog already at home when she arrived. Never before or since had the animal run off and arrived home on its own. Perhaps it had sensed 'the presence' shortly before Barbara herself and immediately bolted for home. Given the basic instinct for pure escape which had suddenly overtaken her, she felt she really could not blame him.

Was this then a ghost, haunting this ancient site and literally making its presence felt? Or was it a more normal human prowler, stalking the night? We would like to suggest another possibility - that of a "thought-form". It has often been postulated that the power of thought is capable of literally creating things. Psychics such as Uri Geller have been credited with starting (and stopping) clocks just with the power of thought. The philosophy called "Positive Mental Attitude" suggests that it is possible to bring into your life that which you powerfully focus on over a period of time: more money, a better job or so on. Occult circles have long talked about "thought-forms" as desires or fears given some sort of physical existence through the power of the mind. (Richard Bach, creator of "Jonathon Livingstone Seagull", gave a wonderfully simple and light-hearted view of thought-forms in his book "Illusions".)

Beneath the area of The Hedgehog and the surrounding fields lies a vein of quartz crystal. Anyone familiar with 'New Age' thinking will know immediately quartz's reputation as an amplifier of healing or psychic energy.

When we investigated the area, Jenny received very strong psychic impressions in the area of The Hedgehog. She clearly 'saw' an event from decades ago, when a young woman was brutally assaulted at knife-point in the cover of the trees. A footpath, used for as long as anyone can remember, passes right by the hedgehog on the south side. Jenny knew that the young woman's male attacker had lain in wait for some time among the trees of the copse. He may have done this on numerous occasions and attacked more than one woman. He was a violent and wicked character, without remorse.

Could this have given rise to the feeling of being watched, which so many people had felt in the area? Amplified perhaps by the 'energy' of the quartz, could the man's evil intent have left a sort of psychic imprint on the copse? Young minds sitting around a night fire, filled with superstition and rumours of the place, might be quite capable of unknowingly creating a form personifying their fears.

Had conditions in some way been exactly right on that particular night for Barbara to tap-in to that energy and create her own thought-form, her own special interpretation of the psychic echos from long ago? We wonder how many phenomena which would usually be called 'a ghost' might actually be thought-forms, created quite unknowingly by the observer. In any event, you are unlikely to find the authors wandering around the phantom fields after dark, thought-forms or not!

THE HOUSE ON BUNKERS HILL.

Another tale concerning the area around 'The Phantom Field' was told to us by someone who used to live on Bunkers Hill, their garden backing on to the haunted fields.

The young woman who lived in the house was sitting with a girlfriend one evening in the lounge, overlooking the garden and fields beyond. It was dark but they had left the curtains open as the property was not overlooked to the rear. While chatting to her friend, she had for some time been seeing small flashes of light, just outside the room, coming from the garden. She had ignored them, thinking they were an effect she had often noticed, due to reflections from the very edge of her contact lenses.

After a time however her friend mentioned the lights, as she could see them too and had been wondering what they were. She did not wear contact lenses. Both women said they felt the atmosphere was 'a bit strange'. They were listening to music playing on CD and were suddenly amazed to hear the CD begin to play backwards. This was only rectified when the power was turned off and back on again.

No sooner had they got the CD working properly again when they both heard the crying. It sounded exactly as if a small baby was upstairs in the house. It did not come from any adjacent house, but from within their own building. But the young lady lived there alone and did not have a baby.

SPIRITS IN THE VAULTS.

"The Cornhill Vaults"

Kate, washing out some glasses behind the bar of The Cornhill Vaults pub, suddenly remembered her cooking underway in the kitchen. She was now overdue to check on some vegetables, this having slipped her mind temporarily as she had been busy serving customers. She immediately took advantage of the lull to rush back to her culinary efforts. Just as she was turning round though to head back to the kitchens, she saw another customer approaching the bar. The pub is entirely underground, with arched brick ceilings giving a cavern-like atmosphere, to which the rather dim lighting adds. Kate could see the young man quite clearly though. He was perhaps in his middle or late twenties and was wearing a collarless, "granddad" type shirt, unbuttoned at the top. The Vaults is a thriving haunt of Lincoln youth, so the young man's appearance was nothing remarkable.

Kate decided however that she was not stopping to serve the man, as that would almost certainly mean the death-knell for her vegetables. She turned and dashed back towards the door to the kitchens and in the process nearly bumped into Norman, one of her colleagues. "Oh Norman, just serve that bloke coming to the bar would you" she said hurriedly as she disappeared through the kitchen doorway.

She had just reached the cooker and begun to examine her cooking when Norman came into the kitchen. "Didn't he want anything then?" she asked. "Who?" said Norman, stealing a piece of cheese while Kate was out of wrist-slapping range. "That young man I asked you to serve at the bar a second ago" she said impatiently. "I thought that's what you said" replied Norman "but there was nobody there".

"Of course there was!" she replied tersely, and being convinced the customer must still be waiting impatiently to be served, Kate turned down the cooker and went straight back to the bar. Less than half a minute had elapsed since she had left, but when she arrived back, sure enough, no one was there. A young lady who was a regular at The Vaults and whom Kate knew well was sitting at the bar with her drink; they had been chatting for some time in between customers. "What happened to that young man who was here a second ago?", Kate asked her friend. "There hasn't been anyone here for a minute or two" her friend said, "not since those two businessmen in the flash suits. I'll tell you what though" she continued "I just went ever so strange, all tingly and freezing cold, just for a few moments. It was really weird".

Even though Kate had long been aware that The Vaults was haunted, it was still a shock when something like this actually happened. And it was her, more than anyone else, who seemed to pick-up on the pub's phantom residents. Then she remembered seeing the young man before.

It had been 6 or 7 years earlier, in the early part of one evening, before the place had got really busy. The young man had been sitting near the bar, deep in conversation with Gary, one of the pub regulars. Kate had seen them talking for some time when one of Gary's friends came in and walked up to the bar, Kate already pulling his usual pint. He had to walk past Gary in the process and Kate noticed him looking at Gary with a puzzled expression. As he was paying Kate for the drink, he asked: "Who does Gary think he's talking to?". "I've no idea" replied Kate, "someone who came in a while ago, I don't know him". Gary's friend looked even more puzzled. "But there's nobody there, Kate. Gary's chatting away to himself. How many has he had?".

"What are you on about!" Kate said. "Of course he's not talking to himself, he's talking to that bloke right next to him. And he's only had a couple of pints yet". The friend now began to get a bit agitated and said: "Look, I've had a hard day and I'm not really in the mood for a wind-up, so why don't you two just knock it off and let me have a quite drink". Now it was Kate's turn to get shirty. "Are you telling me that you think Gary's talking to thin air?" she enquired "you reckon you can't see him?". "There's nobody there!" he insisted, before muttering an expletive and shuffling off to another part of the bar.

Kate called a colleague over from another bar. "See Gary at that table there?" she asked. "Yes" came the reply. "And see that young bloke in the granddad shirt next to him?" she continued. "No, what bloke? Hey, why is Gary talking to himself?" said her colleague. Kate thought fast. "Oh, it's just a wind-up on one of his mates" replied Kate and her colleague wandered back to her own area. Kate then saw the young man leave and she immediately went over to speak to Gary. It seemed that they were the only two people who had seen the young man. Gary at first thought that Kate was trying a joke on him, until he later had a word with his friend who had come in earlier. Although the ghostly man had seemed perfectly real to them, he had simply not existed as far as the rest of the pub had been concerned. Kate recalled that he had looked just like the young man who she had seen advancing to the bar during her rush to the kitchen.

She wondered whether it was this young man who kept turning off the gas taps and beer lines in the cellars, a troublesome but all too common occurrence at The Vaults. Or maybe it was the ghostly old lady, in dark clothing, who had often been seen in the bar and kitchen areas. She was only visible from the waist upwards and Kate had always thought there must have been an old floor which no one knew about, two to three feet below the present one. In the early 1990's, she was proved right; during major renovations in that area of the building, part of the floor caved-in to reveal a second, older level which had not previously been known of - just where the old lady was seen drifting along.

THE HAUNTED FORGEWORKS.

In 1979, Smith Clayton Forge Limited of Lincoln proudly celebrated their 50th Anniversary. In the June 1980 'Anniversary Edition' of "Forge News", the inhouse magazine of the Company, many photographs of the factory over the years were included. One in particular was of the Old Forge building, taken in the 1940's or 50's. The picture had caught bright shafts of sunlight streaming into the otherwise rather ominous factory area and was felt to be rather atmospheric. It certainly did prove to have a very special quality.

During research for this book, the author came across a story published by The Lincolnshire Chronicle in July 1980, concerning this photograph. It said that when the "Forge News" had been published, some of its recipients noticed a ghostly figure in the photograph of the old forge. One of them also happened to have a copy of the original photograph and declared that the figure did not appear on the original. This seemed like a good story, if fifteen years old, so the author contacted Smith Clayton Forge Limited to investigate.

Reality turned out to be even more curious than the Chronicle's story. Derek Chantrey had been Editor of "Forge News" at the time of the Anniversary Edition and still worked for the Company. He had in his files both a copy of the magazine from 1980 and the original photograph which had been sent to the printers who produced that edition. At first sight, the author could not see anything unusual about the picture. When it was pointed out however, the image of a man up to about chest height, semi-transparent, was clearly visible standing in the marked-out pathway of the factory floor.

The figure was wearing a suit, with the shoes and bottoms of the trousers being quite clear. This photograph is reproduced figure 1. The author has seen several so-called ghost photographs, where the supposed ghost is probably no more than a shadow or combination of shapes which the eye could possibly convince itself to be a figure or a face. (In the same way, it is possible to look at a cloud and see crocodiles, trains, mountains and so on, depending on how your mind wishes to interpret the random shapes.) This photograph appeared different. The reproduction shown here has lost some clarity in the copying, but the man's legs and feet are still quite unmistakable, particularly the shine on the shoes. Once pointed out, the figure becomes clear and is evidently not a 'made-up' shape. There appears to be no trace of this figure, in this position, on the original photograph which is reproduced figure 2. But the mystery quickly deepened.

Figure 1

Figure 2

Two discoveries were made sitting in Mr. Chantrey's office that day in January 1995, which had either been missed for the previous fifteen years or else had appeared in the meantime. Firstly, the ghostly figure was on the original photograph - but in a different position! Look in our reproduction of the original shot, just above and to the right of where the man appeared in the magazine picture; an artist's drawing is given to help you find the right place on page 43. The figure of a man is again quite clearly visible, but this time we see his back, his left arm tucked behind him in a typical 'Prince Charles' type of stance. This time we see him up to his shoulders. The legs and shoes are again clear and it would seem to be the very same figure as in the magazine picture, but in a different position.

It is worth here reiterating events. The original print, not it's negative, was sent to the printers of the magazine together with dozens of other photographs. Nothing unusual had been noticed at that stage. The photograph was subsequently returned from the printers and sat in Derek Chantrey's files for fifteen years. A ghostly figure was noticed on the magazine print. What looks like the same figure was then also noticed, in a different position, on the original shot.

If we take the situation at face value, we definitely have paranormal forces at work. But is it all a hoax? Images such as that seen on these photographs would be easy to produce in any basic darkroom. But why would anyone bother?

The story had originally been published in The Lincolnshire Chronicle because Derek Chantrey had contacted them with the story. The image in the magazine shot had been pointed out to him by several readers. He told the author that he had contacted the printers concerning the ghostly image at the time, but they had denied all knowledge of it. They maintained they had simply printed all the photographs as they were received. They had enough to do with printing the magazine to the right quality and on-time without messing about faking ghosts (they said). Mr Chantrey therefore thought it a humorous curiosity, but one which may

Figure 1A - Artists Impression

Figure 2A - Artists Impression

give their fiftieth anniversary a little extra local publicity, so he had contacted the Lincolnshire Chronicle. Sure enough, they got a small piece in the local paper, but that was that. No national exposure, no money in publication fees, and really, very little publicity at all.

If this was a fake to get attention, it did not do a very good job. And why not mention the figure, in a different position, on the original? That would be like winning an Olympic Gold Medal and only publicising the Bronze you also won. Mr. Chantrey appeared to the author to be a reputable and professional gentleman. He denied all knowledge of the origin of the ghostly images. Ruling him out, we are only left with two possibilities; true paranormal influence, or a rather elaborate hoax by persons unknown at the time, including the printers of the magazine, who in fifteen years have failed to take any advantage of their handiwork. Hoaxers usually hoax so that they can dramatically reveal 'the truth' at the moment of most impact. In this case, this would have presumably been fifteen years ago when the story broke to the press. As no one has yet come forward, we rather favour the paranormal explanation. *Particularly so, in view of the other two figures also visible in the pictures.*

The first of these was noticed by the author, at the same time as the other be-suited figure in the original. This figure appears on the magazine copy, just to the left of the suited man, in front of the dark screen (see Figure 1 page 41). It is clearly the upper torso, shoulders and head of a man, wearing a white, probably collarless shirt and with a balding head. He is looking towards the man in the suit. There is no trace of him on the original photo and again, once seen, he is quite clear. But even the author did not spot the second figure.

When a copy of these photographs was given to a commercial artist to produce the line drawings, the artist immediately referred to "these two figures in front of the screen". On close inspection, a second figure, almost like a mirror-image of the first, was then seen over the left shoulder of the white-shirted man. Everyone, including the author during a careful study of both photographs, had so far missed him. If these photographs were faked to such elaborate detail, why has no one ever claimed the credit?

It would appear to us that in the magazine copy, we have perhaps a manager or boss proudly posing in his old factory, with a couple of the workers looking on. In the original, the boss seems to have kept the field to himself.

Was then the Old Forge haunted? We would suspect probably not, in the conventional sense anyway. This photograph was taken of an area which had seen great toil and devotion for over fifty years. Many men would have worked here for most or all of their working life, through the dark days of World War Two and into the "you never had it so good" days of the sixties. Perhaps the feeling of sheer nostalgia present during the Anniversary celebrations would have been enough to allow the imprint of these images of a time gone by. A glimpse of old fashioned times, together with their equally old fashioned sense of dedication and "family" spirit, which many local employers, on whom the community then so heavily relied, often engendered. Or maybe, some of the forge's old inhabitants simply wanted to get in on the fiftieth celebrations, of which they were still so proud, even if they did happen to be 'dead'. We find it unlikely, in any event, that the ghosts of these people were actually wandering around the old forge in such profusion when the shot was taken, to say nothing of swapping positions while the photograph was being printed for the magazine.

Perhaps the workers had simply found a way to forge a link between this world and the next... .

LINCOLN CATHEDRAL.

Walking through Exchequergate from Castle Hill, one is greeted with the magnificent architecture of the West Front of Lincoln Cathedral. The two ends of this Front finish in pinnacles, or very small spires, which have stone figures at their peaks. The northern most one, to the left as you view from Exchequergate, is of a figure blowing a trumpet.

This figure is sometimes called 'the Swineherd of Stow' and is said to depict Bishop Robert Bloet, the second Bishop of the Cathedral. He consecrated the building for the first time, on completion of the original structure in 1092. Legend has it though that Bloet was far more interested in matters of the flesh than the spirit, and his depiction as a swineherd was a symbol of what Lincoln folk thought of him! It has been said that at times, the blowing of his horn can be heard in the Cathedral precincts.

The conventional history of this prestigious building is of course well known, but its paranormal heritage has been less publicised. How many visitors know that the Cloisters are supposedly haunted by ghostly monks, drifting around in silent procession as they would have done in life, as if in solitary prayer? While the Cathedral is rightly known as a place of divine worship, events of a more macabre kind have also occurred there, which the visitor might wish to keep in mind during a tour.

In the late 12th century a sub-Dean named Bromfield was murdered in the Cathedral while praying; his murderer was one of the Cathedral vicars. What events might have given rise to such an act, history has not recorded. Revenge was however swiftly meted out by some of the sub-Dean's servants, who tied the murderous vicar to a horse's tail and dragged him through the town to Canwick Hill, where he was hanged.

In 1392, further inter-clergy skullduggery occurred. On St.John's Day, December 27th, one of the Dean's servants attacked a man called Thomas, who was attached to the Treasury, during the service of Vespers. Five days later, on New Year's Day 1393, the intrigue continued as a group of the Dean's servants attacked a bell-ringer called Simon, again during Vespers (seemingly a dangerous time in those days). Simon was attacked in the precincts surrounding the Cathedral and made a dash for the door of the Church for safety. It is recorded however that the door was locked against him and Simon was seriously wounded in the attack. The Church authorities then seemed to rally themselves, for the perpetrators of this crime were excommunicated, a fate taken as quite literally worse than death, for it meant eternal damnation to hell. The Cathedral was proclaimed tainted by these ungodly acts and closed from holy worship for a suitable cleansing period.

If "Civil War" is mentioned with regard to England, most will immediately think of Charles 1st, Cromwell and the strife of the 1640's. Few are now aware of the devastating conflict under King Stephen, which began in 1139 A.D. and in which Lincoln Cathedral itself seemed to take a paranormal hand.

Stephen was a valiant warrior but a poor ruler and his reign saw much strife; one chronicler recorded that it was a time when "Christ and his Saints slept". The civil war commenced in 1139 when Matilda, Henry's own daughter, invaded the country from her powerbase in Anjou in a bid for the Crown. Two years later saw her holding Lincoln Castle against Stephen. The Castle did not fall quickly as Stephen had hoped. He therefore prepared for a long siege by commandeering the Cathedral, only a bow-shot from the castle, mounting his siege equipment on the walls and archers on the parapets. The clergy and townspeople alike were outraged at his sacrilegious use of their holy place.

Stephen failed to break the castle's defences and eventually reinforcements for Matilda arrived in the shape of her supporter Robert, Earl of Gloucester. Shortly before riding out to meet him in battle, Stephen suddenly seemed to remember the real purpose for which his siege headquarters had been built. It was the morning of Candlemas, February 2nd, and he had Bishop Alexander say mass for him, which added hypocritical insult to injury as far as the people of Lincoln were concerned. During this service, the building itself seemed to take the opportunity to rebuke Stephen for his actions and predict his future fortunes.

As part of the ceremony of Candlemas, the Monarch had to offer a large wax taper, "worthy of a King", to the Bishop. As the Bishop reached out to receive it however, it crumbled and fell to the floor in pieces. No doubt in the Cathedral at that moment you could have heard a pin drop. Above the main altar hung a small round holder called the Pyx, suspended by a chain, which held the consecrated wafer. Later during the service there was a crash. The chain had snapped and the pyx smashed onto the altar, spilling its holy contents.

Few attending that service doubted the outcome of the battle. The day ended with Stephen a prisoner, his army defeated. No subsequent monarch ever dared to commandeer Lincoln Cathedral again.

In 1237 the building seemed to take on a life of its own for a second time. Bishop Grosseteste ascended to his episcopal Seat at the Cathedral in 1235. He was an ardent campaigner for righteousness among the clergy and seemed to be of the opinion that many of them were considerably less than spiritual. He made himself most unpopular by continually berating his fellow clergy for their worldly ways. Two years after his enthronement he was preaching in the Cathedral, again highlighting the ungodliness of his peers. Perhaps by way of apology to his no doubt weary congregation, he begged their indulgence for yet another sermon of 'fire and brimstone' with the words: "... but were I to be silent on these matters, surely the very stones themselves would fall?".

No sooner had the echo of his words begun to fade around the massive stone walls than the Cathedral's central tower promptly collapsed, killing several members of the congregation. Coincidence or divine intervention? Perhaps 'the very stones themselves' could simply no longer put up with him!

In March 1976 the Lincolnshire Echo ran a story about a man who claimed to have witnessed a human head rolling down the hill from the Cathedral. The story did not record the exact location of this gory descent, but as we sometimes point out on our Lincoln Ghost Walk, it was probably "from 'ere to 'ere".

The cathedral has many spires and towers, most now permanently closed to the public. This may be partly due to so many people in the past having chosen to commit suicide by throwing themselves off one of the Cathedral's high vantage points. Some of these suicides have been repeatedly witnessed in ghostly 're-play' form, observers again seeing someone crashing to their death who actually did so years before.

"East Front of Lincoln Cathedral"

The most famous legend concerning the Cathedral, and probably the most famous of Lincoln as a whole, is that of the Lincoln Imp. This is a small stone carving of a mischievous little demon to be found on top of a pillar in the 'Angel Choir' of the Cathedral. Legend has it that shortly after the Cathedral was completed in the mid-13th century, the Wind carried two imps to the building to marvel at its splendour, but also to see if they couldn't do a bit of clergy tempting as well. One imp was so over-awed that he did not dare enter the sacred place and he alighted on a gargoyle above the Judgement Porch. The other imp was braver (or less wise) and finding the South Door open, flew inside. After wafting around for some time he came to the Angel Choir and was so impressed with its splendour that he settled on top of a pillar to admire it more fully. Seizing the opportunity, the angels around him immediately turned both him, and his friend resting outside on the gargoyle, to stone for eternity. The Wind however still haunts the confines of the Minster Close awaiting the return of the imps.

The Cathedral authorities today officially describe the story of the imp as "an early 20th century invention of commercial interest". We rather prefer the legend!

BISHOP KING'S GUARDIAN GHOST.

Bishop King held office at Lincoln Cathedral from 1885 to 1910 and was much beloved in the City. He was very much a "man of the people" and stories of his kindness abound. It seems that in his younger days, he was the recipient of a ghostly helping hand himself.

Long before he rose to the heights of Bishop, the Reverend King was a young Curate in a small village. He had just arrived home late one wet and windy night when there was a loud hammering on his door. His housekeeper reported that a messenger was there with news that a farmer, living about three miles away, had met with a terrible accident. The Curate's presence was requested immediately to perform the Last Rites. King put back on his soaking coat and muddy boots and set off for the farm. As he left his house there was no sign of the messenger and he presumed that the man had hurried back to the farm without delay.

After a dark and wet journey on foot across the fields, King arrived at the farm and knocked on the door. It was opened by the allegedly dying farmer, looking in the peak of health and wondering what had brought the Curate to his door during a storm. King explained about the messenger, but the farmer said he knew nothing of it and was perfectly well. King then returned home and the incident remained a mystery.

Many years later in a nearby town, King was administering to a man who was dying in hospital. "You do not remember me, do you?" asked the man and King had to admit that he did not. The man then identified himself and King immediately recognised him as a man of very bad reputation from the village in which he had been a Curate. The man continued: "Do you remember that night when you got a message about a farmer having a bad accident? Well, it was me that brought that message; I had intended to kill you just after you had left the house. You priests usually have something valuable about you and the clergy are no friends of mine. It was lucky for you though that you had that friend with you, because when I saw there were two of you, I backed off".

Bishop King remembered the incident well and also knew that he had been quite alone on that stormy evening. Or rather, he thought he had been alone; he had evidently had a ghostly companion, who had literally saved him from murder.

TOM OTTER'S GHOST... ?

The smoke from the fire rose up into the air above The Green at the east end of Lincoln Cathedral. The service of exorcism had been a solemn affair, performed by the Bishop himself, who now hoped that the matter would be laid to rest for good. The fire slowly consumed the blood-stained hedgestake, leaving only a small amount of grey ash. No longer would this grisly relic of 'murder most foul' be the centre of superstitious tales and un-Godly whisperings; or so the Bishop thought, back in the middle of the nineteenth century. History was to prove differently.

That the Sun Inn at Saxilby, just west of Lincoln, was haunted, was beyond doubt. All manner of strange noises would disturb the Landlord's slumbers in the early hours. Things would disappear to be found somewhere quite different later on. Ghostly apparitions were seen by many. But the origin of the hauntings was to prove far more mysterious than anyone would have guessed.

Until the latter part of the 1800's, when the Bishop of Lincoln finally intervened, few had any doubt as to the cause of The Sun Inn's mysterious happenings. In 1806, Lincoln's Brayford Pool, as it is known today, was being constructed by the containment of the earlier and much bigger Swanpool. One of the many itinerant labourers who found work on this project was one Tom Otter. While lodging in Lincoln he had an affair with a local girl who became pregnant by him. As was the custom in those days, he was forced by the City authorities to marry the girl, much against his wishes. But imprisonment being his only other option, he went through with the ceremony, under the watchful eye of the local constabulary.

The scene of the marriage is variously recorded as Lincoln or North Hykeham, but all agree that after the nuptials, the couple set out on foot for Saxilby. About a mile from their destination the new (and pregnant) Mrs. Otter sat down to rest at the side of the deserted country lane which was their route. History has not recorded exactly what then occurred; quite possibly the couple had a violent quarrel about their enforced predicament. The outcome at least is certain. Tom Otter brutally ended his three hour marriage by beating his new wife to death with a hedgestake.

Dropping the murder weapon next to the body, he then seemingly just walked away, along the road which is today known as Tom Otter's Lane. When the body was eventually discovered, it was brought to The Sun Inn at Saxilby and laid out on the 'stoop', a raised bank used for mounting horses. It is said that the bloodstains from the body could never be washed off the stoop; it was eventually painted black to hide them. The body was duly buried, but the murder weapon, the blood-stained hedgestake, was kept at the Inn by the Landlord and put on display behind the bar.

Why Otter was not immediately suspected of the murder is not recorded. Some say he fled the district for some months until things had calmed down. The story continued about a year after the murder, when Otter was sitting drinking in The Sun Inn itself. He was sitting next to a window with strong sunlight streaming over one side. The local policeman was walking past the Inn and noticed him through the window. Something caught the policeman's eye about Otter's sleeve. Before becoming a policeman, the man had been a butcher and he suddenly recognised the mark on Otter's sleeve as an old bloodstain. He entered the Inn and arrested Otter on the spot, on suspicion of his wife's murder.

Otter may have still escaped justice but for a young man called John Dunkley. He enjoyed the pastime of a 'peeping tom', spying on courting couples in well known spots of amorous pursuit. The scene of the murder had been in just such a 'Lovers Lane' and on the fateful day, Dunkley had been in hiding there awaiting his hoped-for entertainment. He had instead witnessed the murder, which had terrified him to the core. Otter of course had no idea he had been observed. Dunkley had said nothing of the incident for fear of possibly becoming Otter's next victim. Once however Dunkley heard that Otter was safely behind bars on suspicion of the murder, he felt secure enough to come forward with his eye-witness evidence, which firmly sealed Otter's fate. He hanged at Lincoln Castle shortly afterwards. But that was not the end of him.

Due to the horror of his crime, Tom Otter was "gibbeted" after his execution. This meant that his corpse was not buried, but suspended in an iron frame from a gibbet placed near the murder site. Here the body was simply left to rot, until it fell piecemeal through the bars or was carried away by animals, a grisly reminder of the retribution of the Law. A bird made a nest between Otter's decaying jawbones and it's constant journeying in and out for food for its nine chicks gave rise to the local rhyme:

> *"Nine tongues within one head*
> *A tenth went out to seek for bread*
> *To feed the living within the dead".*

Not surprisingly, after this event it was commonly thought that the ghost of Tom Otter, possibly together with that of his wife, haunted The Sun Inn. Particularly so, as the hedgestake used for the murder would mysteriously vanish every year on the eve of the anniversary of the event. It would later be found at the roadside where the murder had taken place. It would be returned to the Inn, but the following year it would disappear in the same way. Attempts to trick the ghost, by moving the hedgestake to another Saxilby pub shortly before the anniversary, would be to no avail; the hedgestake would disappear from its new location as before. It was assumed that Tom Otter's ghost was responsible for moving the hedgestake, not wishing his terrible deed to be a constant topic of bar-room conversation. If this was the case, his annual efforts must have had rather the opposite effect.

After some years the tales of the disappearing hedgestake eventually became known to the Bishop of Lincoln, who decided to end these ghostly goings-on by exorcising and then burning it. Although it was popularly felt that this must have laid Tom Otter to rest for good, the hauntings at

The Sun Inn continued, although minus the itinerant hedgestake. No longer having such a good story to hang the hauntings on, the ghosts of Saxilby seemed to become less discussed - until very recently.

Shortly before Christmas of 1993, the Landlady of The Sun Inn was going upstairs to get her children's presents for wrapping. Suddenly rushing back downstairs, she told her husband that she had been followed by the sound of stamping, but invisible, feet. She had fled immediately and insisted that her husband go and get the presents from the upstairs room.

One Sunday evening, a pop group were booked to play at the Inn and they arrived before the pub had opened for the evening. Their knockings at the door brought no reply, even though they had noticed someone through the window, in the bar area. When no one answered, they went back to the window for another look and could still see the figure, but their knocks continued to be unanswered. Eventually they were let in by the Landlord and they asked who it was that had been there but would not let them in. The Landlord told them that the place had been quite empty. On going to the area inside the pub where they had seen the figure from through the window, they found themselves by the pool table - but no pool table had been there when they were looking at the figure a few minutes previously.

Three bar stools were once observed to fall over simultaneously when no one was within reach of them. The Landlord's young son could often be heard talking to someone in his room late at night when nobody was with him. Lights mysteriously turned themselves on and off for no obvious reason.

All of these events culminated in the visit of a local 'sensitive' to the Inn in early 1995. Eddie Burks developed his psychic powers relatively late in life. Having retired from his career as a Consulting Civil Engineer, he devoted much of his time to both spiritual healing of the living and in releasing 'earthbound spirits' from haunted places through mediumship. Eddie helped literally hundreds of ghosts to move-on in this way and wrote a book called "Ghosthunter" (Headline, 1995) about his amazing experiences. He identified two ghosts in the building, neither of them apparently having anything to do with the Tom Otter saga. One was a woman, who had died in the 1920's shortly after childbirth. The second was that of a man from the Napoleonic war era, a military gentleman who was very angry and agitated. He had probably been the cause of most of the mysterious phenomena witnessed over the years. Eddie apparently helped them both to come to terms with their situation and finally release their earthly ties, enabling them to leave the building and move on. The process of Eddie's "release" of these ghosts was filmed by a Swiss television crew and since then, all has been quiet.

It is interesting to note that one of the ghosts dated from the time of the Napoleonic wars - almost the same time as Tom Otter's demise and the start of the hauntings.

AT THE SIGN OF THE BLACK HORSE.

"The former 'Black Horse Chambers'"

If you follow the line of the northern wall of The White Hart Hotel along Eastgate, just opposite its end you will see a very old building, with an opening to a small car park behind. In late 1994 and early 1995, this was the Black Horse Chambers, a pub and restaurant. The building has been an Inn of some sort however for many centuries. A little further along Eastgate, on the Cathedral side of the road, there is a section of wall bordering the Minster Close. High up on this wall is set a single gargoyle. Unlike most such stone heads, which tend to look directly downwards, this gargoyle looks to the left - directly at The Black Horse Chambers. Legend has it that in the 16th and 17th centuries, the Inn was much frequented by the local clergy. The Bishop of Lincoln at the time had the gargoyle put in place to remind his clerics that God (and he himself) was always watching. Whether this did indeed discourage their ale-ridden sojourns to the establishment, or simply move them around the corners of Eastgate to the 'White Hart' or 'Lion and Snake', history does not record.

During its time as The Black Horse pub in the 1980's, one of the cleaning staff fled the building after sighting a ghostly 'grey lady' and subsequently resigned her post due to the apparition. In the summer of 1994 the building was completely refurbished inside, including major structural work and complete re-wiring. We have often found in our investigations of haunted properties that building or major redecoration work tends to disturb the atmosphere. Any resident ghosts seem to become unsettled by the activity and haunting phenomena increase. This was certainly the case at the Black Horse.

Some of the tradesmen who worked on the refurbishment told us of many strange incidents which occurred during the project. They would put down a particular tool for a few moments but on going to pick it up again, find it had vanished. None of their colleagues would have been near them in the meantime and a thorough search would reveal nothing. The item would not reappear for hours or sometimes days, which necessitated frequent borrowing, and sometimes replacement, of tools. (After the work was completed and the Black Horse opened for business, it was items such as pens, keys and notepads which tended to vanish and reappear mysteriously in a similar way.)

Footsteps would often be heard by the workmen on the bare wooden boards of the building when no one was there to make them. But the strangest incident was witnessed by everyone in the building, about a dozen in all, shortly after the work had commenced. The manager of the building was standing next to the owner of the Electrical Contracting firm employed to do the re-wiring. The building was fairly dim, with daylight filtering through the dust being created by all the ripping apart. Suddenly, everyone stopped dead as the building became brightly lit; every light in the building suddenly switched itself on. Part of the work underway was the ripping out of the old wiring, a job for which it was obviously essential that all power was disconnected.

The contract's manager shouted for his electrical foreman to enquire, none too delicately, why he had not disconnected the mains, while silently thanking each of his lucky stars that no one had yet been electrocuted. Far from being sheepish, the foreman was indignant that his boss could suspect him of such a basic error. He said that not only had the mains power been disconnected, but he informed his boss that the fuseboxes, through which the power had entered the building, were currently outside in the rubbish skip. Yet everyone there had seen the lights come on. They had remained on for perhaps half a minute before plunging the building back into its former dusty gloom. When the cables were tested, they were of course found to be all 'dead'.

After the building finally opened for business in the Autumn of 1994 the paranormal incidents continued. It became not uncommon for glasses to suddenly fly off tables without anyone being near them, landing on the floor some distance away with a thump, although never being broken. In January 1995, the Landlord reported that several of his customers had complained that the sound of a small child crying was putting them off their drinks. A member of staff who decided to sleep in the building one night awoke in the early hours to the sound of about half a dozen voices chatting away in the downstairs bar. He had been locked in the building and the alarms set, so that anyone moving about downstairs would have triggered the alarm system instantly. Pluckily, he shouted as loud as he could to the ghosts to be quiet, as they had woken him up. The voices continued as before with no acknowledgement that he had been heard. This also seemed a good excuse for him not to go down and investigate. He eventually turned a radio on to drown out the sounds of the ghostly get-together, which is how he finally got back to sleep.

No incident was as eerie however as that experienced by two staff members late one dark, autumn night. The place had closed after a busy evening and everyone had left except them. They had decided to stay on for a time in front of one of the open log fires, to talk in the flickering fire-light. As it was a cold night and the fire was low, they decided to put on some more wood. Normally, the fire would have been damped down for a few minutes until the new fuel began to catch, but tonight was different.

The moment they put the wood on the fire, it flashed into life as if they had thrown petrol on instead of wood. As the flames roared, they heard a low howling sound of wind. It seemed to come down the chimney from above the fire and out into the room. They felt its icy chill as it swirled around them. It then seemed to move across the room towards the stairs. The howling continued more faintly as the movement seemed to go up the stairs and along the upper floor of the building, until they heard the slam of a heavy door. Everything then fell completely silent. Even though the fire continued to burn strongly, the room remained icy cold. They were both convinced it was no ordinary wind that they had felt enter the room. A few moments passed as they stared at each other in the silence. Then they both jumped as a piece of brick suddenly crashed down the chimney into the fire. They locked up and left.

HANGING AROUND AT THE OLD SESSIONS HOUSE.

Hanging was not a pleasant way to die.

Preferable of course to being burned alive or disembowelled, it was generally not however the quick and humane process we might assume today. A swift death by the axe or sword was reserved for errant nobility; the common could suffer. And suffer they undoubtedly did.

Prior to an Act of Parliament in 1868, executions were public affairs, no doubt on the basis of deterring future criminals. The principal effect however was simply to pander to people's limitless appetite for gore and spectacle. Huge crowds would always gather in Lincoln on a hanging day; one chronicler recorded that, at a time when the normal population numbered about ten thousand, a hanging day would see around twenty five thousand people in the City! Rather than a rapid fall through a hatchway to a snapped neck and oblivion, most hangings then took the form of dangling the victim by a rope from the nearest tree or gibbet. Death occurred by simple strangulation, a gradual process governed by a variety of factors such as the width of rope, strength of neck muscles and so on. The average time to expiration was 20 to 30 minutes. It could take as long as an hour.

One can only wonder what might have been passing through the condemned person's mind during their rather lengthy dispatch. Praying for relief from the pain, certainly. Perhaps also the much known "life flashing before them" experience. But they often remained conscious for a desperately long time before death finally claimed them. It does not seem unreasonable to assume that many may have felt intense anger or bitterness as their final emotions. Many executions were for "crimes" which would barely merit a fine today, stealing food for a starving family being high on the list. Our then primitive system of justice left the way wide open for false accusation, mistakes and pure vindictiveness; we all recognise the phrase "a witch-hunt" even today.

Many paranormal researchers have suggested that strong, unresolved negative emotion may be responsible, in rare cases, for preventing a person from properly making their transition to 'the other side'. They then stay close to this level of physical existence and may well appear as ghosts, temporarily unable to either move on into their new world or exist as before in the old. Until, that is, they can find it within themselves to release the emotion which ties them; forgive their false accusers, let their bitterness fade or whatever it may be. They may sometimes be helped to achieve this by a 'medium', a living person who is still able to communicate with them. Then they can move on.

Such a situation, though almost certainly very rare, seems much more likely for those with a prolonged opportunity for such negative emotions to build up. Like dangling from a rope for half an hour, for example. Perhaps this is why so many ghost stories are associated with executions, violent murders and the like, where strong negative emotions are likely. Is this the case, we wonder, with The Old Sessions House?

This still stands in Lincoln on the corner of Lindum Road and Monks Road. In 1810 the City Gaol was moved there from the Stonebow, which had been called "the worst prison in the country" due to its inhumane conditions. Later, the Sessions House was to become a Police Station and the City Magistrates Court, a use it maintained until as recently as the late 1980's. It was also a place of execution and this is possibly why the building is haunted.

In the early 1970's, a policeman was on night duty in the building on security patrol. The building was otherwise empty, being unused at night, hence the need for security. The policeman was used to patrolling the empty building on his own and was unperturbed by his solitude. He was touring the basement area where the cells were located, when he suddenly heard footsteps. Looking quickly around he could see nobody, yet could still clearly hear the footsteps. They paced up the corridor between the cells, went up a stairway and were then heard to go through a door on the ground floor above. Curious rather than frightened, the policeman tried to make sense of his experience, but found he could not. Then it suddenly came to him. He realised that the footsteps had originated from what used to be one of the condemned cells. They had gone along the corridor, up the stairs and out of the doorway, just as someone would on the morning of their execution - on their way to the gallows outside.

Was this a 'trapped soul', forever retracing their final steps on this earth? Perhaps. Or might the intense emotion of that final journey have somehow imprinted itself on the area, like a psychic tape-recording? Conditions may have been just right on that particular night for the 'recording' to replay itself and be witnessed by the policeman. Whatever the reason, policemen are trained to be objective observers and are not generally given to experiencing ghosts; and are even less likely to tell anyone about it, if they do!

SPIRITS IN THE WINGS.

Martin was helping out at one of The Circle's doorways at Lincoln's "Theatre Royal". It was an afternoon matinee in 1974 and the audience was fairly small. Only the first three or four rows of The Circle were in use but a member of staff was always present to help guests to their seats. 'The Circle' was of course more like a crescent moon in shape, the stage being between the two points. There were doorways at each end and Martin was standing just inside one of these.

Glancing round the Circle, he suddenly noticed a gentleman sitting on the back row, end seat, in the corner furthest from him. The back row was not in use for this performance so no one should have been there. The man was somewhat portly in appearance and had a rather large, Edwardian-style moustache - and he was smoking an equally large cigar. Smoking was not permitted within the Theatre's auditorium, not least because the previous Theatre Royal had been burned to the ground in 1892. Martin decided he had better have a quiet word with the gentleman.

He made his way round the back of the Circle, keeping a watch for guests arriving who might need his assistance. When he got near the corner however, there was no sign of the gentleman. The man could not possibly have stood up and walked out without Martin noticing him, yet there was no sign of him.

Martin advanced along the aisle towards the corner seat. He felt he must check, but the gentleman was not of course on his hands and knees hiding behind the seats, the only place Martin thought he could logically be. But the seat in which he had seen the man sitting was in the 'down' position. This was odd, as the seats were always kept 'up' when not in use. Also, the air around the seat should have been heavy with tobacco smoke, yet Martin could only just persuade himself that he could detect the faintest whiff. It was as if the man had never existed ... .

On the wall, immediately adjacent to this seat, the outline of an old doorway could still be seen beneath the heavy wallpaper hung decades ago. Its frame stood proud of the wall and was clearly visible under the covering. No one knew why, or when, the door had been sealed in this way; it had been like that as long as anyone in the theatre could remember. It was known that it led to a small room, the only entrance; a window for the room was visible on the outside wall of the building.

Had Martin seen the ghost of a previous proprietor, or perhaps a wealthy patron, of the theatre? Was the room to which the doorway led an office, or even a private room? The cigar-smoking gentleman, in his own time-frame of many decades ago, may simply have stood up and walked through the doorway to this room. The outline of the doorway is still visible today, and the area it occupies is known by staff as "the haunted corner".

In common with many theatres, strange happenings seem to abound at The Theatre Royal. Theatres exist of course to stir up emotion and create atmosphere and perhaps this has a more general effect than most might guess.

There have been many ghostly sightings in the Theatre on a fairly regular basis. A dressing room right at the top of the theatre has been reported to have a ghostly resident by at least four separate actresses in recent years. The Stage Manager has often had to placate a distressed performer who is demanding a change of dressing room following a phantom visitor. Ghostly figures have been observed in the Theatre's Circle as recently as the middle of 1994. Several members of the stage crew saw someone there, but at the time they all assumed it was another one of their own number. This would have been unusual as there was no work to be done in that area. When notes were compared later, it was found that none of them had been anywhere near.

Strange noises, knockings and footsteps seem to abound in the building. Very clear footsteps were heard late one evening in the lounge area outside the Circle when no one was present to make them. The footsteps were those of someone walking on a bare wooden floor, although the area they were coming from was thickly carpeted. The area known as 'The Flies', high above the stage, seemed particularly affected.

The movement of scenery and the curtains was controlled by a complex system of ropes from this area. It ran right across the top of the stage and could only be reached by two stairways leading from either end of the stage itself. On one occasion, several members of the Theatre's staff were working on the stage when they again heard these strange noises coming from above. Thinking they finally had a chance to catch the prankster who was constantly playing tricks on them, they immediately took action. Some of them dashed up the stairs to the flies from stage-right, while others sprinted up the opposite stairway on stage-left. They thought they were certain to now catch the perpetrator between them in a pincer movement. Both teams quickly met, panting and breathless, in the flies - but with no sign of any prankster. They searched the area thoroughly, but no one was to be found. After resuming their duties on the stage below, they later heard the same noises coming from the flies; but this time they decided to leave the ghost to it.

A knowledge of 'the flies' would certainly have helped a ghost to perform the following paranormal feat. Paul was the chief designer at the Theatre. In the early stages of planning a new production, he would often work long hours designing the scenery. He used to work alone, until he had it all well worked out and needed assistance in simply making it. He would often work late into the night, finding that the peace and quiet aided his concentration.

One night he was still there at about 3am, working on the stage making paper mock-ups of his ideas. He decided that he needed a broader view of things and made his way to the front row of the Circle, from where he had an excellent view of the whole stage. He had been there only for a few moments when he was startled out of his contemplation by a movement. The main curtain was coming down. He watched as it descended, all on its own, right to the stage floor. The curtain operated rather like a giant roller blind; it had ropes at the end which were pulled one way to let it down and the other way to raise it again. The Theatre was locked and he was quite alone, so no one could be there to operate it.

It then occurred to him that if someone had not secured the ropes properly and they had come loose, the sheer weight of the curtain may have caused it to unroll. He stood up, about to go and investigate. His knees had barely straightened however when he stopped dead. The curtain was going *back up again*, an impossible event without someone hauling on the ropes to make it happen. He called out "Who's there?" but received no reply. He dashed down to the stage and found the ropes tied in position as normal. There was no sign of anyone.

Paul concluded that the Theatre's ghost was perhaps wiser than himself and was giving him good advice. "Bring down the curtain on tonight's efforts. You are too tired - go home and rest and you will be fresher tomorrow". He decided to agree and left for home and bed.

A superstition common to many theatres is that if a butterfly appears on stage during a live performance, it is actually the spirit of an actress or dancer, come back to take part in the show. This may seem just a quaint piece of fantasy, until you learn just how often butterflies do appear on stage at the Theatre Royal. A notable occasion was during the pantomime "Babes in the Wood" in the late 1980's, when a butterfly flittered persistently around one of the performer's heads; appropriately enough, during a woodland scene. The actor kept trying to waft it away without success. None of the performers could get their lines out properly and the audience were in uproar with laughter. Eventually it flittered off into the wings and disappeared into the darkness.

Pantomimes are of course held around Christmas time, when virtually all butterflies have long since perished. No one knows how they get into the Theatre. They are never seen anywhere else in the building prior to their appearance on stage. They are also never found after their exit into the darkness of the wings. Several different species of butterfly have appeared in this way, so that a breeding site for a particular type of butterfly somewhere within the theatre seems unlikely.

It is even more curious when you realise that performances have never been interrupted in this way by any other type of insect. It is never a moth, a wasp, a bee or fly which appears. Only a butterfly.

"The Theatre Royal"

MARY AND THE DRAGON.

"Oh by the way, you do know the place is haunted, don't you?", Andy was asked.

It was July 1994 and Andy McLaren had just taken over The Green Dragon Inn on Waterside North. He was in the hand-over period from the previous manager who was showing him the ropes. He knew that the building went back to the 14th century and that its distinctive four "garret" roofs had been added in the 1500's. On the walls were photographs of the major preservation work carried out in 1956, when the building had been stripped back to its timber frame, making it resemble a matchstick model.

"The Green Dragon Inn"

Andy was a no-nonsense Scot for whom the only spirits that had existed in his pubs had been in bottles and decidedly for drinking. "Haunted?" replied Andy. "What, you mean wee ghosties and goblins and such?" he scoffed. "Well, make of it what you will" his predecessor continued, "but we actually had a valued member of staff quit a couple of years ago after seeing a ghost. It was up in the Witham Suite, the function room on the top floor. One of our barmaids said she saw the ghost of an old woman, clear as day. She said the figure was very small, only about four and a half foot or so. The old woman was wearing a grey shawl with broad, black stripes and was smoking one of those old-fashioned clay pipes. Frightened her so much she gave in her notice on the spot".

Andy had never had much time for spooks, and the diminutive old lady seemed one of the least likely he had ever heard of. He had forgotten all about her a few minutes later as he continued learning about his new premises.

Some months later however, in early December, one of his bar staff called him over to meet two ladies who were sitting at the bar. They were in their late 50's or so and had said that they used to live in the building before the 1956 renovations. Andy was actively researching the history of the place, in order to answer the stream of visitors' questions which had been directed at him during his first summer's residence. He became fascinated to learn that these ladies were life-long friends and that one of their grandmothers had been one Mary Cooper - who had kept the middle of the row of three shops that had comprised the ground floor of the building. Mary had sold second hand clothes and had lived above the shop. As young girls, the two ladies had spent a great deal of time with her and had virtually grown up in the building. Mary had also made and sold umbrellas and had been widely known as "Umbrella Mary".

The two ladies had both married and moved away from Lincoln in the early sixties, Mary having died not long after her home was gutted and rebuilt. Neither of them had been back to their home town for nearly thirty years. They were now on a joint nostalgia tour and of course had come to see how their previous 'home' was faring.

Remembering the story of the ghost, Andy thought he would gently probe the ladies for further information. "You know," Andy began "this is a very old building and people are always asking me if it's got a ghost. Did anything happen while you lived here?". The ladies thought for a moment then replied "No, nothing, it was always very peaceful". That's the end of that then, thought Andy. Wanting to make some wall displays of the pub's history, Andy asked if the ladies had any photographs of Mary which he could use. They did send him one later, although they had none with them at the time. Andy therefore thought he would probe a little further.

"I'll look forward to seeing the picture of your grandmother. Out of interest, what did she look like?" asked Andy. "Well, she was quite a distinctive character" one of the ladies began. "You see, a childhood illness had left her with a curvature of the spine, so that she only looked very small, four, maybe four and a half foot tall". Andy's ears pricked. "Really?" he answered. "And what sort of clothes did she wear?". "Throughout the winter months she was never without her grey shawl around her shoulders. It was made in Ireland and had big black stripes on it" the ladies said.

"Did she smoke, by any chance?" enquired Andy, wanting to complete the picture. "No, she never smoked" said one of the ladies. Andy was now confused, but a few moments later all became clear. They had assumed Andy had meant "Did she ever smoke *cigarettes*" and had answered in the negative. As an afterthought though, one of them added: "Of course, she was never without her dojeen". "What's a dojeen?" asked Andy, never having heard the word before. "It's one of those old-fashioned clay pipes" came the reply.

Here then it seemed, was the ghost of the Green Dragon: Mary Cooper. By this time however, Andy had become at the very least open-minded about ghosts, if not an outright convert. He had witnessed so many inexplicable things in his few months at the Inn that his previous cynicism was sorely dented. Like the night of Halloween, for instance.

It had been a busy Monday evening in the pub, with party-goers dressed as all manner of vampires, witches and skeletons, calling in for a drink on their way to various Halloween parties. By 11.30pm the last of the bar staff had gone and Andy was doing his tour of locking

Mary Cooper
"Umbrella Mary"

up and alarm setting. He ended in the Witham Suite, put out the lights and went through the "Staff Only" door into his private apartment. It was about twenty minutes to midnight on that most haunted of nights. Andy sat down on his sofa about to relax, when suddenly he froze, listening. Coming through his private doorway, from the Witham Suite, were noises. It sounded as if about 9 or 10 people were having a merry get-together, chatting and laughing. He had just locked everywhere up and knew no one could possibly be there. The alarms were set. He had just come through that very room, yet suddenly there seemed to be a party going on. Andy was a reasonable man. He decided that if the ghosts of the Inn wanted a halloween party in his function room, well, that was fine; as long as they did not come into his private area. They didn't. And he did not venture into their space, either.

Instead, he listened intently to the sounds coming through the closed door, wondering what would happen at the 'witching hour' of midnight. He did not have long to wait. As his clock began to strike twelve, the noise of the 'party' ceased and did not return.

Strange noises and odd happenings were becoming quite common at the Green Dragon even before Halloween. In all the pubs he had run, Andy had always known the occasional bottle to get broken in the cellars. But here, the number of broken bottles were many times that of any of his previous twenty-odd pubs. He trusted his bar staff when they said, most of the time, that they knew nothing about it; pub managers develop an uncanny judgement of character. On numerous occasions, the staff would be sitting chatting for a few minutes after hours, taking a breather before their journey home, when loud noises would be heard coming from the cellars. The noises would be those of a keg of beer or a crate of bottles being dragged across the hard cellar floor. As Andy put it: "Everybody that I was paying wages to was sitting there staring back at me; so who was in the cellar?". Searches of the cellar always revealed nothing, except occasionally something moved out of place.

The cellar was something of a focus for odd occurrences at the Green Dragon. In the autumn of 1994, the pub had a new 'gas' system installed in the cellar, which controlled the pumping of the beer up to the bars. A complex system of valves and regulators fed the gas from the high pressure cylinder to each of the many different barrels of beer, lager and cider. Within the system was an isolating tap for each individual barrel, to allow for easy change-overs. The system came on-stream one lunchtime on a normally quiet day, but on this occasion it was very busy. Andy had only one member of staff working that shift, so the two of them were kept flat-out. Suddenly, the two beer taps they were both engaged in pulling pints through dried up in mid-pull. They tried the others and found they were all off too. "That new gas cylinder must have been a dud!" shouted an irate Andy to his barman. "Get down there and change it over will you, fast!".

The barman disappeared through the doorway to the cellar stairs, but reappeared again much too quickly, and ashen faced. "It's not the gas cylinder" he gasped to Andy "you had better come and see". "What do you mean?" snapped Andy, waiting to pull the rest of his customer's pint. But the barman was adamant, so Andy put down the half-full glass and went down to the cellar himself. Then he understood.

He found that every tap on the gas system, leading to each separate barrel, had been turned off. They had been in mid-pull when it had happened, so the taps must have all been on and then turned off suddenly. All at the same time. In a locked cellar.

He turned them all back on again and returned to his customers. The barman still looked pale.

But the cellar was not, it seemed, Mary's only sphere of influence. The Witham Suite was used for a variety of functions and its tables and chairs therefore had to be frequently rearranged. On more than one occasion, a member of staff had been mid-way through setting out the furniture when they were briefly called away to help with something else. On returning they would find a table or a couple of chairs a long way from where they had just left them. Checking with their colleagues, they would find they had all been busy and had not been in the room.

Shortly before Christmas 1994, the Witham Suite had been set out for a function and a particular table had been placed by the entrance door. Several sets of leaflets had been carefully arranged on it, so that guests could pick them up on their way in. The staff member left the room for only a few moments. When they returned, the leaflets had been scattered all over the table and floor, as if by a strong gust of wind. But all the doors and windows were shut and there was no air movement.

On Saturday, 28th January 1995, we visited the Green Dragon specifically to 'psyche it out'; that is, for Jenny to use her psychic abilities to see if she could detect a spirit presence. She was indeed able to confirm that Mary Cooper was still paying visits to the Inn and was responsible for many of the ghostly happenings. Jenny reported that Mary did not seem to appreciate that she was dead and would not have any of her suggestions of moving on to a more appropriate abode. Jenny picked-up that Mary had become quite absent-minded late in her life; and of course, still was. She had been forever putting things down and then forgetting where she had put them, and would then turn the place upside down looking for them. It seemed she was still doing just this, hence the noises in the cellar. She seemed to have taken a particular dislike to the new gas system and it was she who had turned off the taps.

After our visit, Andy asked us if Mary was likely to be more active after our psychic probings. "We sometimes find that things may be a little shaken up after our visits" Jenny told him. How right this was to prove. Not only were the more common happenings of noises and things moving much more frequent in the week or two following our visit, but a rather alarming incident occurred the very next day. A member of the catering staff was in the kitchen on the Sunday morning, cooking the joints of meat for the Sunday lunches. They had been cutting a joint of beef with a long, sturdy carving knife before returning it to the oven. Just as they were doing so, Andy shouted to them that they were wanted on the phone, so they quickly shut the oven door, put the knife on the chopping board and went downstairs to the phone.

When they went back to the kitchen some time later, they let out a scream which had Andy dashing up to investigate. The knife had been snapped in two. The two halves of the blade had been placed in an "X" on the chopping board. No one else had been in the kitchen in the meantime and snapping a very sharp knife in that way would have been difficult and dangerous.

Today, you can visit the pub and see this knife displayed on the wall of the Witham Suite, together with other displays covering the Inn's association with Dick Turpin, Henry 8th, James 1st and others. We also end the Lincoln Ghost Walk at the Inn and if you attend, you may even witness the strange event of 'the moving hippo'.

"The Witham Suite"

This is a small stuffed toy in the shape of a pink hippopotamus which sits on top of one of the beams in the Witham Suite. We had not even noticed it until our third Ghost Walk, on Easter Monday, 1995. David had just finished the final story and wished everyone a good day, standing in 'the haunted corner' of the Witham Suite itself. A small boy about 7 years old, together with his father, had been on the Ghost Walk and approached David at the end. "Excuse me" said the little boy, grasping his father's hand "but that pink toy was not there when we came in". The father pointed out the hippo on one of the beams and explained to David that when the group had entered the room a few minutes before, the hippo had not been there. They had not seen it actually move, but by the end of the stories it was in a different position.

David nodded politely, but did not give it a great deal of credence. He did ask Andy about it later though and Andy confirmed that the hippo did frequently seem to move positions around the room. We were still reserving our judgement when another of our Lincoln Ghost Walk guides reported the same thing. It apparently happened quite often, to the degree that he began pointing out the hippo's position when first entering the room, explaining the reason why a little later on. On one Saturday evening Walk, a group of several young ladies had attended who had been good natured, but rather (noisily) sceptical about many of the stories. The guide was reaching the end of his presentation in the Witham Suite when one of the women literally screamed and grabbed her nearest companion. She had just noticed that the pink hippo had indeed moved from where it had been at the start of the stories. The group of sceptics then suddenly became a group of 'believers' and rushed to the bar for nerve-calming refreshments.

One of the displays currently on the wall of the Witham Suite is a photograph of Mary Cooper, a copy of the picture provided by her granddaughters. Andy personally took the original to a processors for copying to ensure its safety. The man at the shop experienced great difficulty however in getting his electronic wizardry to work and copy the photo. Normally, he said, the equipment worked perfectly, first time. But it took him five attempts to copy Mary's photograph. On the fourth try, he exasperatedly asked Andy "This has never happened before. This isn't a photograph of a ghost or anything, is it?".

EPILOGUE - THE NATURE OF GHOSTS

We hope you have enjoyed our haunting tales of Lincoln. A very brief description of the field of ghosts and hauntings is given below, in order for the reader to put the stories into greater perspective. We are currently preparing another book in which we discuss this field in much greater depth.

Most experts in the paranormal agree that while probably the majority of all reported, so-called paranormal occurrences can be explained in ordinary terms, a significant proportion defy rational explanation. That is, explanation within the terms of what is commonly regarded as "science". However, professional scientific researchers, and those with a more amateur interest in "studying" hauntings and the like, seem to have an in-built reluctance to suggest explanations for ghosts which are beyond the bounds of science. If you are a medium however, the situation is quite different.

As a medium, it is not necessary for you to measure temperature drops or set up video cameras to detect the presence of a ghost. You simply talk to them, albeit perhaps through thought rather than spoken words, and attempt to find a reason for their presence. Asking a medium whether they "believe" in ghosts is rather like asking them whether they "believe" in their next door neighbours. We know our next door neighbours well; we speak to them regularly, see them over the garden fence and hear them coming and going. We therefore accept they exist, because of the evidence we experience which demonstrates their presence. It is just the same with ghosts. We do not believe in them, so much as simply experience that they are there.

Genuine "hauntings" can have a number of quite different explanations. We give below the most commonly accepted explanations, amongst those with mediumistic ability. We appreciate that we are to some degree crossing over into the area of philosophy and "religion", but it is impossible to talk about ghosts without doing so. We are not attempting to preach or convert anyone to anything. We are simply presenting consensus opinion based on actual experiences, not on any faith or dogma.

1) THE ACTUAL PRESENCE OF A "SPIRIT". Human beings are not simply a bag of bones and chemicals called a body. They have another component, which is not physical in the normal sense. Call it a spirit, soul, personality, essence, life-force, prana, ki, chi or what you will. This component survives what we call death. Think of the body as a car, with the spirit being the driver. At "death", the driver gets out of the car and the used-out vehicle rots away. But the driver carries on. The driver may remain about the "roads" they "drove-around" in life, for a variety of reasons; they may not wish to move on, they may not realise what has happened to them. They may be seen, felt, heard or otherwise sensed by the living. They may turn house lights on or off, slam doors, or a myriad of other things. This type of ghost may well interact or communicate with their living observers in some way, as they are a sentient, if sometimes confused, being.

2) THE RE-RUN OF A "PSYCHIC TAPE-RECORDING". It seems that on rare occasions, events can get "recorded", by some process that we do not understand, onto a building, location or object. These events are often highly emotionally charged, such as murders, battles and times of great distress. At some future time, when perhaps the "atmosphere" is just right, or someone with the appropriate degree of psychic ability is present, the event can reply itself and be witnessed as a ghostly happening. Roman soldiers are seen to march along their ancient road, the screams of a lady ring out as her false lover takes her life. But their is no actual spirit presence there, anymore that Arnold Schwarzenegger is inside your TV set when you watch a video of "The Terminator". This sort of ghost is often called a "time-slip". They will be witnessed in exactly the same way by different people over a wide period of time, because it is the same "replay" being activated. This type of ghost will not interact with their observers in any way, because there is no consciousness present to do so.

3) SUBCONSCIOUS ENERGY OF A LIVING PERSON. Most people will recognise the term "poltergeist" to describe a haunting where typically things are thrown about, vases smashed, loud noises heard for no apparent reason and a wide variety of other physical disturbances. Poltergeist means "noisy spirit" in German, and it is popularly assumed that such occurrences are due to a malevolent or mischievous ghost. The vast majority of the time however, this does not seem to be the case.

While there are "evil spirits", in just the same way as there are evil people, they are extremely rare. (How many really evil people have you ever known?). Most so-called poltergeist activity seems to be due to a type of energy, undefined as yet by science, which living people can vent off, rather like steam bursting out of a safety valve. The person concerned has no idea that they are responsible and are probably just as frightened by the events as anyone else. They do not always have to be physically present at the time that things happen. The person concerned is often in their teens or early twenties, and going through emotional stress of some sort; relationship difficulties, trouble at school, family upsets. As a way of coping with the built-up of internal, stressful energy, they somehow "dump" it onto the environment around them, which may be at their home, work or school. No spirit activity is involved, and the solution to the haunting is for the living person who is causing it to take a different perspective on their problems, perhaps through counselling or relaxation techniques.

In addition to the above, it is very well documented that ghosts of people who are still very much alive have been seen. There are also a number of other types of apparitions and hauntings, such as thought-forms (see "The Phantom Field", p.29) and paranormal figures on film, such as in "The Haunted Forgeworks" on page 40. Our further book will deal with these in more detail. We hope that the above descriptions have been interesting and have perhaps given you more information with which to interpret the stories given in this book. The Phantom Rider of Castle Hill and the footsteps at the Old Sessions House are probably time-slips or recording-type ghosts. Mary Cooper at the Green Dragon and the child at Browns Pie Shop may well be actual spirits. At least one thing seems certain. Mankind will remain fascinated by the nature of his existence for as long as he exists. Which would seem to be far longer than his "three score years and ten".

OTHER PUBLICATIONS BY CASDEC LTD

GHOST STATIONS SERIES
by BEST SELLING AUTHOR
Bruce Barrymore Halpenny

GHOST STATIONS 1 £5.99 The first book to bring you TRUE stories about the old abandoned airfields. The book has now reached cult status.

...In the still morning are the faint throb of a Lancaster Bomber could be clearly heard ... the dog ... runs to greet his Master. A light flickers from the derelict Control Tower and in the distance ... the sound of young men laughing and singing is carried on the wind as the mist rolls in across the deserted airfield ... these are the Ghost Squadrons.

GHOST STATIONS II £5.99 Sets the scene of those who wish to visit, whether on foot or, from the safety of their armchair ... the haunted airfields.

... In this volume you can read about the phantom aircraft and more about the Montrose Ghost ... the most famous ghost in the Royal Air Force. And weaving a sinister spell over deserted airfield ... the Keeper of Memories. The Lightning XS894 Mystery ... and the Harrier Jet mystery will give you food for thought.

GHOST STATIONS III £5.99 The truth about the 'Z' Men. Proof beyond any doubt that Glen Miller never died in December 1944 as the world was led to believe.

A spine chilling mystery ... Spirit of the Air Hero Ghost ... told in this volume for the first time. The truth about the Devil Dogs ... the hauntings of RAF Bentwaters ... Flying Saucers and Psychic Forces. And read why Borley Church is the most haunted church in the world. The Sentinel and the Ghost Squadrons ... Do the old airfields abound with Ghosts ...?

GHOST STATIONS IV £5.99 The concluding part of the Glen Miller Myth ... Was Miller a spy ...? Now told in THIS volume for the first time ... The Truth.

... The truth also about the Hess mystery ... the truth will shock you. The Loch Ness Ghost ... told for the first time in Ghost Stations IV. And official mythology exploded which could explain why the old airfield are haunted.

GHOST STATIONS V £5.99 Read about ... the phantom bed-checker of RAF Hereford ... Nigger - The mystery lives on ... the ghost squadrons of RAF Scampton ... the truth about the Lancester R5894 in Devil's Hill Field ... the ghosts of RAF Bawtry ... strange happenings in the South China Seas ... the Red Four mystery.

GHOST STATIONS VI £5.99 The lights were out in 1939 and 'Put that light out' was heard throughout this then green and pleasant land. A Christian Land. Bomber and Fighter airfields mushroomed overnight ... it was the spirit in these airfields and aircraft that fought to keep the world free. Many brave ... very brave, young men and women died.

GHOST STATIONS VII £5.99 Ghost Stations VII is brought out in December 1995 to meet the demands of Halpenny's readers who never seem to tire of his books on airfield ghosts, UFO's and mystery.

CASDEC HERITAGE SERIES
3 books by Clive Kristen

GHOST TRAILS OF NORTHUMBRIA £3.99 This trend-setting title remains as popular as ever. The ghost-hunter is invited to follow five trails that lead to some of the region's classic haunts. Award-winning pictures, maps, and a full historical glossary complement the lively and entertaining text.

MORE GHOST TRAILS OF NORTHUMBRIA £3.99 Following the spooktacular success of Ghost Trails of Northumbria it is not surprising that this second foray into the world of the supernatural became an instant best seller.

MURDER AND MYSTERY TRAILS OF NORTHUMBRIA £3.99 This companion volume to the Ghost Trails books develops the tour and explore the theme against a background of dubious departures, early exits and horrible happenings. Murder and Mystery Trails again features the award-winning team of photographer Duncan Elson, and illustrator Mark Nuttall.

by Chris Rooney

A PEDALLER'S TALES £2.25 Popular postie, Chris Rooney leapt into the Casdec saddle with a book that has found favour with all those who enjoy classic countryside and the freedom of the road. So why not join Chris and his cast of colourful characters as they set off in search of adventure?

by Jill Harrison

TASTY TRAILS OF NORTHUMBRIA £4.99 Northumbria has a culinary heritage that can be traced back more than 1000 years. Farmer's wife, Jill Harrison, has woven her account of the very best of Northumbria fare into the popular CASDEC trails format. If you enjoy the taste of tradition and all that is best today you will find FOOD TRAILS is the gourmet's delight. Wonderfully illustrated by Jill's Aunt.

by Clive Kristen

GHOST TRAILS OF THE YORKSHIRE DALES £6.49 Following the success of the Ghost Trails of Northumbria series, author Clive Kristen invites you to explore the supernatural world of the delightful Yorkshire Dales.

by David Johnson

CYCLING TRAILS OF THE YORKSHIRE DALES £4.49 Veteran cyclist David Johnson, helps you to enjoy the byeways of the Yorkshire Dales. Certain to become a favourite with cyclists of all ages, the book is packed with anecdotes and advice as well as the customary maps and pictures.

by Andrew Waterhouse

VILLAGE TRAILS OF NORTHUMBRIA £4.99 Northumbria's villages are an Aladdin's cave of hidden delights for anyone interested in local history and the great outdoors. Join Andrew Waterhouse on his tours of some of the most attractive and fascinating villages in Britain.

OTHER TITLES

by John West

STUDIES IN SCARLET £4.95 "The man's body was lying on the bedstead in a state of nudity, its left hand pressed to its heart and the right hand convulsively clutching the hair. And oppressive odour as of scorched fat prevailed the room. No wound was obvious upon the body but the chest was transversally barred in several places by dull red stripes. A deep and broad burn was exhibited in the middle of the back and the spine was found to be completely carbonised".

The horrific tale is just one of the many true life stories that form the basis of a fascinating and gruesome study into the darker side of Victorian society.

by E Radcliffe

THE SECRET OF LIFE TBA This true story tells of the teachings brought by these dear friends and of the effect on Eddie's life and upon the lives of so many around him. From simple healings to helping many through the veil of death, so called. For those who are already mediums, those aspiring to be mediums and those just interested in the possibility of a spirit world, this unbiased account is a must.